If I Stop I'll Die:

The Comedy and Tragedy
of
Richard Pryor

John A. Williams
and
Dennis A. Williams

Thunder's
Mouth
Press
New
York

First trade paperback edition, 1993

Published by Thunder's Mouth Press
632 Broadway, 7th Floor
New York, N.Y. 10012

Library of Congress cataloging-in-publication data:
Williams, John Alfred, 1925–
    If I stop I'll die : the comedy and tragedy of Richard Pryor/by John A.
    Williams and Dennis A. Williams. — 1st ed.
    Includes index.
    ISBN 1-56025-062-3 : $13.95
    1. Pryor, Richard 2. Comedians—United States—Biography.
    3. Motion picture actors and actresses—United States—Biography.
    I. Williams, Dennis A., 1951– . II. Title.
    PN2287.P77W54 1991
    792.7'028'092—dc20
            [B]   91-14225
                                                CIP

Text design by Kathryn M. Abbott.

Printed in the United States of America.

*To Margo Carolyn Williams and David Justin Williams
and in memory of John Henry Williams*

Acknowledgments

The authors wish to thank the following recording companies, artists, technicians and staffs who have made it possible for us to use some of Mr. Pryor's materials in this book:

Andresol Records, Ltd./Cinema Finance Assoc., Ltd.
Dade Records, Ltd.
Laff Records
Northern Voices, Ltd./Lighthouse Partnership
Partee Records
Phoenix 10 Records
Platinum Voices, Ltd.
Reprise Records
Roulette Records
Stax Records
Tiger Lily Records Corp.
Warner Bros. Inc.

We also thank the people in all parts of the country whose anecdotes, comments, observations, research and technical assistance helped to make this book possible.

Preface

It's only after I have laughed until my belly hurts that I realize just how great a feeling it is, how wonderful it is to sense a curious relief, as though unseen and unfelt, I had been carrying a great burden that has just been lifted from my back.

For this afterglow of good feeling we all owe comedians more than we can imagine.

I was blessed, as my son was not, to have seen the last vestiges of black vaudeville, with its great bands, vocalists and comedians, some of whose names are noted in this book. Much later came Richard Pryor, and he is being followed, if not chased, by still another generation of black comedians.

This is a work about Richard Pryor, whose art and life made such an explosive impact on the American scene from the early 1970's through the mid-1980s. If we agree that race or ethnicity is a crucial element in American politics, we can then consider Pryor's humor to have been political—though he was preceded in political humor by a multitude of black comedians whose audiences until relatively recently were all black. As such, the comedian related to the already committed, people whose lives were not then so terribly removed from the comedian's. Those times—the twenties, thirties and forties—did not lend themselves to direct attacks on the system that had made them less than complete citizens. Dick Gregory's arrival on the comic scene in the late 1950s began to change that when he left South Side Chicago to perform in the Loop and across the United States before white audiences. (Greg, in fact, preceded the term "crossover," though the designation would most be used with Pryor and later Eddie Murphy.)

By the time Redd Foxx hit the big time, propelled by his success in black clubs—like comedians before and after him—the best of his material had been well-worked. Bill Cosby chose to be more political offstage than on, a decision that undoubtedly insured his longevity as a comedian. Others, perhaps seeded in the shifting currents of opportunity, peaked then faced decline, sometimes rapid, sometimes not. Cosby's life was but a small part of his act.

Over twenty years ago, during a three-day interview with Cosby, who was starring at Harrah's Club in Lake Tahoe accompanied by Ray Charles and his band, Cosby talked to me at length about the importance of Richard Pryor to American comedy in general and to black people in particular.

He finished at the club at three in the morning; the interviews started at noon at breakfast and continued until late afternoon. We also talked between sets in his dressing room—if he was not playing dominoes with Ray Charles, whom he frequently and loudly accused of cheating. The interview was for *Amistad 3*, of which, however, there were to be but two issues.

We talked of the way much of white America mistakenly compares black writers, singers, actors, athletes, and, most certainly, comedians to one another. Cosby, for example, was compared to Gregory, even though their comedy was completely different. And then Pryor early in his career was compared to Cosby. Yet, however true that may once have been, it is clear that differences emerged between their comedy, beginning with language and ending with public politics. But it was the standard opinion of influential figures in the entertainment industry that Cosby and Pryor were alike because they were both black, and this blindness helped Pryor along his way. Black was in and that now also included Pryor. Once he got in, though, it was hard to get him out, since Pryor was not, like Cosby, the kind of guy you want to have over for dinner, as one of our subjects said.

Nevertheless, Pryor was a gut-buster. Most black people were glad he made the observations he did. That they were accurate can be determined from the audience response at the box office and at his club and concert appearances. Pryor was the other side of the preacher, who historically had done most of the talking for us because he was the kind of black man the white folk liked. Turn the other cheek. Forgive. Christian charity. Pryor took that preacher, turned him inside out, and in the process became a folk hero.

Whatever his topic, he spoke the unspeakable. When *he* said what *we* were thinking, he lifted our burden of murderously vengeful thoughts we'd buried without laughter deep within ourselves to his own shoulders for preciously few moments that seemed a lifetime. He gave us motive for feeling and behaving the way we did. That created laughter. We also knew Pryor opened windows on our existence for those who could never have understood it without him. With Pryor around, we certainly came to know the difference, if we had not before, between white-bread and black-bread comedy.

If Pryor's comedy gave us magnificent lift of heart, most of his forty-one films gave us serious heartburn. We wondered at his pronouncements about the deficiencies of American filmmaking and his penchant for helping to solidify those same deficiencies, perhaps even magnify them. We were not concerned as much with box-office grosses as with meaningful representations of ourselves on screen. We knew he could do better, thus wondered why he didn't.

We may have known or at least suspected why. Still, as with ourselves, we hoped for the miracle to reoccur. We still do, feeling what Pryor himself said: "If I stop I'll die." And, I believed, that when he stopped some part of us would die too.

J.A.W.

JOHN A. WILLIAMS

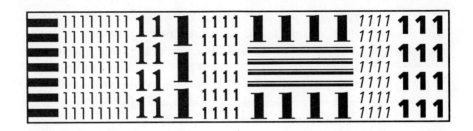

One

Comedy may be considered the opposite of tragedy, but the most ancient of peoples recognized and appreciated laughter more than they did sorrow. For a while in ancient Greece, comedy was held to be a higher form of theater than tragedy, which in fact may be the maturation of comedy.

Richard Pryor was, of course, one of the several gifts left in the wake of the tragedy of American slavery and racism. There is an irony here that Pryor seemed very much aware of (He once said, "I can't help feeling that my life is a cosmic joke.")

The irony extends beyond Pryor and black people to the white world. In Poland's Gdansk shipyards, when Solidarity mounted its first strike, workers sang "We shall Overcome," and then marched off to worship the black Madonna at Cestowa. (This would not wash in Polish Chicago or Detroit.) Students in the People's Republic of China have also sung this anthem of the civil rights movement of the 1960s, and during the Easter 1983 antinuke demonstrations at the Greenham Common missile base in England, there came wafting over the fields social messages dressed in reggae music. And in June 1990, the citizens of Hong Kong, protesting the scheduled annexation by China in 1999, also sang the civil rights anthem.

Irony is the humor of satire, and the stroke of the "Great Humorist," said George Meredith in his 1877 "Essay on Comedy and the Uses of the Comic Spirit," "is worldwide with lights of tragedy in his laughter."

Hardly anyone argued that Pryor was more Dionysus than Robin Goodfellow, or that satire was more his best weapon than the cute prank. Min of the Egyptians and Dionysus of the Greeks were gods of luxuriant fertility, wine and harvest. The son of Zeus and Semele, Dionysus was raised on Mount Nyassa, which, according to legend, was located somewhere near present-day Zimbabwe*, or in "Aethiopia near Meroe." In old Greece, plays were offered to Dionysus.

The earlier Egyptian Min is usually pictured with an erect phallus, while Dionysus's signature in Greek is φαλλός (*membrum virile*) which seemed most apt for much of Pryor's comedy. ("If I ain't horny, I check to see if my heart's beatin'. I am a *pussy man*. Give me the pussy and I'll deal with the rest of the shit later.")

In ancient Egypt, the comedians laughed at their heroes instead of honoring them; the Greeks, on the other hand, began by honoring, then ultimately came to degrade them. Today's comedians continue the tradition; they are often abusive, grotesque, absurd. They attack folly, vice (even if their own, as in Pryor's case), weaknesses, the manners and mores of the people and the institutions of the state. This didn't change when the comedies of Epicharus and others up to Aristophenes gave way to the Latin works of Plautus and Terence. And when mime (mimus) (of which Pryor is a master) became the favorite type of comedy, Publilius Syrus, like Terence a former slave, became its foremost playwright. Dionysus became Bacchus in Rome, and the festivals in his honor degenerated into orgies that had to be banned or monitored by the authorities. Lost was the old Greek concept of Dionysus—also called Zagreus ("torn in pieces")—in which Dionysus was born anew every third year—as Pryor seemed to be born anew after each crisis or incident that brought him again into the public eye.

On stage and apparently, one supposed, in private life, Pryor seemed to be very concerned with sex, which is a concern well within the Dionysian tradition; even the suggestion that having sex is a two-way tumble, not just a male prerogative, is in the tradition. Pryor was the comedian who most aptly applied the Dionysian signature to work and life, sometimes using the most basic Anglo-Saxon language juxtaposed with Black English.

It was not only the demystification of sex that enlarged his comedy (though the wonder is that it still requires demystifying, but audience reaction implied that it does), but the demystification of the corrosive mythologies whites have created around blacks as well. It is not surprising that the creation continues, but was altered to fit the times.

* *Pryor has visited Zimbabwe at least twice.*

IF I STOP

It was said in black neighborhoods, for example, that Elvis Presley made millions of dollars doing what hundreds of young black men did every day on the street for nothing more than the sheer joy of doing it. (Rappers seem to be the latest performers in this evolutionary development and glorification of traditional street performing.)

If Presley (and other white musicians) served as the conduit to white audiences for a music that was traditionally fixed in black life, we might view Richard Pryor as having been the conduit to mixed audiences for humor that is also traditionally fixed in black life.

But, if we pass through any cluster of black people at that magical time when "lying and crying" commences, the story-telling begins, we can find Richard Pryors on every corner, in every barbershop or pool hall, combining humor and folklore, creating original material, and causing laughter to explode over experiences which if not shared are at least known; experiences many Americans conveniently forget, which are the result of a peculiarly American tragedy, a "coming and going at the same time," as Pryor said about his father's death. LeRoy Pryor, Jr. (also known as Buck Carter) is supposed to have died while making love.

The quality of being in limbo—of being from Africa and never quite being accepted as Americans—also precisely defines the position of black people in the United States today, so the wonder is that they have anything at all to laugh about. Yet, black humor, that is, humor related by black comedians about people who are black (and white and brown), only began to enter directly into the American consciousness with people like Slappy White ("Father of the Integrated Joke") and Dick Gregory. However, black humor of course existed long before, in Africa and probably on the way to America in the ships. Black people had always at least known of its existence.

They may not have been aware of Plato's view that comedy contains essences of both pleasure and pain, because Plato's opinion as well as that of Aristotle and others simply could not have encompassed the experience of the black man in America.* That experience was yet to come. When we consider that our literature and history, two of the greatest catchall disciplines not obliged to submit to the empiricism required of science (not always so good itself at deriving conclusions from fact), deal only marginally with black people, it is not surprising that their humor/comedy likewise has been relegated to a subgenre for more convenient dismissal.

*Pryor knew, instinctively or otherwise: "Like you need pain to be funny," he told Stephen Farber in a soggy interview in The New York Times, June 12, 1983.

Along the way, however, something happened, and as we peer from back to front, we see it was predictable. It is impossible for us to have traditions running parallel to each other for a couple of hundred years or more without discovering that each is meaningless unless it borrows from or admits to a relationship with the other, particularly when both undergo portions of the same experience in the same place. Indeed, from almost the beginning, blacks were present in American theater, but as objects of ridicule. *The Padlock* played in 1769 and featured a "West Indian slave," Lofton Mitchell reports, "who was a profane clown of little authenticity." The changes in American theater were minuscule for two hundred years, but there was a tradition that preceded Bert Williams, whose career peaked mainly while he was with George Nash Walker during the Jazz Age, coming just before the Harlem Renaissance of 1925.

W.C. Fields said Williams was the funniest man he'd ever seen—and the saddest. He recorded songs like "I'm in the Right Church , but the Wrong Pew," "Come After Breakfast, Bring Along Your Lunch and Leave Before Supper," and his famous, deeply pathetic "Nobody." During his tours with various editions of the Ziegfield follies—as the first black man so featured—Williams played opposite Eddie Cantor in a blackface father-and-son routine. Cantor, of course, and Al Jolson, carried blackface into the decades of the twenties and thirties after Williams died in 1922.* It was Jolson who, as the title character in *The Jazz Singer* (1927), announced the birth of sound film in a pseudo-black voice, "You ain't heard nothin' yet!"

Until the Roaring Twenties much of America's humor/comedy fit precisely into Herbert Spencer's now discredited dictum that humor makes us laugh when we are "prepared for a large perception and arrive at a small one." Humor was found in clumsy comic strips, infrequently on the stage. (American theater tended to borrow "serious" work from Europe, or replayed the classics, or played American melodrama, much of it consisting of relations between pioneers and Indians, blacks and whites, or whites and whites. Minstrelsy and vaudville combined to give humor/comedy its origins.) If we reverse Spencer's notion, we might reach a more logical conclusion about later American comedy, and it is that we laugh when we expect small perceptions but discover large ones. We are then, as when confronted by remarkable

---

* *The Walker and Williams routines spawned "Amos 'n' Andy," Freeman Goodson and Charles Correll in blackface. They were hits on radio, made some terrible movies, and lasted into the age of television.*

4   JOHN A. WILLIAMS

poetry, surprised and delighted, but since we have come to see comedy, we laugh; it is a way of offering up praise. This largeness of perception is based on an understanding and acceptance of the American experience, with all its colorings, contradictions and capabilities. Religion, politics and education have failed to bridge W. E. B. Du Bois's color line; humor /comedy might.

Two factors embrace "capabilities," those goals the United States can achieve through the elimination of racism. The first is the understanding that black comedy has a long tradition, which was perhaps formalized by people like Bert Williams. The bearers of that tradition include John "Bubbles" Sublett, and Ford "Buck" Washington, of Buck 'n' Bubbles, Butterbeans 'n' Susie, Jackie "Moms" Mabley, Dewey "Pig Meat" Markham, Lincoln Perry (Stepin' Fetchit), Willie Best, Mantan Moreland, Eddie "Rochester" Anderson, Willie Washington, Willie Lewis, Timmie Rodgers, George Kirby, Redd Foxx, Slappy White, Nipsey Russell, Dick Gregory, Bill Cosby, Flip Wilson, Richard Pryor, Eddie Murphy, Arsenio Hall and others. Like all lists, this one is woefully incomplete, but it does provide the shape of a long and viable tradition.

The second factor that informs "capabilities," perhaps unfortunately for some, is cultural exchange, or as some have more precisely put it, cultural theft, for in thievery there is never any acknowlegdment that what was stolen ever belonged to anyone else. To confess that is to admit to a criminal act. Besides, you cannot gracefully acknowledge the theft of what you have ridiculed for so long. Nevertheless, the acceptance of Pryor's comedy by large numbers of contemporary Americans of all colors and creeds indicated that we are capable of understanding, empathy and maybe action that might lead to something better than we now have. Pryor himself had asked of the racial climate, "So what's changed?"

The phenomenon of "borrowing," "stealing," and "exchanging" has been observed and extensively commented on. No one was more succinct, however, than Truman Capote, who in an interview with Cecil Brown, also a writer (*The Life and Loves of Mr. Jiveass Nigger*, 1970 and *Days Without Weather*, 1983) noted that "about sixty percent of everything in America originated with black culture. That's why I get so absolutely furious with the whole cult of modern music—starting with practically anybody, because its's *all! all! all!* taken from black people! I can't think of anybody in America who isn't ripping off black people."

Musical borrowing is the most obvious, with dancing not very far behind. The Beatles, whose music seemed to mark a clear departure from rhythm and blues as far as whites were concerned, in reality traced from Bo Diddley through Chuck Berry, and admitted an indebtedness to Little Richard, James Brown and other black musicians. But a declaration of dependence is rarely made.

Perhaps the use of things black has become a way of American life itself. Leslie Fiedler, in his *Waiting for the End* (1964), oberved that

> There is scarcely a father of an adolescent in the United States who is not presently becoming aware (though he may feel it as a pain, rather than know it as a fact) that his son is in his whole life-style, his speech, his gait, the clothes he wears, the music he loves, as well as the vices he emulates, closer to the life-style of Negroes than he could have foreseen on the day of his son's birth. He may find him, in fact, in posture and in gesture, in intonation and inflection, perhaps even in the deepest aspirations, which, after all, control such outward behavior, closer to the great-grandfather of his Negro friends, or at least to what those great-grandfathers have meant to the white imagination, than to their own great-grandfathers.

What explains this phenomenon of the oppressor adapting the mores of the oppressed? Usually, psychiatrists tell us, it's the other way around. In his book about comedians, *Funny People* (1981) Steve Allen calls the phenomenon "hipness," citing Lenny Bruce's success as being a result of America's taking "a long lurch toward hipness . . . In the late thirties hipness was limited to a minority percentage of the urban black population," he says, "and to jazz musicians, white and black. Some forty-five years later, a much larger segment of our population has become hip to one degree or another."

However, Allen never defines "hip." He vaguely equates it with black hostility toward racism. But most contemporary dictionaries define the term as being wise, sophisticated, knowledgeable, aware. Appropriately enough, the term originated in Harlem, where, in the beginning "one pulled on hip boots" to protect against water.* Originally the offending element really was not water, but human waste. Shortened to "hip," the term has obvious metaphorical meanings about the world in which we live and how to protect oneself from it. The hip boots shield one from the surge of the fluid that flows down the gulf between national dictum and lack of deed. While most of us are powerless to do anything about the situation, we are by now nevertheless aware of it, crowded in the same listing vessel.

---

* *Robert S. Gold,* A Jazz Lexicon *(New York: Alfred A. Knopf, 1964).*

Today's comedians perform in highly charged political circumstances. Some deal with the situation and others do not. Of course, the worldwide racial situation has also been considered a ticking time bomb. Aside from the late Lenny Bruce, most white comedians have steered clear of racial issues (perhaps feeling that it's not their prerogative). Some black comedians have boogalooed neatly around it as well. But the awareness of these issues may have accounted for Pryor's wide audience—even though race was not his single nor even his major topic. People and their foibles has been the Pryor topic. Academics would tend to call this a universal view, except that black people are not supposed to have one. Nevertheless, his topics and antics created a multiracial audience, one that was nurtured through the tradition of black comedy, countless comedians on the corner and on the stage, and the inevitable cultural borrowings, of which Pryor himself was a culprit. In his routines he's done Chinese waiters, Japanese actors, hillbillies, middle- and upper-class whites, women—and himself. "I am everybody I can create," he said. "I'm somehow a part of them. I've got the same things in me, no matter how terrible they are."

"Terrible" would not accurately decribe the events that were to occur; nightmares would be more precise. Or holocaust, that sacrificial offering that is consumed by flames. "Terrible" would almost be the fulfillment of a Sagittarian note in Pryor's horoscope: "There is a liability to accidents and a sudden or violent end." But, like Zagreus-Dionysus, Pryor would be reborn, perhaps not so much because of any mystical destiny, but out of his own strong instinct for survival, a courage he may not have known he had.

Two

The suburb of Northridge, about twelve miles northwest of Los Angeles, is near California State University, Los Angeles Pierce College, Los Angeles Valley College and a Veterans Hospital. Although there are many modest homes in the region, there are also estates whose swimming pools and tennis courts are sheltered from sight and sound by walls, tall shrubs, trees, and lawns sprouting neatly groomed Saint augustine grass; these are tended mainly by Mexican-Americans. The San Diego Freeway runs northward beside the Van Nuys Airport after crossing the Ventura Freeway, and merges with the Golden State Freeway above the San Fernando Mission.

On the Monday evening of June 9, 1980, a slender black man lurched out into broad, quiet Parthenia Street. Traffic moves at a brisk pace along the street, almost apologetically for having to go through it, with its walled homes on either side.

The man staggered for nearly a mile, ending up on Hayvenhurst Avenue, alternately running and walking, almost aimlessly it seemed, but nevertheless with a vague, desperate determination. Motorists saw him; he appeared to be in extreme pain. They stopped and tried to help. They called to him. The man, who smelled like cooked meat—the motorists saw that he'd been burned—would not stop.

Two Los Angeles cops, Carl Helm and Richard Zielinski, were on duty when they saw the cars and the man who was moving in a shocked parody of a man running; Officer Helm recognized the man as Richard Pryor. Pryor's shirt was burned and in smoking tatters; his chest looked like a steak that needed turning, quick. Pryor's hands, left cheek, nose and lips were already swelling. Zielinski got out of the car.

When he saw the extent of the burns Pryor had, Helm called an ambulance. By this time, Pryor's Aunt Dee, who had been chasing after him, arrived panting and frightened. She'd already called an ambulance.

(Fire was already a Pryor trademark of sorts. His album, *Is it Something I Said?*, released in 1975, carries a photo of a woeful Richard Pryor about to be burned at the stake. In the second "Richard Pryor Show" on NBC in 1977, Pryor plays a caveman who discovers fire and is then burned at the stake. On the jacket of his 1978 album, *The Wizard of Comedy*, Pryor is pictured in the background surrounded by fire and smoke.)

This strange group now consisted of: Officers Helm and Zielinski, Pryor, who was refusing offers of help from the cops, and Aunt Dee. Also proceeding down the street were various pedestrians and motorists who'd happened by on this pleasant evening. It was about 8:15 P.M.

"Stop, Richard," Zielinski said again. "We gotta get you to a hospital."

The next second, Pryor managed to juke out of Officer Zielinski's grasp, saying, "If I stop I'll die."

The ambulance came wailing up the street, lights pulsating in the dusk. Pryor and Aunt Dee got in; the attendants placed a fluid-treated sheet over him. "Oh, Lord," Pryor moaned. "I guess you got me now." (He had, of course, already "met God" in his monologues—one of Pryor's characters often said he'd met God in 1929 in Baltimore, while eating a tuna fish "sammidge.")

The ambulance hurtled east and south to Sherman Oaks Hospital and Burn Center, a complex of yellow and brown buildings near the Ventura Freeway. Pryor would not notice the yellow and beige walls for a couple of days; it is possible that not even the presence of a closed-circuit TV camera in his room offered comfort. In the blue-walled nurses' station, another monitor in the Sanyo system would now tell the staff how the newest patient was doing.

Officer Zielinski said Pryor had groaned in agony as they trailed along Hayvenhurst, "Oh, Lord, give me another chance." If there is a God, then he/she heard him. Immediately after Pryor had been brought in, a team of four nurses and technicians began working on him; this was before Dr. Jack Grossman, who had just finished a long and complicated operation, answered the summons for his help. The burns, many of them third degree, covered about 50 percent of the comedian's body.

Quickly, fluids were pumped into him, then he was given drugs for the pain and oxygen to help him breathe. Antibiotic-laced dressings were swiftly applied to kill off the deadly bacterial infections. Within an hour of his arrival at the hospital, Pryor was wired for his blood pressure, heart beat, temperature; he was placed in a special bed over which hung a Plexiglas heat shield that radiated warmth and made unnecessary any body coverings.

Doctors Jack and Richard Grossman, who run the largest private burn center in the country, together with an excellent staff, concentrated on a 100-percent recovery for Pryor—at about the same time the obituary writers on the newspapers and magazines must have been wondering just how much space they'd be given for the death pieces they were up-dating. Pryor fooled them. Six weeks later, after two debridements—the surgical removal of dead skin tissue—and three skin grafts, and following a series of mixed reports of his imminent death or slow recovery, Richard Pryor was out of the hospital with not a keloid showing.

Before he left the hospital, his ex-wife, Deboragh McGuire, had said, "This [the accident] is his next album." Pryor had always used life as he saw and experienced it in his monologues; why not his holocaust? McGuire was almost right; his holocaust did become the centerpiece of his next concert film, *Richard Pryor Live on the Sunset Strip* (1982); but by the time it was released, he was back on the set of *Bustin' Loose* (originally called *Family Dreams*) and moving, moving on.

Before his immolation, Pryor was on his way to becoming the biggest black name in Hollywood since Sidney Poitier. The fact is, bigger than many white names. He'd played, been featured, or starred in some twenty-five films; his club and concert dates, twenty-three years of them, were events not to be missed. Grammy awards and an Emmy rolled his way as if set on some mysterious schedule. He wrote for Lily Tomlin, Redd Foxx, Flip Wilson and himself. He had emerged as *the* scene thief in *Lady Sings the Blues*, *Car Wash* and *The Bingo Long Traveling All-Stars and Motor Kings*. Although he was originally cast in only a small part in *Silver Streak*, Twentieth Century-Fox kept writing more and more of him into the script, until he rode the train into Chicago—and saved the picture. He'd become to acting in films what Abe Burrows was to mending plays. He began an NBC-TV series that proved to be short-lived, but left his mark on the medium forever. Then there was the triumphant film *Richard Pryor—Live in Concert* (1979). He was one of the brightest lights—black, white or brown—to have successfully stormed the Hollywood Hills.

"Pryor," said Thom Mount, a leading executive at Universal Pictures, "is the most significant crossover artist in the history of the movies."

Pryor did not like the term. In any case, he'd done it all his way; he'd lined his route up the Hills with street talk and body moves right off the block. He spoke Black English with unadulterated joy and uncommon vigor. Epithets in his mouth became nothing more than the stops, glottals, and sibilants used so automatically in everyday speech, or they became punctuation. Pryor's pauses and emphases were one-syllabled, tried-and-true Anglo-Saxonisms, or the quadro-syllabic, black-affiliated, "mother—" word that with tonal variations becomes damnation or praise or just another form of punctuation. Through dozens upon dozens of interviews, some of which became cover articles in the nation's most prestigious popular magazines, and also because of private escapades—fights, arguments, shootings, earthy *bon mots* in public places, tax problems, business manager problems, marital beginnings, endings and disputes in the middles—Pryor became enfolded in a reputation. He was *weird*, crazy, explosive, unpredictable; he was brilliant and a junkie; he was generous, vindictive, and insulting. He tired quickly of people, especially if they were women. He was snarlingly guarded about his private life, which made people wonder what that was *really* like, since so much of it was public anyway. He talked too "nasty" and instilled fear in people. He often misled writers who interviewed him; sometimes, as a result, it was difficult to tell where the put-ons ended and the truth began.*

There seemed at times to be something religious about him, but he worked up monologues that twitted and satirized the everyday purveyors of religion, the black preacher, the white middle-American evangelist. And staring blasphemy dead in the eye like a child challenging God to prove Her/His existence, Pryor created some of his most explosive comedy around God's relationship to himself in particular and to people in general.

He carried all this off because he looked pretty ordinary, like the rest of us. He doesn't have the athletic, cocky good looks of Bill Cosby, and he doesn't have the angular, sleepy-eyed expression of Dick Gregory. He was not as belligerently self-assured as Redd Foxx. Pryor appeared vulnerable. His eyebrows were fixed to fly upward in fear, surprise or useless protest; his arms flailed in defeat. He was that lean-shanked, sensitive being to whom almost anything could happen.

It was Pryor's face, tracing an unprecedented range of human and animal expressions, that marked him as a major mimic of our time.

* *In 1982 an entertainment lawyer involved in litigation against Pryor said of him, "He is an incredible writer, and incredible creator of stories. I don't know that he knows the difference between truth and fantasy."*

There were other greats—Jonathan Winters, Sid Caesar, Carol Burnett, Robin Williams, Lily Tomlin, Steve Martin—who could slip like oil from one character to another. But none of them had that extra dimension of being black.*

Black comedians like Russell or Foxx were not mimics to the degree Pryor was. We always saw them as they were. And they certainly didn't display tenderness or vulnerability, the way Pryor did, which may have been the reason he could do a stalked deer or squirrel monkey or a dog so superbly.

Pryor acted out his materials; there had to be movement, and as women noted, he moved well. He had a sinewy body, more half-miler than boxer. It seemed wind-resistant, light-boned. He was on the stage what Dr. J was on the court; he mimicked middleweight boxers, the smooth gait of Billy Dee Williams, the cowpoke saunter of John Wayne, the stutter step of a drunk.

The acting out was pure black. "I'll be willing to bet," Bill Cosby said two decades ago, "seventy-five percent of the black kids in the ghetto can act, man, 'cause they want to perform and they do it anyway. You stand around firing the finger at a cat . . . and wish you could be a star . . . I don't know if it's [acting out] found in all races; my idea is that in lower economic groups where people don't have the attention and also where they don't have the things that take away from their imagination—in other words, the more bread you get, the less you have to play act about what you are and who you are. Richard Pryor is perhaps the only comedian that I know of today who has captured the total character of the ghetto."

Much of that character was body movement, an explosive addition to the contemporary comic art. Of course, Cosby, Winters, and others had *moved*—but not like Pryor, whose arrival put the motionless, cerebral-appearing stand-up comic in the shade. He also broadened the effectiveness of mike-sound acoustics in his monologues. Winters and Cosby, of course, were but two of the innovators of mike sound; in their hands the mike became a prop as well as an electronic gadget to carry their voices.

Pryor was, almost everyone seemed to agree, stupendous, the kind of raw star talent that image-makers were unused to. Not even Flip Wilson or Redd Foxx, with their television shows, had prepared Hollywood for Pryor. And in addition, he was a money-making motherfucker! The comedian's personal holocaust proved beyond a doubt that

A number of comedians, including Robin Williams, Tom Dreesen, and several others, did mini black monologues or used "the language." Unlike older comics, they were never derogatory with such material.

all kinds of people—and not just black people, who had given him his mandate over the years in hundreds of clubs—had been listening to him. The mail that poured into the Sherman Oaks Burn Center was torrential. If Pryor ever had reason to doubt that his humor was getting over, that he was loved and admired, he now had overwhelming proof to the contrary. It may have been this great outpouring for a man who perhaps felt unworthy of it that brought him out of the ashes, moving him over the bricks almost without having missed a stride.

Three

While Pryor may have rushed light-years away from Peoria in many ways, nevertheless the place still rode shotgun on his memories, which appeared to be more bitter than sweet, even if they had given him a mine of material for his monologues. Any man is a product of his place; he may indeed grow out of it, but the cocoon remains.

For some travelers through Illinois, Peoria is a place to avoid. Chicago, they say, may be the only place in the state for nightlife. Optimists say there are two: Chicago and Springfield. There's not much mention of East St. Louis or Cairo. They're tough places, usually making the news through violence. We almost never read or hear about Peoria—or didn't—until Richard Pryor came along to put it on the map with a vengeance. Some people pronounce the name of his hometown the way they would pronounce pyorrhea.

Long, long before Pryor came along, a black man had lived there trading with the Indians and cutting out a farm for his family. He was the ubiquitous (for Illinois) Jean Baptiste Point du Sable, who arrived about 1760 and then moved north to open another trading post in what is now Chicago. Later, Peoria became one of the many stations of the Underground Railroad through which slaves escaped from the South to the North in a slow-moving, steady stream. Illinois, like several other northern or border states, had a fugitive slave law; the runaways, if captured, could be returned south. Abolitionist newspaper editor Elijah Lovejoy was killed in Alton, a distance north of Peoria, by an antiabolitionist mob in 1837. Abraham Lincoln and Stephen Douglas held their first debate in Peoria, on October 16, 1854, a year after the state had passed a law that called for the fining and imprisonment of any black person, slave or free, who entered Illinois with intent to remain. Peoria's Anti-Slavery Society, as elsewhere, was overwhelmed by pro-slavery groups. It brought Frederick Douglass to town to speak, but it could not get him a room in the local hotel; he walked the streets all night to keep from freezing. That there was a perceived difference between the abolition of slavery and equality for the black man, which produced a problem still unresolved, was made clear by the failure of any of the Anti-Slavery Society's members to take Douglass in out of the cold. But the blacks themselves were led in their efforts to secure equality by men like Thomas Lindsey, George Janver, Augustus Dobbins and David Strother. A tiny black school had been maintained for the Afro-American population which, by the end of the Civil War, numbered 115 pupils, but during the postwar period that school was closed and the Peoria school integrated. It was run by a Miss Duffy who earned thirty dollars a month, and there were no reported major incidents of racial conflict there.

As the tumultuous nineteenth century ended, with a horrendous twentieth century looming ahead, some sixty-five miles south, in Decatur, Richard and Julia Piper Carter had a daughter. They named her Marie. She would be one of twenty-one children—and Richard Pryor's maternal grandmother. At that time, 1899, there were only 900 blacks out of a population of 41,000 people in Peoria, which, for Marie Carter, was still a distance away in miles and in time.

Most of America lived on farms, although the cities were beckoning. Twenty cents an hour was considered an average wage. The train was the king of transportation, and education was just starting to come into its own as the ladder to a better life. In Decatur and Peoria, the blacks as well as the whites could not have known that W. E. B. Du Bois was the most educated black man in the United States; he was, in fact, one of the best educated men in the world. But most of his people, less than a quarter of a century out of slavery, did not count education as an immediate need.

American families were large, moving here and there with wagons and horses and perhaps bicycles. While yellow journalism began to crest, black people in Peoria and Decatur sometimes read the conservative papers of their towns; there were almost no black weeklies then. Church was at the core of all social activities. Life was slow and deliberate, and offered not much promise of anything, especially if you lived in Decatur. If you were black you also moved with circumspection, for there had been a dozen known lynchings of blacks in Illinois from 1893 to 1915. In Decatur, the people recalled the lynching of Sam Bush on June 3, 1893. The Civil War was over, slavery had ended; Reconstruction, that brief symbol of hope for the entire country, had faded. Racism in its ugliest, most deadly form had taken over.

White people lived on average fourteen years longer than black people, but some recognition was given to the black presence: Booker T. Washington was appointed the Negro Leader, not so much by the black population as by white public opinion. (The habit of white opinion-makers anointing black leaders has been practiced and refined to the present day.)

However, the movement was hardly noticed in Decatur and the surrounding farmland, where the grain grew tall and the red-brick factories stood. Near where the Sangamon flowed lazily into Decatur Lake, the Carter clan persevered. Marie took up with LeRoy Pryor, and children followed soon after—three sons and a daughter. LeRoy Junior, who was known for quite some time as Buck Carter, was born June 7, 1915; he would be Richard Pryor's father. Marie's other children were Richard, John and Maxine.

The small black populations in Central Illinois, already heirs to a legacy of violence against them, were stunned when the East St. Louis rioting broke out July 1 and July 2, 1917. Six thousand black people were run out of their homes and places of work by a white mob that killed about fifty blacks and wounded uncounted others. Two years later in Chicago, twenty-three blacks along with fifteen whites were killed in rioting; there were 520 injuries to blacks and whites. In the center of the state, the black people were acquiescent; they created no waves, demanded little, for fear that they, too, would be inundated by mob violence. Ever wary, they slumbered, scaled down their dreams, drew tighter the reins on their children. Marie Carter was no exception.

She was an attractive young woman, her head topped by curly, sparkling hair. She had exotically slanted eyes and a light complexion that indicated a not unusual mixed heritage back down the family roots. Marie was about five feet seven inches tall. Over the years—and there would be sixty-three more of them following the birth of Buck when she was sixteen—she would grow, in the view of some, almost as wide as she was tall.

Marie Carter arrived in Peoria in 1929, when her son Buck Carter was fourteen. It is difficult to discern if any of the other children

16   JOHN A. WILLIAMS

arrived with her. Thomas Bryant, whose name was to be intimately associated with Marie's, and who would become known as "Pops" in the community and as Grampa to Richard Pryor, appeared on the scene at precisely the same time.

The old names for the black neighborhoods were wearing out. Soup Alley, Tin Can Alley, Pig Ear Alley, and Watermelon Wards were not used quite so frequently by the time Marie arrived, but the neighborhood stigma remained.

Thomas and Marie Carter Bryant were listed in residence at 2510 South Washington Street. A Dee Pryor, a mechanic, also lived at that address. There is no indication, however, that LeRoy Pryor, Sr., was there as well. Thomas and Marie remained at this address until 1932, when they moved, according to the Peoria City Directory, to 205 South Globe Street. Thomas was then employed as a butcher at Armour and Company. One Gertrude Thomas, bookkeeper, lived at 2215 North Jefferson Avenue, not far away. This Gertrude Thomas, eight years later, became Richard Pryor's mother.

Times were so hard in Peoria during the Depression that even its chapter of the National Association for the Advancement of Colored People, which had originated in 1915, folded; its members were more concerned with the basic elements of survival. "These early years of the Depression were times of economic stress among Negro residents and through lack of support permitted the Branch to die," wrote local historian, Romeo B. Garrett. That lack of support would continue. The Branch would not become active again until 1938, when it would die once more. In 1940 it would again be resurrected, only to fade until 1944, when, with new leadership, the Branch focused on the crunching need for jobs in Peoria.

When times are rough, tenants usually move often. Thus, after one year at Globe Street, Thomas and Marie moved to 206 1/2 Hancock Street. He then worked for the Wilson Provision Company. Buck Carter—LeRoy Pryor, Jr.—a tough, streetwise kid, was then eighteen and a fighter good enough to win a Golden Gloves tournament in Chicago. Meanwhile, Gertrude Thomas lived at the same Jefferson Avenue address, in the same neighborhood.

Thomas and Marie lived at 206 1/2 Hancock Street for two years, then moved to 108 Hancock, where one child was recorded as living with them. For the next five years they and the family reappeared in 1940 at the 205 South Globe Street address, and with them was

LeRoy Pryor, laborer. "Carter" had been dropped, but LeRoy was still known as Buck. Marie was forty-one and Thomas ten years older.

As the fourth decade of the twentieth century began, not quite 3,000 black people lived in Peoria; there were 102,000 whites. Gertrude Thomas, Pryor's mother, remained in North Jefferson Avenue.*

(There is a photograph dated March 9, 1969, of Pryor holding hands with his mother, Gertrude Thomas Emanuel, in Peoria Methodist Medical Center. She lies in a hospital bed looking past him into the camera. Some of her front teeth are missing. her right eye is half-shut, as though from a stroke. Pryor stares slightly downward. There is a blankness on his face that does not quite conceal a suggestion of primness; also present is a hint of sadness or resignation or pity. Much later he would say, "My mother went through a lot of hell behind me, because people would tell her, 'You don't take care of that boy.' She wasn't the strongest person in the world. . . . At least she didn't flush me down the toilet like some do." Gertrude Thomas—"Miss Thomas"— died not long after her son's visit.

It was fifteen degrees above zero in Peoria on December 1, 1940, the day Richard Franklin Lennox Thomas Pryor was born.** The local paper, The Peoria Journal Transcript, was filled with news of the war in Europe, which was then fourteen months old. German submarines were torpedoing ships in the Canadian-American convoys at a fearful rate; France and England were under heavy attack.

In the second section of the paper, Myrtle Meyer Eldred's column, "Your Baby and Mine," was subtitled, "Parents Can Help a Child Develop a Likable Personality." It is not likely that Pryor's parents read that column.

Not only was Pryor born into a world that was at war, with the worst yet to come, but things had gone from bad to worse within Peoria itself. The Civil Liberties Committee, a subcommittee of the Peoria Advisory Committee of the State Commission then investigating the condition of black urban populations in Illinois, came up with these statistics concerning the city:

---

* The Peoria Journal Star (June 6, 1977) reported: "The self-styled stroker [Pryor's chosen nickname alluding to his pool-hall swagger] from Peoria (born here to a broken home in 1940) has a closet full of gold records, Grammys and Emmy Awards.

** The Superintendent of the Office of Catholic Education of the Diocese of Peoria said: "The County Clerk has no record of his [Pryor's] birth, and the parishes in which he might have been baptized do not have a baptismal record for him."

IF I STOP

• Forty percent of the black population was unemployed.*

• Thirty-two percent of the remaining 60 percent held only part-time jobs or worked for the federal government's Works Progress Administration.

• The average annual wage of heads of households with four people was $1,300.

• Sixty-seven percent of the people questioned complained of police brutality and injustice.

•Sixty-three percent reported unfair treatment at the hands of public relief office workers and doctors designated to serve indigent victims of the Depression.

• Ninety percent of the people questioned believed they had been denied work because they were black.

• Seventy percent of Peoria's black people lived in substandard housing in extra-legally segregated areas of the city—on the north and south sides.

• Only two restaurants in the downtown area served black people.

• Black people were barred from all hotels.

• Black people were denied entrance to two downtown theaters, not permitted into residential theaters, and restricted to the rear sections of another.

• Recreational facilities on a full-time basis were available only at the Negro Community Center, which became Carver Community Center three years later. Blacks were allowed limited use of facilities at three other locations, and could use the city swimming pools only one day a week.

The subcommittee that had amassed these statistics was dissolved before it could provide recommendations to improve a situation that had been more or less static for close to a century. Peoria, activist John Gwynn was later to note, "civil rights–wise, was behind other cities."

Harry Sephus, a member of this committee, in a parting shot at local businesses that seemed to be right on the mark for the Peoria of 1941 and for the decades of the future, said:

> Our employment group, headed by Father Farrell, director
> of Catholic Charities for the Diocese of Peoria, is seeking to

---

* *In 1983 it was 38 percent unemployment for black adults and 74 percent for black youngsters.*

find out why the Negro is barred from employment by a great majority of the industries, businesses and public utilities of Peoria. They seek to find out why the Caterpillar Tractor Company, the largest employing unit in Central Illinois, can find no place for Negro labor. They seek to find out why the Keystone Steel and Wire Company, employing hundreds, can find only a few places for colored men. They seek to find out why retail businesses soliciting colored patronage consistently refuse to accept Negro employees. They seek to find out why the Iowa-Illinois Power and Light Company, both furnishing service to 90 percent of the Negro population, are carrying only one Negro on their payrolls. These are only a few of the many cases which the Employment Committee has under investigation.

Of course in 1941 such findings were not uncommon. But Peoria was in that region which was to become known as Middle America, one of a few "ideal test market" cities for new products; its way of life was a national norm, including what was then an apparent pervasive racism. According to Madison Avenue, if a product plays well in Peoria it may be a winner in national sales.

In 1941 Gertrude Thomas lived at 109 Jackson Street, not far from the Globe Street address of Thomas and Marie and her daughter, Maxine. Mother and daughter gave their occupation as waitresses, and both used Bryant as their surname. William L. Carter was in a business briefly described as "Liquors." His presence indicated that some of Marie's family had become established in the city. In North Washington Street, there lived Harry Allen at 313, Mamie More at 317; American Freight Lines was located at 322. No 324 is listed. These are the addresses, with the exception of 322, where, according to Pryor, brothels were located. His family, he says, owned or ran at least one of them. Although not far away, no Pryor is recorded at this time as living in North Washington Street.

It does seem to be clear, however, that the extended family of Carters, Bryants, Pryors and Thomases ran through the community thriving as best it could, carving out for itself an existence that defied the grim statistics compiled by any committee that could be mustered. Marie Carter Pryor was the sun around which the entire family orbited; she was the strong one. "Everybody jumped when she spoke," a Peorian noted.

Cast by a series of events and the time in which she lived as the legendary black matriarch, Marie Carter Pryor on December 20 or 22, 1942, went down to St. Louis with Thomas Bryant and married him

JOHN A. WILLIAMS

some thirteen years after public records first linked them. That was also the year when LeRoy entered the public statistics as a bartender at the Famous Door tavern, undoubtedly on the watch for the heavy breathing of the draft board. William Carter's "Liquors" was at 223 Smith Street, and Gertrude Thomas, after having been at 109 Jackson, in 1943 was back at 2215 North Jefferson. Compared to many other black folks in Peoria, the Bryant-Pryor clan seems to have been surviving if not well, then adequately.

Between 1943 and 1944 the Army did catch up with LeRoy Pryor, while his mother took over as waitress at the Famous Door. It was at this time that the clan moved to North Washington Street which was, Sander Vanocur wrote after an interview with Richard Pryor in 1977, "noted for its string of whorehouses."

In 1946, the war over, LeRoy and Gertrude Pryor lived at 317; according to the City Directory, so did Dickie, who worked as a bartender at the *Famous Door*. Marie and Thomas were at 313, and nothing changed much except that young Richard was growing older and, if not wiser, more observant about life in the Peoria "fast lane."

If Peoria was a country town, it managed like all other towns to have its share of the bawdy life, hustlers and whores and others. For entertainers who couldn't make it in Chicago or St. Louis or anywhere else, Peoria was prime, like the steak. It was away from the main roads that led to Springfield or to St. Louis or beyond; it lay somnolent beside the slow-flowing Illinois.

But not very far from the river and the midwestern life, so clean and vigorous on the surface, was the underlife, and apparently it flourished during Pryor's boyhood, before the reformers moved in. "Jefferson was one whorehouse after another. There were B-girls trying to hustle customers into buying them drinks, overpriced and watered down at least. . . . And there was gambling, slot machines. The Old Faust Club, they used to have slot machines in the dressing rooms. The boss wanted his money back," says Ray LeRoy. LeRoy, who is white, worked the Peoria turf for twenty years. He once lived next door to the Pryors on Millman Street, when Richard was starting out.

Given the economics of the situation that seems to have always prevailed in Peoria, one might be able to understand the underside of life that Pryor spoke about so often in the 1970s.

But there had to have existed, also, side by side with it, another facet of life—the black church. Much of Pryor's work has dealt with that, too, and most pointedly with the black preacher.

Although Pryor has told some interviewers and friends and audiences that he and his family were Catholic, and even that he had been an altar boy, this does not seem to be the case at all.

His grandmother, Marie, who exerted the greatest influence on his young life, was a member of two fundamentalist churches. She belonged to the Morning Star Baptist in Peoria, the largest black church in town. (Another, Mt. Zion Baptist, in 1925 bought the klavern headquarters of the disbanded Peoria KKK for its new quarters.) Marie Carter Pryor Bryant also belonged to the Church of the Living God in Decatur, where she was buried at her death. She was also a member of the advisory board of the United Neighborhood Corporation and a member of the Nora Field Taylor Temple 270, IBPOE (Improved Benevolent Order of Elks).*

Both the Baptist church and the Elks have been basic institutions in the black community, drawing more from the masses than from among those who considered themselves to be middle-class or on the way up. Pryor came by his satires on black life quite naturally.

Even if true that his family was engaged in prostitution, even if true that Marie was a madam, and that he saw "his mother go into rooms with men," and saw "his aunties go into rooms with men," there was that necessary separation of those instances from those of periods of worship and communal relaxation—a not unusual accommodation found among all people everywhere. However, to make those distinctions clear to a child, discipline was strict. Pryor's skit of his grandmother whipping him with a switch is but one example. Such discipline also served to remind youngsters that the white world outside the door, if crossed, might claim more than the youngsters were willing to pay. To obey, to not get into trouble, to be able to tolerate various aspects of everyday life was the central message in the harsh disciplining. Pryor, of course, was not the only black youngster to have undergone such an experience.

From 1946 until 1950, LeRoy and Gertrude, Uncle Dickie, Thomas and Marie were all located on North Washington Street, at 313 and 317. The Santa Fe Trail Transportation Company had taken over the American Transport Co. Richard Dewitt Pryor, Uncle Dickie, was also bartending at the Famous Door. The black population, now numbering about 5,000, was still pressed close to the lake and the railroad tracks. True, Nat "King" Cole had a radio show, and Ralph Bunche had won the Nobel Prize for his peacemaking efforts in the Middle East. Even in Peoria, Bradley University had hired is first black

*A throwaway line in a 1970s Pryor monologue was: "Your mama... she a Elk, ain't she?"

faculty member. Marie opened a beauty shop on Adams Street in 1950; LeRoy and Gertrude were recorded as barkeeps; Uncle Dickie was listed as manager and all still worked at the Famous Door.

That year must have been traumatic for young Richard, then ten. On August 16, his father married Viola Hurst. If LeRoy had ever married Gertrude, records do not reveal it.

In Pryor's May 29, 1979, interview with Barbara Walters, she asked: "Were your mother and father married?"

Pryor's response: "After I was about three, they got married." Thus, Pryor's mother, Gertrude Thomas Pryor, drifted out of the records as quietly as she had entered them.

During this same interview, the comedian said of his father: "He had a child [Pryor]; he didn't need a child. It was hard for him. He was placed in that position ... wasn't no planned parenthood." Pryor said as well as implied that he was an only child—which may be true as far as Gertrude and LeRoy were concerned. He did not talk about siblings, but there were two sisters, Barbara Pryor Mayfield and Sharon Pryor, both well-known as his sisters in Peoria, according to long-time residents.*

The comedian implied the existence of a large extended family while putting on New York *Daily News* columnist Sidney Fields in 1966: "Richie was brought up by his mother, grandmother, father, uncle; whoever wasn't busy. They all lived in the same house with the 12 Pryor kids. Richie was the seventh."**

Talk about the whorehouses Marie Carter Bryant was alleged to have run led to Pryor's dismissal from Catholic school. There are a number of such stories about these brothels. In 1977, the comedian told Sander Vanocur that his parents "owned one of the houses on the block." That is, the 300 block of North Washington. He told Barbara Walters that his grandmother ran, not owned, "three houses of prostitution." With some embellishments added or subtracted, this view of his life was passed along to friends and acquaintances, along with his claim that his family's involvement with prostitution got him expelled.

The Catholic church, as one Peorian put it, "was the only church that did not segregate" in Peoria. "It was either Catholic or Baha'i. There was nothing in between."

* *LeRoy and Anna, reported the* Peoria Journal Star *in 1966, have a daughter, June. But she may be Anna's daughter from a previous marriage.*

** *New York* Daily News, *March 5, 1966. In a monologue on the record* Are You Serious? *Pryor has a family consisting of eleven kids, two grandmothers and a "Miss Thomas." Pryor disclosed in 1982 that in adulthood he discovered "half-brothers. Two that I know of."*

The Catholics had been involved in community action in the 1940s: the employment group of the Peoria Advisory Committee had been led by Father Farrell, director of Catholic Charities. Father Thomas Henseler had been the first white person to head the board of directors of the Carver Community Center. ("That caused some problems," Father Henseler said. "My car was broken into and so forth ... and Richard was in town for a benefit to try to raise some bucks ... that was during the sixties and things were hot. He spoke to me briefly, at that particular point.")

The Pryors came into contact with the Catholic church through "a lady who supposedly was [Richard's] grandmother.* She had cancer and I did a lot of ministering with her," Father Henseler said, "and ultimately received her into the Church. I had that funeral in St. Patrick's at the Parish. I believe that was the reason for the door opening. And it was not too long, within a matter of months, that the father, LeRoy, died. The family came to me because I'd done the other funeral, and they asked if they might have the funeral at St. Patrick's. I was not the pastor, so I had to consult the pastor in charge. It is very unusual that you'd have a non-Catholic funeral in a Catholic church because of the Mass and all ... so, he offered something I'd never seen before, the pastor in charge. He said, 'I don't think this is appropriate, but, if it's to your liking, we would allow you to have the funeral in St. Patrick's gymnasium,' and the family accepted that and the funeral was very well attended. The Church ministered to Richard's family and I think he was deeply appreciative of that. No, they were not Catholic."**

Time was running out for the old neighborhood down near the lake and the railroad tracks. The infamous addresses of the houses of ill repute, run or owned by the Pryor's, were earmarked for urban renewal.*** There is, however, some question about those addresses, variously cited as 313, 317, 324 North Washington Street; 322 was always listed under a name other than Carter, Bryant or Pryor, and 324 did not exist. At 322 there was always a freight company and, toward the end, Continental Bus Lines.

* This was Pryor's stepmother, Viola Anna Hurst Pryor.

** James Alan McPherson wrote in his New York Times Magazine piece (April 27, 1975), "He [Pryor] says his family ran whorehouses. His grandmother, a Creole and a Catholic, was the owner. ... He attended Catholic school, receiving all A's, he says, until the business activity of his family was discovered and he was expelled."

*** Joyce Maynard noted in the New York Times (January 9, 1977) that Pryor has been given to saying that he was raised in a brothel, which is evidently not the case." She does not explain the statement.

By now Thomas and Marie were not only running Pop's Pool Hall at 618 West 6th Avenue, but a tavern at 405 North Washington as well. Young Pryor was already, as his father said, "getting into trouble at school. His mother was always getting notes from school and visiting the teachers. He wasn't mean, but just upset the classes with his funny faces and his comedy."

Pryor attended many Peoria schools, none of them for the retarded, as he has claimed. They included: Irving, Lincoln (where the "State Park" monologues come from), and Blaine Sumner, where he ran into teacher Marguerite Yingst Parker. She remembered him "not as a wisecracking funny kid, but as a perpetually exhausted, sometimes lonely, always likable twelve year old kid who tactfully avoided using any of the profanity that would later help make him a big star and lots of money, too.

"Had he applied himself," she said, "he could have been a very good student. He was a poor black kid in what was then a predominantly white school, who didn't mingle with his classmates on the playground."

Miss Parker and young Pryor reached an agreement that would get him to school on time: She would let him have a few minutes each week to do a routine if he arrived in class promptly. The deal worked. A larger performance area was about to be made available to him, for the old landmarks were everyday being vacated. The North End, with its substandard housing, the cause for "a high social pathology incidence," was to be mostly demolished.

Thirty years ago, the phenomenon of demolishing the poorest sections of towns and cities, where black people almost invariably lived, was called by them not Urban Renewal, but Negro Removal. This may not have been an altogether bad thing, for it disrupted old restrictive housing patterns and made it possible for some people in Peoria—and elsewhere in the nation—to live where they otherwise couldn't.

However, those old restrictive patterns in larger northern urban centers were used by white ethnic groups to consolidate their political power. A dispersed black population, on the other hand, that was just arriving at the point of exercising similar clout, in the end found it had very little. Peoria's South End, where former North Enders moved to, was at the time fairly well integrated. But for Peoria, white flight was in the future.

The North End is the more picturesque of the two sections, being almost flat down beside where the Illinios River widens out into Illinois Lake. There are only a few hundred feet between the water's edge and what remains of North Washington Street, and the Peoria and

Western railroad tracks slice through this space. North Washington Street now ends quietly at the foot of Fayette Street, and is a series of off-ramps facing Hancock and Eaton. Only great, gray concrete supports loom upwards to contain the roadways leading to the Murray Baker Bridge to East Peoria, across the lake, and to Interstate 74, and routes 24, 29 and 88, over which traffic thunders steadily.

The red-brick H. S. Beeney and the white-painted R. E. Commons Equipment buildings, both abandoned, stand like weary guards over the corner Pryor must have known like the back of his hand. Rusted rail sidings lay like dead brown snakes between the weeds, and the half-dirt, half-brick road through Hancock Street evokes an abandoned past. The South End today reflects a more modern kind of abandonment and seems emptier than the crumbled nineteenth century section near the river and rails. There is no hum of traffic; block after block unfolds, inhabited only by weeds and rubble. One or two structures, sometimes lived in, but more often not, occupy an occasional block. Where there are homes, blacks and whites share a common vista of urban desolation. A housing complex for elderly people now takes up one corner of the emptiness; it is called Heartlands and the inhabitants live in comfort, if not elegance. The newest incarnation of Carver Community Center is not far away, but gone is the communal sense of shared experience, good or bad, the old sense of neighborhood that no doubt characterized the center in earlier days, such as when young Richard Pryor met teacher Juliette Whittaker.

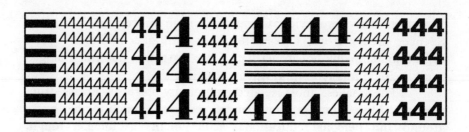

Four

In the mid-1980s, Miss Juliette Whittaker was a small, fast-talking, forceful lady. She was the director of The Learning Tree, which boasted a tough, accelerated—not remedial, she pointed out—private school for gifted pupils. Richard Pryor came to her attention in 1951 when she worked at the Carver Center.

The daughter of a lawyer and a teacher of drama at Bradley University in Peoria, Miss Whittaker had brought a dash of professionalism to Carver, which was the offspring of Peoria's old Negro Community Center. It is she to whom Pryor and nearly everyone else gave credit for having harnessed his energies and seeing behind the clownish facade he had already built up in his eleven years.

The comedian did not forget. Miss Whittaker appeared on television shows with him, and he rarely talked about his beginnings without mentioning her name. Over the years he gave more than eighty scholarships for deserving students to attend The Learning Tree. The Emmy that he gave her was her greatest pride. In addition, Pryor contributed directly to the school and to various other organizations in town as well. With nearly all of his immediate family dead, Miss Whittaker remained the most important link in Pryor's relationship with Peoria. Some of the children who appeared in his film *Bustin' Loose* were Peorians, selected and chaperoned to the West Coast location and back by Miss Whittaker.*

The Carver Community Center was founded in 1922 on Globe Street, which later became a part of Pryor's boyhood turf. When Miss

---

* *Old Peoria buddy Matt Clark also appeared in the film.*

Whittaker and Pryor met, Carver had been moved to Third and Spencer streets. It was a year after Miss Whittaker had arrived, her degree still smoking hot in her hand, in a town that had not changed since the Commission report fifteen years earlier.

The smallest, most isolated community possesses a class structure, and Miss Whittaker commanded respect as much for her background and personal educational achievements as for her tough, take-charge manner with children and adults alike.

"Peoria," she explained, "is a place of paradoxes. The people who succeed here did not come from Peoria; they did not come through the school system. They all came from someplace else." Miss Whittaker came from Iowa.

"Caterpillar still imports its blacks from southern colleges, people for the management and engineering levels. They've got to have blacks, because they have government contracts. The number of black students who finish high school here is very low." She paused and glanced through the one-way glass out into the nursery, just outside her office. "Big drop-out factor here." The Bach violin concerto playing on her radio ended and the news came on. You know that she would have been one of the Peoria blacks who attended the Marian Anderson concert, the Bayard Rustin and Langston Hughes lectures, the exhibit of Edouardo Scott's murals and portraits during the forties, had she been in Peoria then.

There were two gathering places for black youth when Miss Whittaker arrived: Proctor Center, run by the city and chiefly for athletics (it had a gym), and Carver Center, where the emphasis was on clubs, education and theater. It was the latter that drew Pryor to Carver, though he was involved in the sports at Proctor as well.

"He was about eleven, but looked younger because he was such a skinny little boy. And very bright," Miss Whittaker recalled. "We were rehearsing *Rumpelstiltskin* and he was watching. He asked if he could be in the play. I told him we only had one part left, and he said, 'I don't care. I'll take anything. I just want to be in the play.'" Miss Whittaker smiled.

"He took the script home and unbeknownst to anybody, he memorized the entire thing. One day the boy who was playing the part of the king was absent from rehearsal. Richard said, 'Oh, I know that part.' I said read it for us. He got on that throne and started doing the most hilarious business. He had the kids just rolling. So, when the boy who had the part, Joe Harper, came back, the kids would tease him, and say, 'Man, you ought to see the way Richard does it!'"

JOHN A. WILLIAMS

Joe Harper watched the young Pryor perform and agreed he was the one for the king's role. But Pryor insisted that Joe keep it, and he did.

Rumpelstiltskin was the turning point. (In 1978, Pryor included a *Rumpelstiltskin* routine in his monologues for Laff records.) Miss Whittaker's drama class had scripts, costumes, scenery, and music, and the young actors were expected to know their lines during rehearsals. Sometimes she had to go find the actors and escort them to rehearsals.

Pop's Pool Hall, everyone agreed, although listed under Thomas Bryant's name, was really managed by Pryor's grandmother, Marie Carter Pryor Bryant. "From time to time," Miss Whittaker said, "I'd have to go down there and get Richard, because he was racking the balls. When I'd go in, it would get very, very quiet. His Uncle Dickie would say, 'Just take him, take him,' and I would and they'd go back to whatever they were doing.

"Later Richard told me, 'Miss Whittaker, you'd walk in the door and they'd be cussin' and they'd freeze when they saw you.'"

The pool hall denizens respected Miss Whittaker. "There are," she said, apropos of something else, but applicable here, "levels in Peoria." There was an atmosphere where, as Civil Rights leader John Gwynn said, "Negroes who had college degrees isolated themselves." Miss Whittaker maintained no such distance from the rest of the black population.

The area north of town, around Lake Sparland, was not as developed as it now is. Judge Billy Joe McDade recalled that "even now, north of War Memorial Drive, there are only a few houses. There's fishing at Rice Lake, and they still hunt duck there." It seems certain that Pryor went along on hunts with his older relatives, and heard and saw deer during his boyhood. The result: his skit of the deer and the deer hunters in *Live on the Sunset Strip*. It is an exceptionally tender, precise and comical mime-monologue. Hunting was a class thing; those who didn't need the meat or who were not drawn to the outdoors, didn't hunt. They had learned what Pryor had yet to learn.

In school he had the usual boyhood crushes, one of which was with a white girl. "I brought her a scratch board, one of those gray cardboard things you draw on, and then lift up the plastic and the picture's gone? The next day her daddy comes to school and says, 'Don't you dare give my little girl a present.' When I told my father, he just shook his head. Nobody told me about racism, but he knew."

The story illustrates what cannot be really illustrated. A child cannot understand hate, and the manifestations of racism are easier discussed than racism itself. Yet, a child can perceive currents in the air an adult will not. The comedian used to call himself "Sun," because he thought he was the color of the sun. Pryor later recalled that a white teacher told him he was black, a Negro, and he became upset. "I didn't want to be this Negro," he said. (Some Pryor watchers believe this still to be the case.) But something had sunk in and perhaps even been underlined when Pryor was a schoolboy, for Peoria always had its boundaries, its history, its agreements, between black and white, and they were not going to be changed just because of a quiet, skinny, sensitive black kid named Richard Franklin Lennox Thomas Pryor, who was not thinking about color. His "heroes at the movies were the same as anyone else's," he said.

Along came Juliette Whittaker, who swept him up and beyond these considerations far too harsh and heavy for any child to bear without some secret, perhaps irrevocable change. The amount of psychical breaking and hurt racism causes has only been guessed at; we use names for its results that are nothing more than that. The Shadow does not know.

Perhaps Miss Whittaker did.

There is always at least one in every black community, one person who recognizes that any status achieved in the white world may in some superficial sense place him in another class, on another level; but they are also perceptive enough to understand that in America the final determining factor of its class structure is based upon caste. A cop looking for a black bank robber does not care if the alleged criminal is wearing jeans or a suit; a mound of evidence suggests that one black person is interchangeable with another. (Unless he is, of course, Richard Pryor.)

Miss Whittaker's plays whetted Pryor's appetite for heroism. All things revolved around the hero; all things were resolved by him. The hero was the center of attention. "This child," Miss Whittaker said, "had a drive to be; he loved making people laugh, the spotlight, the attention you get. He needed that, the feeling of self-esteem he got. He was somebody."

For kids whose afternoons and evenings were spent in State Park or for kids who at the most spent a weekend in St. Louis or Chicago visiting relatives, Miss Whittaker opened doors on the universe. "They performed in plays that were set all over the world. I wrote the plays. I got them into tights. They *loved* sword fights set to Bizet's music. It was romantic. I offered something through the theater program that Richard wanted."

However much respect Pryor got, his abilities created some envy. Other kids wanted to beat him up, but in order to prevent that, "he cracked them up with jokes. The Clark family pushed people around, but not Richard, because he had them laughing," Miss Whittaker continued.

Fueling Pryor's secret but awesome hunger for attention was television, on which he saw—and imitated—Red Skelton. The young Sammy Davis, Jr., who often appeared with the Will Mastin Trio, became Pryor's target. He was going to be a better performer than Sammy, as he would want to be better than Dick Gregory or Bill Cosby when they came on the scene.

In 1955 "there were restaurants you couldn't eat in or be served," Miss Whittaker recalled. "and no one lived above the Bluff" (a section that overlooks the river). And Pryor remembered that he "used to go to the theaters in Peoria, and if you were black you had to sit upstairs. But I refused. I used to sit downstairs, and they'd throw me out."

The 1954 Supreme Court decision that forbade segregation in schools and places of public accommodation did not much alter attitudes in central and southern Illinois; the Montgomery Bus Boycott of 1955, led by Martin Luther King, Jr., created no waves. Perhaps there were some small ripples in the black neighborhoods of Peoria.

Many white students at Bradley University, a twenty-minute walk from the nearest black community, "came from towns in the state where blacks were not permitted on the streets after sundown. Bradley was not a politically active campus," Nicholas Scoppetta said.

Scoppetta, who lived on the other side of town and never met Pryor, describes a Peoria the comedian never knew. Scoppetta himself grew up in a tough, "disadvantaged" New York neighborhood, was an engineering student at Bradley from 1955 to 1958. A former New York Assistant District Attorney, member of the Knapp Commission and New York City Investigations Commissioner under two administrations, he found Peoria a welcome change after New York and service in the Army.

At the time Scoppetta arrived, Pryor was almost ready to cut loose from Miss Whittaker's talent shows. She began these when the comedian was in his early teens. He was the emcee at first, and did five-minute introductory skits. But after a while, Miss Whittaker "started designing the shows around Richard's acts. He became the premier performer. The kids would come to rehearsals as though they were coming to a performance. The auditorium would be packed with kids waiting for Richard to come on for *rehearsal*."

What happened at Carver was all insular, community stuff; Bradley University students, then numbering about 2,500, didn't know or care about it. There are some small towns in which the college or university becomes the advance guard into reality, but Peoria was not one of them. Its students found the town to be "a nice, clean, bustling" place. It had just won an award as a "Model City," and was experiencing, with urban renewal, a resurgence. Those addresses on North Washington Street were no longer in existence, and when Nicholas Scoppetta arrived, Pryor was in the ninth grade.

The Jefferson Hotel was still a great place; the Pére Marquette and the movie house next to it were places where the Bradley students hung out. They also went to one "great restaurant in the black community—a ribs place." Harold's Club, one of the spots where Pryor later worked, "was a place with music and hookers—the kind of action that'd be beyond most college kids," Scoppetta said. "And there was the Flower Shop, a place to make contact with hookers. Bonnifleck's, around Washington Street, had a big-city atmosphere; some blacks went there and to Sy Maroon's."

Mostly, though, black and white maintained their distances. Blacks only worked in the old mansions and large homes on neat lawns near and beyond Bradley. "It was the wrong part of town," Scoppetta said. "That was the worst you could say about the black neighborhood, but I never heard of any student getting into serious trouble, fights or muggings. That was not the question. You didn't go to the black neighborhood. You just didn't do it."

No stranger to the ugly correlation, which he himself escaped, between environment and behavior, Scoppetta mused, "Pryor can be angry and he's had a lot of early experiences to make him that way."

Still not really interested in school, Pryor, as his father observed, "was beginning to run around with the wrong group." But as far as Miss Whittaker was and still is concerned, she "saw the best of Richard . . . only that child's positive side."

What Pryor was recognizing, and what Scoppetta and to some extent, Miss Whittaker never would see, was the universal humanity in even the most commonplace folk in the black community in Peoria, and Pryor's allegiance to it. Some of his skits are universal: "State Park," "Pimples," "Fartin'," "Have Your Ass Home by Eleven," "Our Gang," "Saturday Night," "Girls," etc. These related experiences are the norm for all boys pushing through puberty—black, white or brown—but draw heavily on the particularities of life in black Peoria. And the characters who people other monologues—Mudbones especially, Grandmother, LeRoy, Jesse, Big Irma (or Big Bertha), Weasel, Officer Torsey (once said to be a captain on the Peoria police force), the winos, cowards, crazies, gays, toughs whose heads were routinely softened by cops' billy clubs—all these, said Miss Whittaker, "are still walking around Peoria."

Like Bill Cosby's characters—Rudy, Nolan, Dumb Donald, Old Weird Harold, Fat Albert, Weasel* and Russell—Pryor's people allowed us a look-in at boyhood peers, heroes, neighborhoods; however, there was not the undercurrent of fear and violence in Cosby's life that we find in Pryor's. That fear and violence lingered longer in the comedian's life than might have been expected. "I'm supposed to be dead by now," he said in 1977. "The cops are supposed to have killed me a long time ago, just on GP (general principles)." That "long time ago" might have begun in Peoria, when his father observed the company he was keeping.

(In the spring of 1983, Stanton, California, police officer Anthony Sperl shot and killed a five-year-old boy who had pointed a toy pistol at him. The boy was alone. Pryor asked permission to attend the funeral and did. The cop was exonerated of criminal wrongdoing, and he retired. In July he was awarded $35,000 workmen's compensation for "psychological damage" related to the shooting. It may be that in that young, violent death, Pryor saw what he believes was one of his escapes from a similar fate.)

The distance between Pryor's neighborhoods and the Bradley University campus could not be measured by any standard yardstick. The farther he was to travel physically and psychologically away from Peoria, the more in fact he would grow closer to it. The gifts, the return visits, the attention he would bring to all its residents, students or not, would indicate that a bond did exist. Perhaps much of it had to do with Miss Whittaker, who, exclusive of his family, asked and demanded nothing more than the pleasure to have known him. There was once a concerted effort on the part of some of the Bradley faculty to confer the honorary degree of Doctor of Humanities on Richard Pryor, but nothing came of it.

When he entered his teens, the family moved to 723 North Goodwin. Pryor was impatient with school, perhaps bored with it. He began to spend less time in classes and more in the streets, where he

_____

* *Pryor also had a "Weasel" character.*

managed to escape the scrutiny of his extended family. He hung out, moved with a gang, came to know firsthand the characters who, full-blown, lusty and often obscene, would leap into prominence in his routines. "Have Your Ass Home by Eleven" must have been a phrase his father grew tired of repeating. Both father and son affirm that Pryor was thrown out of the house where LeRoy lived with Anna. His father said, "That's probably the best thing we ever did for him—make him go out on his own and seek his place in show business."

For among many of Pryor's haunts were the Famous Door, Harold's Club, and Collins' Corner. And he used to stop next door, skim through his neighbor Ray LeRoy's nightclub material, and "ask for advice on how to walk out in front of an audience," according to LeRoy. Some interviewers have quoted Pryor as saying that he was dancing, singing and playing the piano about this time; he had played drums as early as age seven.

Another move settled Anna and LeRoy at 2418 Southwest Adams. Pryor may have simply shifted quarters to his grandmother's. His father and Uncle Dickie had their own business, the Pryor Trucking Company. And young Pryor finally dropped out of school; the age has been reported at fourteen, but was in fact closer to sixteen.*

There is not much in the comedian's boyhood to suggest that it was a life of grinding, unrelenting poverty, in spite of what one of his teachers, Miss Parker, said about his being "a poor black boy in a pre-dominantly white school." White Peorians had a predisposition to think that anyone who was black was poor, because that was almost always the case in their town: the fruits of racism. And some of Pryor's own comments about his early life appear to be designed to elicit sympathy or to play arpeggios on the standard stereotypical opinions held by most white people. The fact is, however, that bartending, waiting tables, owning a beauty shop or a billiard parlor—the alleged owner-ship or management of brothels aside—tended to be ventures of some measurable solidity. In addition, Marie Carter Pryor Bryant was known to be a sharp and shrewd business person. The extended family of the Carters, Bryants and Pryors was probably well enough off, compared to the average black Peorian.

That Pryor did not like school enough to stay there was rather predictable, given some of the family history and the lamentable qual-ity of education observers say existed in Peoria. In and out of the home there was very little encouragement. As Miss Whittaker pointed out,

---

*Who's Who *lists him as a "grad. high sch." Pryor's limited education seems to bother him more than it does his admirers.*

the black people who made it in the city were not residents. The male role models were not the men who had achieved a great deal of education in a formal sense. Over the next couple of years, Pryor maintained himself, when he was not absorbing human nature in all its elements, by working "part-time jobs at the Armour meat-packing plant, truck driving for his father's carting firm, and racking balls in his grandmother's pool hall," the local paper later reported.

Of course, he found time to be with girls, as most boys will. A great deal has already been written—and broadcast—about how young he was when a young woman, who through Pryor's own consideration today remains unnamed, delivered their first child.* Pryor was not that young. He was seventeen instead of the fourteen or fifteen years usually ascribed to him when his first child, Renee Pryor, was born in 1957.

The following exchange, which could not have pleased Pryor's eldest daughter, took place on the air with Barbara Walters in May 1979:

> WALTERS: You were fifteen when your first—
> PRYOR: Fourteen.
> WALTERS: —child was born?
> PRYOR: Yeauh, yeah. Yeauuuh . . .
> WALTERS: How could you? I mean—
> PRYOR: It was fun.
> WALTERS: Was it?
> PRYOR: Oh, man, are you kiddin'? In the garage?
> WALTERS: And then after she was born?

At this point Pryor related that his father had first made love to the girl.

Pryor joined the Army the next year. It must have been somewhat of a relief for him, relief and escape from the unending small-town nightlife that had so attracted him. He undoubtedly perceived its limitations. It was an escape—from his child and its mother; escape from his own mother, stepmother and father; escape from his grandmother and stepgrandfather; from the entire family that extended down to Decatur and back. Joining up was escape from the pressures, from the scrutiny of everyone, but mostly escape from the kind of local stardom that Ray LeRoy enjoyed. Outside of Peoria, no one ever heard of Ray LeRoy. Pryor was hungrier than his neighbor had been, more determined. No doubt, he also sensed that the time had come when, through

---

* *She has married and has at least one more child.*

the accumulation of experiences, that adulthood was closing in on him faster than he wished it to. He was a father. He had been bounced out of the house by his father. There was Illinois Lake on one side of him and the prim, fastidious, monied Peoria on the other. Pryor challenged the squeeze by slipping into a uniform—quite probably with the encouragement of family, for the Army has always been the court of last resort for young men who could not be disciplined in civilian life. And at seventeen, he had grown away from Miss Whittaker, and was in limbo, neither boy nor man, his infant daughter notwithstanding.

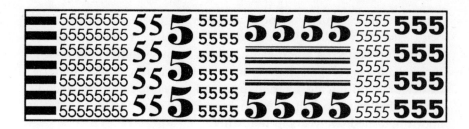

Five

War, whether politics should continue as usual or not (there were frequent demonstrations against the Vietnam War and the politics of Johnson and Nixon), and race were the big issues of the 1960s. By the end of the decade, there were murders of people in high places, and Vietnam had changed from an obscure outpost for U.S. military advisors to the scene of over 50,000 American deaths. And also at the start of the 1960s, race and the law, race and the future—impelled by the 1954 Supreme Court decision outlawing segregated schools and public accommodations, and also the Montgomery bus boycott—grabbed center stage.

Older than America and all the wars it had fought, racism was a shape-altering malignancy that required immediate attention. For a short while it was literally a burning issue from one end of the country to the other, an issue that would compete neck and neck with the Vietnam War—which some people saw as the great racial equalizer, since so many young black men were fighting in it. Then it would be shoved backstage, along with other concerns that had grown up around it or because of it. The women's movement would survive. Demands were made of the society during the 1960s that had never been made before, and the responses came only after extensive upheaval. One of the responses was the white acceptance of the black comedian, whose performances had previously been limited in the main to black audiences in clubs and theaters.

A comedian, as Pryor and his younger contemporary, Eddie Murphy, were to agree, is somehow less threatening than, say, a talented dramatic actor. Few of those emerged during the 1960s. The black exploitation films did not arrive until the final year of the decade, and none produced a talent as durable as Sidney Poitier's; at least no such talent was recognized. No matter how serious a comic's material, he was first and foremost a funnyman and therefore not to be taken literally. That was the drill when Richard Pryor returned home after an undistinguished two years in the Army.

Dick Gregory in 1959 was already the emcee at Robert's Show Club on Chicago's South Side. His Army service had been from 1953-1955. Bill Cosby, after four years in the Navy (1956-1960), was a bartender in Philadelphia who cracked jokes and was on the verge of going into show business. Redd Foxx, approaching forty, was just beginning to get some television spots, his reputation having been made in the black communities where his "blue" recordings had sold in the millions. Flip Wilson was a regular at the Apollo Theatre in Harlem where, Pryor later said, "Them niggers'll eat you up if your shit ain't right." Godfrey Cambridge, winner of a 1961 Obie Award for his performance in Jean Genet's *The Blacks*, was going into comedy, also at the Apollo. Jackie "Moms" Mabley, who'd made her debut thirty-seven years earlier at Connie's Inn in Harlem, was about to do her first great gig in Carnegie Hall, with singer Nancy Wilson and alto-sax man Cannonball Adderley. Slappy White and Nipsey Russell were only months away from spots on "The Tonight Show," hosted by Jack Paar. In the early 1960s, the black comedians all seemed to be bunched up at the starting line, which is always white, like distance runners waiting for their careers to go into high gear.

There were other comedians, of course, and they were sharp departures from previous white funnymen; they bit faster and more savagely with their comedy. Foremost among the standup satirists were Lenny Bruce and Mort Sahl. They rode the crest of the irreverent moods of the young, lunging at the topics of race, war and politics; they established a manner, but they were not the only comedians who shaped these issues into comedy. Dick Gregory did too. Serving as a replacement for a comic at Chicago's Playboy Club, Gregory became an overnight success. His trenchant material consisted of commentary on race, politics and the Army, but he had to contend with the introduction he was usually given at the start of his career—"The Negro Mort Sahl."

With his success Gregory incurred the envy of an older black comedian who was not pleased with his own level of success. Gregory had made *Variety*, and it had said that he was "the first standup comedian of his race to crack the plush intimery circuit, and in such force." That envious comedian recognized America's one-at-a-time program for black success, as Pryor was to recognize it in a couple of years. Watching Cosby at work on television one night, Pryor said, "Goddamn it. This nigger's doin' what I'm fixin' to do. I want to be the only nigger. Ain't room for two niggers."

Bill Cosby was the other black comedian to break out of the pack using material that attracted the young and the hip—the same crowd that liked Gregory, Bruce and Sahl. Unlike much of Gregory's comedy, Cosby's did not touch on race. But when the inevitable, because essentially racist, comparisons were drawn between him and Gregory, Cosby emphasized his nonracial comedy from a perspective that anyone could identify with. Nevertheless, the fact that he was black, and had arrived at the time he had, colored the "colorless" material and helped him along the road to success.

When Pryor was twenty, he was still living within the circumscribed world of Peoria. He had yet to work his way beyond the fifty or seventy dollars a week he was paid at Collins Corners or Harold's Club. The black population had grown to about 8 percent of the population, which was 103,000.

Pryor returned to the familiar. "He worked at Caterpillar for a while," Miss Whittaker said. "That's when he decided that he could no longer put the widget on the digit. That was not what he wanted to do. He wanted to perform." He worked with his father and uncle in the carting business; it was a living, but not the one he thirsted for. And he had a child to help support; by 1961 it was children to support. The second child was by another woman. There was no marriage this time, either. The child was named after his father; Pryor's first marriage would be sixteen years away. His life was in limbo, neither a coming nor a going. His main occupation seemed to be watching the other black comedians who were appearing sporadically on the tube. He realized that Peoria simply was not the place where one got discovered. That realization was step one; step two was shaking loose from the family which, with LeRoy and Uncle Dick, was starting to move into the small construction business.

Of course, it is arguable whether or not any kind of career is worth the hardship caused to two children in the absence of their father. Cosby and Gregory would have several children, but wouldn't run out on them, and Gregory came from a family even more fractured than Pryor's. In any event, Pryor was not the first star-struck kid, nor would he be the last, to run to fame leaving behind those who would claim, for a time, anyway, that he had instead run away from responsibility.

Stories of "the way up" in show business are legendary. The route is often a series of nightmares and occasional glimpses of light. For black performers it has long been a segregated route. Only relatively recently have young black comedians, some for the first time, found themselves before all-white or mixed audiences. One of the stops on Pryor's path was St. Louis, which had produced Redd Foxx and Dick Gregory. The Faust Club there, and other rooms in East St. Louis, Chicago, Windsor, Buffalo and the rest in that class, were tough. They were a proving ground, if not a killing floor. If some material didn't work in Youngstown, maybe it would play in Buffalo. Why didn't they laugh in Cleveland? Why did they fall out at the Shalimar? In that season Pryor learned to handle hecklers, pick up timing, measure his audiences. He also learned that in show business, as in other endeavors, one hand—so to speak—washes the other: "Like you'd suck the fire-dancer's pussy in the dressing room, and her next job, she'd try to get you as the emcee. Shit, if I hadn't been able to give head, probably still be in St. Louis, at the Faust Club," Pryor said in his "Mafia Club" monologue.

Much of Pryor's material was topical. He latched on to Edward R. Murrow's TV show, "See It Now," and worked up a routine:

"This is my table. This is my chair. You've seen my table, and you've seen my chair. Now, this is the wallpaper. . . . " Reduced to monologue without pictures, Murrow's show became a parody in Pryor's hands, the reverse of watching a picture without sound.

Army service also provided comedians with materials. Pryor often zeroed in on the commissioned and noncommissioned officers. In these monologues, the commissioned officers invariably had effeminate voices. Pryor did a monologue about cadence calls—he called them—and the inability of soldiers to understand the commands they were intended to convey. In time the thrust of the routine changed to become an example of the way soldiers swing when a black guy calls cadence, and how nobody can swing when a white Middle American twangs it out. Pryor would have a few monologues develop as he matured, would add more follow through, as in a sport, to bring the monologues into the time in which he was relating them.

His early routines were done without Black English; he wasn't into "the black thing" yet. The Mafia routines, however, have come a long way with Pryor. Even before it attained yet another level of the legendary through Mario Puzo's novel and Francis Coppola's subsequent film, *The Godfather*, Pryor had Mafia material in his repertoire. Someone arranges to have Ho Chi Minh killed. The hit man says, "Chief, it shall be done." There is a long pause, and the hit man asks, "What's a Ho Chi Minh?"

Less fascinating, less terrifying than the Mafia monologues the comedian would do twenty years later, the lines and time were pure Cosby. Some of Pryor's one-liners, however, possessed more smoke than fire, for example:

"You know how to give Mao Tse-tung artificial respiration?"

"No."

"Good!"

Pryor's early style sometimes resembled that of Slappy White or Nipsey Russell who, among other black comedians, must have been wondering how Gregory and Cosby were managing to sprint past them. Gregory's success, though, would help them, and Pryor, not unaware of him, from time to time slipped into his style, too: "Peoria's a model city, you know. [*pause*] That means they've got the Negroes under control."

Gregory must've smiled with pleasure; he was riding high with his sleepy eyes, ashtray and pack of Tarryton cigarettes. Most of all he loved the response he got after he was introduced as "The Negro Mort Sahl." He'd snap back: "In the Congo they call Mort Sahl the white Dick Gregory."

The Red Skelton style Pryor had admired and imitated in grade school was all but dead. Skelton's comedy was, all in all, too gentle for the times, not right for Pryor. For if Peoria had served him a strange psychological stew, the world was more than willing to give him a second and bigger helping. Pryor jettisoned all the white comedians; he and they shared few experiences. Pryor even dismissed some of the black comedians in order to concentrate on front runners Gregory and Cosby. Lurking nearby was Redd Foxx, but he wasn't getting the big play. No, it was Greg and Cos, Cos and Greg.

Pryor moved on, impressing the writers who were beginning to interview him with his soft-spoken, gentle manner. Some noted a "mystical" quality about him. There was something not quite shy about Pryor. And he was courteous. The explosions that were to characterize periods of his life would be unexpected because of that apparent, gentle exterior. A woman entertainer in Pittsburgh may have been one of the first to experience this unexpectedly violent side of his character, as far as the public record reveals. In an interview, Pryor said he "really assaulted . . . really battered" her. If she was surprised, so was Pryor. A judge handed him time for assault and he did thirty-five days before he could raise the money for the fine to get out. He moved on to New York, where he worked the Cafe Wha?, The Improv, The Living Room, the Bitter End, Café Au Go Go, crossing paths with people like George Carlin, Gloria Lynn, David Steinberg, Denise Darcel and others. New York then did not divide its title as entertainment capital of the world with Hollywood as much as it does now, so it was always possible that in the audience there might be sitting a person worrying about filling a bill on a show, the stage, a club or television. Certainly there had to be some interest in someone who was not unlike Bill Cosby, as *Variety* noted when Pryor played The Living Room: There was "much in Richard Pryor's routine to remind us of Bill Cosby."

As in the best of fairy tales, there was a person in the audience who was casually looking the talent over. He was Rudy Vallee, and it is to him that Pryor gave credit for the second boost to his career. Vallee preceded even Pryor's father's generation; he was the original crooner with a megaphone, with roots in Island Pond, Maine, and Yale University. Vallee was of stage, screen, radio and now television fame. Their lives—Vallee's and Pryor's—could not have been more different, yet there he was, Richie Pryor, being booked on Vallee's television show, "On Broadway Tonight," even though the producer, Irving Mansfield, thought he was "way out."

It was, yes, 1964, and white America was trying to play catch-up on the issue of civil rights, being temporarily goaded by guilt. Perhaps media executives had the feeling that if you put enough black folk on television, funny people particularly, maybe whites would start to think that everything was okay, after all, in spite of Birmingham police chief Bull Connor's image on TV news. Didn't Nipsey Russell have a near-permanent spot on "Car 54, Where Are You?"

On August 31, 1964, Richard Pryor made his national television debut in "On Broadway Tonight." Of course, one television appearance does not usually a success make, but for Pryor it was the beginning of the yellow-brick road; the appearance symbolized success, acclaim, achievement, triumph—all of which Pryor himself would later define as "a sham—a trick that deludes." He also came to say of television that

"Basic truths are not told on TV . . . it's a bunch of bullshit, it's evil. The top-rated shows are for retarded people, but it could be such an informative medium. One week of truth on TV could just straighten out everything."

Pryor was a processed-haired (or conked) kid back then. Nearly all the black showfolk had conks. They set you in a special category. Didn't Sammy Davis, Jr., have one? Pryor was a stringbean with the energy of a live wire. Adolescence hovered about him. He had no mustache, no beard. And he was a good-looking kid who moved athletically. Could "eye-fuck" well. Women glanced at him—and then looked again. They wanted to protect and mother this shy, vulnerable, young-looking man. He hadn't yet mastered that smile that was mostly teeth, and that bold, open, I'm-looking-you-directly-in-the-eye look. Light shimmered off his "whitefolks" hair. TV and Richie Pryor—it was a match. Television exuded either youth or graceful aging, as with people like Robert Young and Lorne Greene. Television had selected Cosby over Gregory because Cos looked better, was more straightforward with that strong jawline and closecut hair with the neat little part on the left side, that cool voice.

New to it all, Pryor was grateful. He said to his audiences, "Thank you very much! I'—I'm really glad to be here in—show business, 'cause it's exciting, you know. . . . " He was happy. It was exciting. However, it was the time when make-believe revolutions bounced like scattershot off the TV news, TV dramas, and Superfly-style films, the time when the first real rebellion would burst out in New York, along the spine of Harlem, Seventh Avenue, now renamed Adam Clayton Powell, Jr. Boulevard.

Being on the tube in guest spots certainly gave Pryor more money than the few dollars he earned in the hip little pocket clubs in Greenwich Village; they paid less than chump change. One night, accompanied by a girlfriend, he doubled back to the Improv to talk to the owner, Budd Friedman, about his low wages. Pryor accused Friedman of taking advantage of him because he was black. Friedman, upset, angrily denied the charge, and when he got home he told his wife about the confrontation. She said, "You should have told him that you take advantage of all performers, regardless of race, color or creed." Friedman and Pryor remain friends.

Having tasted the tube, Pryor recognized, if only subconsciously, that if it provided exposure, it also demanded the new, the different, the unusual (but not *too* new, not *too* different, not *too* unusual). He began poking around inside himself. Maybe the zeitgeist behind the

"Tell it like it is" had something to do with the search for himself. But he must have sensed, being no fool at all, that the same forces controlling the airwaves over which the daily obscenities of war, killing, murder and corruption were viewed by millions would censor *him*, if he did tell it like it was. The others out there, well, if they were telling it, they were telling it too gently; there was a lot of bad stuff going down out there.

Racial injustice was undoubtedly on Cosby's mind, too, but he dealt with it in private, not in his routines. "Dick Gregory," he said in an interview in 1970, "was like the big number-one cat, and all the publicity written about me had to do with my being his shadow. I'm still working basically the same way I did when I was at the Gaslight. I couldn't see anyway that I could be similar to Dick. At the beginning, he was one-lining. My thing was stories, long stories and vignettes. I decided to take out the racial angles. That was a conscious decision. It would've been very difficult to pass Dick, anyway. And it wasn't the thing you wanted to do."

Ironies abounded. For, while Cosby was commandeering the attention that would lead to his co-starring role with Robert Culp in the "I Spy" TV series (1965-1968), and Pryor was scrambling and scuffling for new toeholds that would take him to the top, "the big number one" was perilously close to tossing it all away. Gregory was spending as much time as possible with the soldiers and leaders of the civil rights movement. A close friend asked why he was so involved with Southern Christian Leadership Conference (SCLC) and Martin Luther King, Jr., why he was canceling club dates in order to meet with the Student Nonviolent Coordinating Committee, why he was turning down offers to appear on TV in order to safeguard James Meredith when he traveled away from the University of Mississippi. Gregory answered in a classic but seldom remembered line, "They didn't laugh Hitler out of existence, did they?"

In 1966, seventeen years before Harold Washington, Gregory ran unsuccessfully for mayor of Chicago, and in 1968, with attorney Mark Lane, he ran, again way out of the running, for president on the Peace and Freedom Party ticket—eleven years before Shirley Chisholm, fifteen years before Jesse Jackson. Gregory pretty much left center stage to Cosby and to a Richard Pryor who was still in the shadows and in imminent danger of becoming what Cosby once was thought to be in relation to Gregory. "Yeah," Pryor said. "I used to do Cosby's material, and it was unnatural." Maybe. When Cosby was

JOHN A. WILLIAMS

doing "Noah," Pryor was doing "Adam and Eve." When Cosby was doing "Medic!" Pryor was doing "The Movies," or as it is sometimes called, "Fantasy Films." Both monologues cast the narrator in the service, Cosby in the Navy as a corpsman and Pryor as a grunt in the Army. In both there is an invasion; both comedians made tropical bird sounds; both skits were extremely irreverent monologues about patriotism and war; both effectively used mike sound to set the scene. Pryor aped Cosby's phrasing and timing.

The "borrowing" was not unique to black comedians. Bob Hope spawned many imitators, and so had "Fat Jack" E. Leonard, most prominently Don Rickles. In the early days of comedy, whites with burned cork had borrowed from blacks, and then blacks, mimicking dances like the Cakewalk, imitated whites who had imitated them, and 'round and 'round it went. Pryor borrowed from Cosby not only the techniques of the trade but "The Family," "The Gang" concept, that cast of characters that was to become so familiar to Pryor fans ("Do Mudbones, Richie!"). Flip Wilson, for whom Pryor would write in the 1970s and on whose TV show he would appear in sketches in his Peoria pool-hall persona, had observed that "the comedians who have done characters have had the longevity. Gleason, Skelton had characters to help them carry the weight on TV." And, yes, it was because of television that Pryor was on the verge of one kind of success. He hated TV, but he tolerated it because he understood what a powerful medium it was. It could be used, however; if you were clever enough, you could use it. (Almost twenty years later, Cecil Brown, novelist, friend and scriptwriter, would have a character say in *Days Without Weather*, a novel of black comedians in Hollywood: "For them the stage is only a way of making it on the 'Tonight' show, and the 'Tonight' show is only a way of making it on some sit-com, and the sit-com is only a way of making a couple of hundred grand a year, which is a feasible plan. But me?" says the character Billy Badman, who is modeled on Pryor, "Fuck, I couldn't even dream that way, those are white dreams." For most of the colored people in America, not to mention the world, the dreams had been colored white; their own more ancient and perhaps more viable dreams had been cast aside throughout more than five hundred years of oppression and exploitation.

Even so, television's gossamer dream obscured the history of racism with the showcasing of a few well-chosen black stars: Diahann Carroll as a nurse ("Julia," 1968-1971) opposite Lloyd Nolan, Cicely Tyson in "East Side/West Side," with George C. Scott (1963-1964). Perhaps even more heartening to black actors and writers were the rumors: of Cos being considered for a series, of Greg doing a movie, and wasn't "N.Y.P.D."'s Robert Hooks hot after doing LeRoi Jones' play, *Dutchman*?

By 1966, Sidney Fields reported in the New York *Daily News* that Pryor had been "all over TV, a Merv Griffin guest twenty-six times. . . ." *Current Biography* of February 1976 noted that Pryor's appearance on the Vallee show was followed by one on the "Kraft Summer Music Hall" and "A booking on 'The Ed Sullivan Show' was followed by a quick succession of other television spots . . . Johnny Carson, and other programs, which led in turn to $3,000-a-week engagements in Las Vegas."

Pryor had been into his now-famous street comedy—not steadily, but now and again—for about two years. It didn't start after the celebrated "crisis" he had in Las Vegas, it began before. Joan Thornell, a writer-filmmaker, recalled seeing him in 1965: "I saw him on this afternoon talk show, and I was really taken with his presence, his humor and his appearance. He was a striking-looking person. He had a way of using his body when talking. He was having difficulties on the show. They were bleeping and bleeping him, but he was dauntless; he just kept doing what he was doing, and I thought 'Go 'head on.'"

The rumors were growing in 1965, the year after Slappy White because the first black performer in the Playboy Club in New Orleans, that Pryor was difficult, troubled, and perhaps even dangerous; there was talk of dope use, heavy boozing and abusing women. But he was still young blood, new blood, and television needed him as much as he needed it. So he missed a date once in awhile, even missed Ed Sullivan's show; hell, in show business a little eccentricity was admired. Good for the underground publicity mill. And who would not want to watch talk shows where Pryor would be *bleeped!* all afternoon?

The bleeping did no harm to his career through most of 1966, when he returned home in October to visit his family. The *Peoria-Journal Star* carried these captions:

FIRST MOVIE ROLE JUST ENDED
YOUNG TV COMIC RICHARD PRYOR VISITING FAMILY HERE

The visit was sort of a triumphal return. The film just finished was *The Busy Body*, a comedy with Sid Caesar, George Jessel, Dom DeLuise, Godfrey Cambridge and Jan Murray. It was released in 1967. Pryor confided to *Peoria-Journal Star* writer Jean Budd that he was "working hard to get the opening to be [in] Peoria."

His father and stepmother then lived at 1319 Millman Street. The interview was notable because one part of it strongly implies that the comedian was using the materials that would later make him famous, at least four to five years before 1970 when it is widely believed he began to use the monologues based on his Peoria experiences.

"I have a lot of people to thank for these funny bits," he told Budd. "My grandma, the boss of the whole family, has lots of material there. I've got a thirteen-year-old cousin, Denise, who they say is just like me.* My uncle, Richard, and my grandpa, Tommy Bryant—what they do gives me material. It took me a few years to accomplish this, but now I can find it and can write about it."

In the same interview he put Miss Whittaker into the record: "It all began right here at Carver Community Center and with Miss Juliette Whittaker."

Pryor had brought to the interview a cat he'd bought for twenty-five cents in New York. If today that seems to have been done for effect, the way Eartha Kitt's leopard cubs were used for publicity, Pryor's contemporary monologues indicated that he was an astute student of animal behavior. He owned malamutes and a Samoyed, among other pets. He may have liked animals, but he wasn't crazy about flying: "I don't dig that flying," he said. Fifteen years later, however, he would own and fly a plane. How'd he like show business? Acting especially? It wasn't as easy as he'd thought, but it was a good business "because you don't have to be flying around all the time."

The comedian's relatives were pleased with his success, and "the thrill of our son making it good tugged at our hearts and brought a tear or two," LeRoy Pryor said.

But what did Pryor want most of all?

"To get married," he told the reporter, "live in a house, have kids; enjoy life—not have to work ever—anymore—at any thing, shape, form or fashion."

Bill Cosby, Pryor said, along with Danny Thomas and Bob Hope, was one of his favorite comedians. Lenny Bruce "was the brightest of them all." It was Cosby, though, behind whom Pryor hid the most. Cosby-style was "safe" and good for bookings. Pryor must have resented needing Cosby so much, and there were times when the resentment showed: "Bill Cosby," he said, "is the only pure comedian around. His material is completely nonracial, nonpolitical and, if you will pardon the expression, never off-color." More frequently, however,

---

* Denise Pryor was sometimes listed as a production assistant on Pryor's films.

Pryor shrugged off Cosby's influence, and Cosby remembered one night when he did: "I was in the audience when Richard took on a whole new persona—his own. Richard killed the Bill Cosby in his act, made people hate it. Then he worked on them, doing pure Pryor, and it was the most astonishing metamorphoses I have ever seen. He was magnificent."

Perhaps the folk in Peoria, which Pryor left for California, had always known how swiftly he could change, but other people were still to discover how suddenly the comedian could switch from one character to another, one mood to another, and become quite something, quite somebody, other than who he'd been only seconds before. Some people were apprehensive.

Just a few years later, Joan Thornell caught Pryor at the Cellar Door in Washington, D.C. "He did a series of sketches that culminated in a portrayal of Nixon as the devil. When he did that, the lights went red, and he got into it as an actor would get into a role. He out-Laurenced Olivier. The transformation visually was something, and he was right on it." Thornell was with a friend, a psychiatrist who, declining to join a party after Pryor's last show said: "That man is so disturbed that he frightens me. He's extremely troubled. I fear for him. I fear for his safety. He doesn't have any personal defenses. These have left him. He's very interesting, but very frightening."

Writer James Alan McPherson also observed the transformation: "Suddenly the face releases its age; the puckered lips move outward revealing strong teeth, and Richard Pryor permits his real self to appear." Other observers described Pryor as "one of show business's most volatile personalities," or likened getting emotionally close to him as not being far from a viper. Not many people were put off, however. His antics, whether or not indicative of deep problems, made good copy. And after all, a fighter who showed some minor signs of being punch drunk was never so labeled while he could still make a buck for his managers or while he himself insisted that he was okay.

Six

Nineteen sixty-seven was the year that Al Freeman, Jr., got a role originally slated for Pryor (he said) in *Castle Keep*, with Burt Lancaster. "The Big Number One," Dick Gregory, had paused in his dartings and dashings long enough to do a film, *Sweet Love, Bitter*, playing a Charlie Parker-type character with Don Murray, Diane Varsi and Bob Hooks. "We got the script in his [Gregory's] hands four times," the producer of the film said, "but it appeared that Gregory never knew it existed, between his managers and his bookers."

Copies of the script were also sent to Cosby, but he, too, never got them; they never seemed to get beyond his managers. Cos was busy anyway with the "I Spy" series, and no one thought of sending the script to Richard Pryor. The producers had never heard of him. Everyone had heard of Cosby, who was, one club owner is said to have told Pryor, "the kind of colored guy we'd like to have over to the house." Not anyone like Pryor. If this attitude mattered, Pryor didn't always let it show. For in something under four years he had moved swiftly from being the tolerated, barely noticed local entertainer in Peoria, where he couldn't buy a headline, to some national prominence. Life was sort of cool with the TV spots and the club dates paying better. He was being more and more accepted by other performers *as* a performer, not an upstart. (It has been reported that some of the black entertainers who raised money for civil rights were visited by the FBI. The agents wanted to know who was giving money to the Black Panthers.) Everybody was helping the Reverend Martin Luther King, Jr., but no one was helping the Panthers. So they said.

That was the time when Redd Foxx said that white people better get off black people and keep an eye on the Chinese (who had tested their first nuclear weapons), "because, when the Chinese dropped the bomb, everybody's ass was gonna be black; nobody would be able to tell one color from another." (Pryor would later use a variation of this pop after his 1980 fire: "In a burn ward everybody's the same color—pink.") But in the United States, most white Americans seemed to be more concerned about what black Americans were thinking and doing than about the Chinese nukes. The entertainment industry was skittish, and there were times when it blasted the civil-rights movement, organized or not, calling it racist itself.

But the performers knew of course that the industry was "drafty," prejudiced as hell, and had always been that way. One felt, however, that this just might *be* the time when all things might work. Clearly, among all black entertainers, Sidney Poitier—not to demean one bit of his enormous talent, which the industry never really acknowledged—was cast as the HNIC (Head Nigger in Charge). Fully one-half of all the films Poitier made up to 1984 as an actor were produced during the period from 1960 to 1969, after which he directed as well as acted.

There had been great concern about the scuffling and scrambling for the top spot among the comedians, too, Cosby said. "But if number one is really cool, like Dick was, he'd go around and talk to club owners, say, 'There's a cat over at so-and-so,' and then the club owners themselves began to take care of business. When Dick heard me, he went and talked to different club owners about me, so I did the same thing in turn when I played someplace."

Word of mouth is the traditional method for discovering talent, exposing it, among show people. It skirts the vested interests of the publicity flacks and critics and reviewers.

"In the sixties, "angry" or "militant" became the adjectives that most often preceded "Negro" or "black." For most of his career, Pryor was considered "angry," which is not unusual when a black person speaks the truth. Dick Gregory was always applauded for keeping his "anger" within bounds; Cosby was applauded because he rarely even discussed the situation that gave rise to the emotion at all. From time to time Pryor brought it right down front—though he was equally capable of satirizing those who didn't play for keeps, those who were jiving about the whole racial climate, as it were; were using it, not for all, but for self. Black entertainers, like other black people in America, still have reason to feel—well—*hostile*. In commenting on Redd Foxx, *TV Guide*'s Hollywood bureau chief Dwight Whitney made an observation relevant to understanding the attitudes of many other black performers: "Anyone who feels as deeply and gets as angry as Redd Foxx does, you don't have any [inteviewing] problems with. And Redd is an angry man. I mean he really hates whitey. He may make jokes about it, but he's still making whitey pay for all the indignities he suffered in those two-bit nightclubs where he had to dress in the toilet." How simply Whitney stated the problem. All have suffered more than mere indignities, humiliation, abuse; racism encompasses far more because, unlike an indignity, it is forever in the American experience. It never quits. "Below scale" is the middle name of all too many a black performer who, struggling from plateau to plateau, finds on each that he has escaped nothing—just as Pryor found, even though he's said, in order to make the pain more bearable, "Kiss my rich, black, happy ass!"

In a *Playboy* article, William Brashler characterized the comedian as being "a man torn between his resentment of being black—and what it means to be black in this country—and his desire to be big, the biggest in a white-oriented, white-run industry." This was, of course, Brashler's opinion; it was what *he* thought or believed about Pryor. The causes of Pryor's resentment at being black—if he *was* resentful (there were many extraordinary statements and examples to the contrary)—and what it *does* mean to be black, were not presented, though everyone knows. The fact of racism is omitted; polite people do not write of it or speak of it, which means then that it does not exist. But it did. The Committee on Integration of the New York Society for Ethical Culture reported thirty-five years ago that "In a five-hour viewing period, three Negroes are likely to be seen [on television, Pryor's favorite medium then], two for less than a minute."

One could grow resentful, even angry at the cause of such statistics, though they have improved. Over the years, though, Pryor's "anger" or "militance" was not tempered by what is generally considered to be success; they have not been mellowed by money or fame as much as by age and perhaps illness. It is easy to forget how young he was when he first leaned into the curve, racing for the top. Cosby was closest to him in age, being three years older; Foxx was eighteen years older, Flip Wilson seven, and Dick Gregory eight. Forget Nipsey Russell and "Pig Meat" Markham; they were of a previous generation. There must have been things a kid in his mid-twenties—a black kid from Peoria, not St. Louis or Philadelphia or New York—simply could not handle, like not comprehending why *his* material could not always be done in certain clubs and certainly not on television. Coupled with whatever problems were packed in his luggage when he left Peoria, it was almost predictable that there would be explosions.

Also, beside people like Dick Gregory, who'd attended college, and Bill Cosby, who was a college graduate, there were times when Pryor must have felt inadequate.

In 1967, changes reflecting civil conflict shook the country. The hippies joined the swelling crusade against the Vietnam War. Representative Adam Clayton Powell, Jr., was denied his seat in Congress because of a contempt of court citation and "deceptive" practices in arranging vacations with a staff member. The year before, the Associated Press revealed that at least fifty other Congressmen had engaged in the deceptive practice of nepotism by hiring their relatives at public expense. "Keep the faith, baby" Powell was denied his seat more for his exercise of power as Chairman of the Education and Labor Committee than for sunning in Bimini with a staff member. That was the opinion of most Afro-Americans, and they boiled. Stokely Carmichael (not yet Kwame Toure) was on the stump, and rebellions followed him across black college campuses in the South. The police responded murderously at Jackson State and Texas Southern, and black people boiled. The World Heavyweight Boxing Champion, Selective Service number 15-47-42-127, refused to take the traditional step forward into induction. "Them Viet Congs ain't done nothin' to me," Muhammad Ali said, and black people cheered. Major Robert Lawrence, who'd studied at Bradley in Pryor's hometown, was selected to be the first black astronaut. (He never made it. He died in a plane crash.) Thurgood Marshall became the first black man appointed to the U.S. Supreme Court, and Richard Hatcher became the mayor of Gary, Indiana, as Carl Stokes became the mayor of Cleveland, Ohio. Claude Barnett, founder of the Associated Negro Press, died at seventy-seven; John "Sheets of Sound" Coltrane died at forty; Langston Hughes, prolific and much-loved writer, died at sixty-five. Other black people were dying, too, even as James Meredith returned to complete the march he'd begun the year before when he'd been shot and wounded. In a hundred American cities black rebellions broke out, rambled through flaming buildings, and shattered shop windows, and many of the rebellious died, some by accident—but in Detroit and Newark particularly, it was charged and claimed, stated and restated, to be by design. It was a hard time to be funny. Richard

Pryor was boiling, too—and not only because of what was going on in the country. His own life was in turmoil.

He was hauled into court in Los Angeles in July by Maxine Silverman and charged with failure to help support the child that had been born to them April 24, 1967. They had lived, she claimed, as man and wife from February through March. Silverman told the court that Pryor went to her house and removed the stereo, tape deck, couch and other items. In addition, he borrowed $5,000 from her which he had not repaid. Out of work at the time, Silverman, a legal secretary, was asking expenses amounting to $575 a month. The Silverman-Pryor case was not resolved at that time. Pryor was busy, moving from club to club in city after city, until in September he arrived in Las Vegas at the Aladdin Hotel.

Godfrey Cambridge topped the bill there just before Pryor arrived. The Wednesday, September 20, edition of *Variety* listed Pryor coming into the Aladdin in the number-two spot on the bill behind Pat Collins; the Brazilia Jazz Review rounded it out.

The Richard Pryor "breakdown" in Las Vegas has become a legend, a legend that has the comedian reaching a watershed in his career; it says that at this point he rejected the pap comedy he was doing to please white audiences; that it was then and there, in the Aladdin Hotel, that he chucked the routines of the past and walked off the stage in mid-performance, after which he went into "exile," or woodshedded, or was blackballed from the clubs. When he came back, he came back smoking, a new, dynamic, outrageous Richard Pryor. So the legend goes, so it is repeated, although the year when this metamorphosis is said to have happened varies from 1969, 1970 and 1971.

It is evident, however, that Pryor was often doing his thing, had been rapping "street" for at least two and perhaps three years—picking his time and spot, of course—before the Las Vegas "rebirth." The comedian may have been in performance before the September 20, 1967 *Variety* came out. Indeed, the writer on the publication who signed his Vegas pieces "WILL" said that Jim Seagraves was the PR man at the Aladdin then, and "Dick Kanellis booked him into the club." "WILL" stated with certainty that "Pryor opened and closed" at the Aladdin on Friday September 15, 1967. Nevertheless, *Variety* continued to list Collins, Pryor, and the Brasilia Jazz Review until October 4, when they were all replaced by singer Billy Eckstine and comedian Herkie Styles. Harry Belafonte was playing Caesar's Palace;

the Mills Brothers were at the Fremont, and Nancy Wilson was at the Sahara. Bill Cosby, who is not publicly associated with Pryor's debacle, was not listed as being anywhere in town on the fifteenth—but he does figure in the untold story of what actually happened. On the basis of "WILL"'s information and Bill Cosby's version of the story as related by author Claude Brown, September 15, 1967, would seem to be the most accurate dating of this incident. However, as a result of interviews that Richard Pryor has given to journalists, different versions of this story have emerged, occurring variously through the years 1967-1971. A sampling follows:

From Mark Jacobson, *New West*, August 30, 1976:

> It was an evening in 1970 when Pryor—then thirty—was telling jokes at the Aladdin Hotel in Las Vegas. Richard was doing a typical show for him in those days: fairy-tale parodies, army jokes, talk-show routines. It was the way Richard had worked since coming out of Peoria in the early sixties except that he had dropped his second-rate Sammy Davis, Jr., impression. . . . The craziness built inside of him until that night at the Aladdin when Richard blew it, or so it seemed. What happened is the pitch of Pryor legend, a great Richard story, better because it's true. Someday after Pryor becomes a major movie star, someone will paint it as part of a series entitled "Showbiz Nightmares." The picture will have Pryor reeling around the stage in his evening clothes, asking himself aloud, "What the fuck am I doing here?" and then walking off in the wrong direction. The tourists, all wearing corsages in the shape of cabbages, will look confused and horrified. The cigar-chomping owners will be screaming, telling Richard he'll never work Vegas again.

From *Current Biography*, February, 1976:

> "It wasn't me," Pryor has said of his early appearances in Las Vegas. "I was a robot. Beep. Good evening, ladies and gentlemen, welcome to the Sands Hotel. Maids here are funny. Beep." When he rebelled against the format forced on him, he was fired by the management of the Aladdin Hotel in Las Vegas in the middle of a seventeen-day engagement in October 1967 on the ground of obscenities he allegedly directed against the audience. . . . Pryor had returned to Las Vegas and was conforming to the dictates of those who, in his words, were trying to help him "be nothin' as best they could" until, one night in 1970, again at the Aladdin, he "went crazy" and not only walked off the stage in mid-act

but walked off the wrong end of the stage. "The panel at that end was like two times smaller than I was," he has recalled, "and the guy's saying, 'No, you can't go through there.' And I'm saying, 'Yeah, I can' . . . and I squeezed through . . . 'cause I wasn't going back across that stage."

"WILL" also said that Pryor played Caesar's Palace in 1968, but *Variety* does not list him in the bills as being there *or* at the Aladdin that year. The comedian is not listed in *Variety*'s bills for 1969, either.

From James Alan McPherson, *The New York Times Magazine*, April 27, 1975:

> In 1970, he [Pryor] says he experienced what might be called a breakdown on the stage of the Aladdin Hotel in Las Vegas. . . . The current characters developing in his head could not "go" . . . restricted as he was to the expectation and tastes of a white nightclub audience. He walked off the wrong end of the stage, leaving Las Vegas and encouraging predictions that he would never again hit the big time.

From William Brashler, *Playboy*, December, 1979:

> "His [Pryor's] walking nervous breakdown culminated in a sudden exit from the stage of the Aladdin Hotel in 1970 in mid-performance. He simply had had it. Even that story carries a typical Pryor embellishment. When telling a *Rolling Stone* writer [David Felton] in 1974 about the incident, Pryor said he walked off the wrong end of the stage and had to squeeze past a panel to get out. (The wrong end of the stage and squeezing past a panel seem to be the only constants in the story which, apparently, had always been told one-on-one, Pryor to interviewer.) In 1977, however, *Newsweek* writer Maureen Orth wrote that not only did he walk offstage, he also stripped and jumped onto a table in the hotel's casino and yelled 'Blackjack!' 'That's a joke I always told,' he says now. 'She must have believed it.'" (See *Craps After Hours*, Laff Records #A146.)

From Steve Allen, *Funny People* (1981) where Pryor gives his accounting of performing in Las Vegas:

> I [Pryor] was on stage doing my comedy act [one night in 1971] when I said to myself, "What am I doing here? I'm not happy—so I'm leaving." So I walked off the stage. The audience sat there for a few minutes after I was gone. I guess they thought I was joking. But I just went out and got in my car and drove back to L.A. . . . After I walked out, I really got

to know the people I was working with. I needed some com-
passion right then, but they were all thinking about themselves. They were saying, "What are *we* going to do? What
about *us*? They weren't concerned about me. I was tired of
that whole atmosphere.

Allen says that "according to witnesses, Pryor's act was not
going over well."

The recapitulation of the birth of the legend goes on, each
somewhat different from the one before. The best possible reconstruction of what happened, according to Claude Brown, among others, is
this: Pryor might have been high and-or undergoing some rapid metamorphoses. There was a special show. (Somehow, Mother's Day enters
into the story, but Mother's Day is not in September.) A group of Very
Special People had invited family members and close friends to the
show—which was specifically for them. Pryor began rambling through
a routine. As Jacobson put it, the audience was "all wearing corsages"
(why corsages unless the show was special?)

Pryor looked confused and horrified. He disrobed. Perhaps he
seized his member and shook it at the audience composed of wives,
mothers, daughters, sweethearts, nieces and husbands, fathers, brothers. . . . The Very Special People became upset, violently upset, murderously angry, and they pounced on Pryor, determined to end his
insane ways once and for all; they pronounced a sentence, and it was
death. He was wrestled offstage or through a panel or off the blackjack
table . . . whatever. Pryor's ass belonged to the Very Special People.

Somehow, this story goes, word got to Cosby, who although
not on any bill, may have been in town anyway. Or perhaps he rushed
to Vegas from Los Angeles. In any case, he *did* show up and passed the
word to other black entertainers in town. The delegation appealed to
the Very Special People for a reversion of sentence; the appeal was
rejected. It was Cos "on his knees, his eyes streaming with crocodile
tears." author Claude Brown related during an interview, whose sum-
mation saved Pryor. Oh, Cosby cried, it is said; oh, man, he pleaded
and cajoled with all the slickness of wit and desperation at his command. "The boy is sick!" he is supposed to have said. "We'll look after
him. *I'll* look after him. He won't do it again. That's a promise." On
and on the scene played, and it turned out to be the best scene Cosby
would ever play; no one else would have been able to do what he did
that day, that night, whenever, at that particular time. Cos's reputation
was bankable. The Very Special People reversed their decision, shoved
the jittering, out-of-it Pryor into Cosby's arms. "Okay," Brown says

they told Cos. "You can have him, but if he crosses the state line again, nobody'll ever see him."

There are those who say that despite the confusion in fixing the date of this incident, Richard Pryor has not played Vegas since, although by late 1983 there was an unconfirmed rumor that a deal had been worked out for the comedian to appear at the MGM Grand Hotel in 1984. He did not.

Pryor is supposed to have quit the entertainment scene after the Las Vegas incident, but from November 9 to 18, he played in Columbus, Ohio, and was paid $3,500. For one performance at Brooklyn College, he got $2,000, and *Cue* said of his act that it was "Sharp without being angry, rooted in his background, but essentially nonracial in character . . . . " and also that his performance was fast and topical."

On November 14, a Los Angeles court ordered Pryor to pay attorney fees for Maxine Silverman amounting to $4,000, and to pay her $300 a month based upon his stated salary of $4,000 a month. But Pryor didn't pay Silverman's attorneys or his own, according to court records, and the court ordered that his earnings be garnisheed. In the meantime, Pryor had done a punch-out on a hotel clerk and had some problem with possession of grass. Court officers were told when they chased down Pryor's paychecks that the comedian hadn't worked in this or that club in ages. But, in fact, Pryor had earned $6,000 for a December 17 appearance on "The Ed Sullivan Show," the records reveal.

But the year wasn't over yet.

Back in the harsh, windswept, riverside flatlands of Peoria, his stepmother, Viola Anna, was dying. She had requested that she be indoctrinated into the Roman Catholic church, and Father Thomas Henseler ministered to her. (Pryor told a reporter that "his mother, a Roman Catholic, died in 1969," but his father's obituary lists her death date as December 31, 1967.) The December date of Mrs. Pryor's death suggests autobiographical connections to the comedian's monologue about the funeral, the cold, and his father's grumbling about how long the service was taking (Richard Pryor—Live in Concert, 1979).

As David Felton and other writers have noticed, Pryor tends to be evasive about the details of his family, and its members and their relationships. Gertrude Thomas Pryor Emanuel seems to have slipped out of his life just as quietly as LeRoy Pryor, Sr., slipped out of Marie Carter Bryant's life. Confusing too is Pryor's knack for interchanging Gertrude with Ann, when convenient. All of this may seem to an observer to be pointless, perhaps more a quirk of the comedian's than anything else, since millions of black people have been victims of or participants in similar situations or worse—and have handled it with far less fancy footwork. It is possible that the desire to be accepted, which is still close to impossible if one is black, may be the cause of the date, name and place confusion. Maybe.

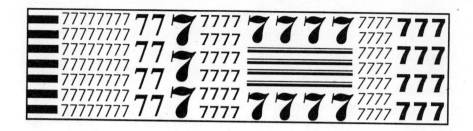

Seven

A few years before he died, John Wayne was asked during a *Playboy* interview if he limited the number of blacks in his films. "Christ, no," he answered. "I've directed two pictures and I gave the blacks their proper position. I had a black slave in *The Alamo* [1960] and I had a correct number of blacks in *The Green Berets* [1968]." One of those blacks was Richard Pryor, who does a fine impression of Wayne, even though, as the comedian put it, "Wayne hated my guts."

Other people, however, seemed to love him madly. He was in another picture, *Wild in the Streets* (1968), and it would later turn out that between 1967 and 1970 he earned a reported quarter of a million dollars.* This included in 1968 a $10,000 week's pay at the brand-new $10 million Playboy Club in Lake Geneva, Wisconsin, seventy-five miles north of Chicago. A representative of the Windy City nightclub called Mr. Kelley's, was there at Pryor's opening night, prepared to offer him $10,000 to $15,000 for a week in Chicago. (The offer was far more than what had been proffered to another black comedian who had done two shows a night and three on the weekend for a seven-day stand. The owners only gave him $750 for the gig—along with a watch the comedian thought worth $60. That comedian had then brought in the biggest crowds ever at Mr. Kelley's. He threw the watch into the Chicago River.) With the civil uprisings after Martin Luther King, Jr.'s murder, the money seemed to be flowing rather loosely, perhaps because of guilt.

---

* *California Labor Commission Hearing reports state that he earned more than $68,000 for 1967 and that from then until 1970 failed to report total earnings of $181,000.*

"My name is Richard Pryor," the comedian said when he opened at Lake Geneva's Playboy Club, "and I come from Peoria. [pause] I'm a Negro. [laughter] I didn't tell that to anyone till I was eight years old. [laughter] They said, 'Oh, we thought you were Polish. [much laughter]."

After one performance, which contained much more, Pryor submitted to an interview with *Peoria Journal Star* associate editor Bill Little, who observed that Pryor's "wife," "a white girl from Los Angeles," was accompanying him. In his article, which appeared Saturday, August 24, 1968, Little criticized Pryor's use of "blue material," calling it "dangerous . . . because it isn't all that funny—although it elicited loud yuks from a handful of people—and it might cost him bookings. And it doesn't take long for a comic to go downhill once his bookings slacken." The comedian, as nearly always now, was mixing his material as a good pitcher will mix his pitches: a little "blue," a little "white." Lake Geneva, after all, was not what anyone would call one of the swinging centers of the country.

Whatever Little's opinion, which seemed peevish, Pryor was on his way to becoming what Cos warned against—wealthy. "In this business they'll let you do almost anything. They just don't want you to become a millionaire, that's all." (In light of Cosby's current status as a millionaire, able to gift a college with $20 million, it is fair to assume that the rules have changed somewhat.)

Just about one month later, on Friday, September 27, Pryor's father died of a heart attack; he was dead on arrival at St. Francis Hospital at 11:35 p.m. The cause of death, according to the coroner's report, was a "left ventricular infarct." But he had had a "coronary insufficiency for several years." Services were held in St. Patrick's gym, and LeRoy was buried in St. Joseph's Cemetery on October 4. Pryor's father's death, like his stepmother's death, cleared the way for the use of new material using family characters. Much of this, however, was not used until the 1970s, which indicated some degree of private pain and long consideration as to whether he should use it at all.

For many people who were not club-goers, their introduction to Pryor's comedy was through his first record, *Richard Pryor*, which was made in 1968 and released, some sources indicate, that same year, while other sources fix the date of release in 1969. The comedian's discography, in any case, is a mess, including bootleg copies being issued by what Jacobson termed "fly-by-night" labels. While statisticians place the number of his recordings at about twenty, a shopper can easily find double that number, what with the monologues juggled back and forth to hell and back, misnamed and no-named. This was a situation that Pryor attempted to rectify in 1976.*

Old Pryor fans now consider the record *Richard Pryor* to be a collector's item. It's a kind of log that marks certain beginnings. His raunchy language, which became almost effusions of endearment, is now unremarkable. "Nigger" is used on some monologues, but in retrospect, one senses that, like an elevator going down while the weights are silently going up, there was a new perception about not using the word that Pryor did not then recognize.

Some of the material is old and "whitebread," and badly recorded. Pryor, echoing the intonations of the Catskill comics, fires off pallid one-liners and limping innuendos. And there are times when he sounds like Redd Foxx—clear-voiced, with almost inflectionless patter. (He became so fond of the Foxx style that Cosby once warned him that he couldn't do "Redd Foxx all his life.") And, of course, there were the Cosby-style routines.

Still, in Pryor's tonality and timing on the record, we can find the origins of some of his later characters. But not until much later did we come upon the comedian who was capable of moving four or even six characters (e.g., *Black Ben the Blacksmith*, 1978) through a skit, laughing all the way, to its logical conclusion without a false step. This kind of versatility was never matched by his performance as a movie actor—only one of which even attempted to utilize this skill. That film, *Which Way Is Up?*, was released in 1977. Pryor was reported as saying that he deserved an Academy Award for playing three roles in the picture: a young activist farm worker, the young man's father, and the Reverend Lennox Thomas (two of Pryor's names). That the film preceded the record argues that the comedian was into multi-monologues for some time earlier.

The enshrining of the black preacher by Pryor began in the earliest records, and what he did with the character on discs, film or videotape is to extend the rascally behavior of the jackleg and the study of his inevitable relationship to the black community that was begun by Zora Neale Hurston during the Harlem Renaissance. She wrote of characters named Uncle Monday, High John de Conqueror, and Daddy Mention. On Pryor's early records we also come upon a prototype of the character Mudbones, who evolves from a skit about a father

* *About a dozen years later Pryor complained that "Laff Record Company did several albums off of one. They take and they package, repackage an album and sell it."*

who is forced to chase hot-blooded boys away from his daughter and is transformed into a belligerent old curmudgeon, brimming over with nuts-and-bolts wisdom about life, the streets, Hollywood, women, the white man, and the world. Mudbones is probably based on Pryor's Grampa Thomas Bryant.

Pryor saw Grampa Tommy—"Pops"—when he visited Peoria on March 8, 1969, at the invitation of the Afro-American-Black People's Federation. He was also midway through another film, *The Young Lawyers* (1969), and ready to begin another, *Carter's Army* (1969). He also told the *Peoria Journal Star* reporter C. Verne Bloch and the photographer, who were rushing through town with him that he had also begun shooting on a third film, *The Trial*, which was being produced by his own company, Black Sun Productions, and "an angel." (This picture, if begun, was not finished.) Within a month of the comedian's visit, the court issued a bench warrant for his arrest, but it was not quashed for still another year.

Pryor went home again not to bury anyone this time, but to help raise funds for community programs. He did a twenty-minute skit in the Carver Center auditorium before Miss Whittaker and an audience of 175. He did the show gratis and paid his own expenses. The reporter asked a peculiarly provincial question about the amount of money Pryor was able to earn, which the comedian did not hesitate to answer. "I can make whatever I want—$300,000, $400,000 a year," he answered, also allowing as how his current take was in the neighborhood of $100,000. The photographer snapped Pryor in his grandmother's pool hall with Mr. and Mrs. Bryant ("Pops" is crouched over the table selecting a shot), Uncle Richard, and the comedian in a Nehru jacket. Another of several photos shows Pryor holding hands with his mother in Methodist Hospital.

A part of the story ran this way:

Arriving shortly before noon at Greater Peoria Airport, the young comic was taken to Methodist Hospital for a visit with his mother, Mrs. Gertrude Emanuel, who is seriously ill. His father and stepmother both died here within the past year.

He popped into his mother's room, gave her a hand mirror for a present, then a big hug and kiss. She had known he was coming and had primped ahead of time awaiting his visit.

Normally soft-spoken despite the roars and shrieks he throws into the mike to accompany the weird gyrations he goes through in his numerous comedy routines, Pryor said, "Hiya, Mom" as he embraced her.

The good that his brief visit did his mother was obvious, and he had confided in an earlier interview that he plans to have her come out to California and live with him in about a month, if possible. . . . *

Pryor also visited his great uncle, Herman Carter; an aunt, Maxine Johnson; sister Sharon; and cousin Denise. "I'm so happy," he said, "so excited. Nobody ever asked me to come here before." And off he rushed by plane back to Chicago, where he'd had a concert at the Hilton the night before. From there he returned to California and "his present wife [who] is expecting their first child in June."

The child, a girl, was named Rain.

Pryor told the reporter that he was "canceling a lot of nightclub work" and "trying to go more and more into the movie business, both with his own company and at other studios." This may help to explain why he seemed to have vanished from the nightclub scene during the second half of 1969 and 1970—although the tax case that came up in 1974 revealed that whatever people thought or believed, he was making a considerable amount of money at this time—not to mention income from motion pictures—before he moved to Berkeley.

By 1969 the San Francisco Bay Area was the hippie capital of the universe. National attention was drawn to student protests in the area in 1960, during the House Un-American Activities hearings, the student rebellions at U.C. Berkeley, and in 1966 by a series of stormy conflicts between students and U.C. Berkeley regents, one of which was over the presence of U.S. Navy recruiting tables in the student union. Across the bay, marching out of Oakland, came the Black Panther Party. Cops and youthful protestors were already eyeball-to-eyeball in the region; now cops and blacks stood nose to nose, ultimately with disastrous results for the Panthers. And at the same time, a drug culture flourished in the Bay Area. LSD may have been the most publicized drug, and grass the most common, but there were others, including cocaine. Pryor said it was the availability of coke that attracted him to Berkeley in 1969. " . . . like I bought Peru, you know? And booze, and in general I wasn't taking care of business." He was not in forced exile. Rather, he may have exiled himself in order to write screenplays. And he may also have been avoiding the Los Angeles courts and the newest responsibility, Rain Pryor, only a few months old, and the wrath of Rain's mother as well. From living in an $80,000 home in Beverly Hills, Pryor moved to a small house renting at $110 a month.

* Pre-performance copy in the Peoria Journal Star (February 25, 1969) included this description of LeRoy Pryor, Jr.: " . . . a former vaudeville comedian. . . "

In Berkeley, Pryor met black writers who walked and talked and acted as though they had digested whole the words of one of their heroes, Chester Himes:

We are a new face in the world's culture.

We are a major influence in the world's civilization.

We are a guiding beacon in American literature tomorrow.

We are the most imitated people in the world . . . .

All young, the writers stood with their feet planted in the streets and their heads in the skies. They were hip, brash, talented and tough. Two were from the Umbra Writers Workshop* that had been formed in the early 1960s in the East Village: David Henderson, with whom Pryor once talked down the night in San Mateo, and Ishmael Reed. Henderson had published *Felix of the Silent Forest* (1967), *De Mayor of Harlem* (1970), and other major works of poetry. Ishmael Reed's *The Free-Lance Pallbearers*, a novel, had come out in 1967; his next book, *Yellow Back Radio Broke-Down* (1967), would have similarities with the 1974 film, *Blazing Saddles*. Claude Brown's *Manchild in the Promised Land* (1965) was known around the world. Cecil "Broadway" Brown had just finished *The Life and Loves of Mr. Jiveass Nigger* (1970) and also a play, *The African Shades*. Reed was editorial director of a new publication *Yardbird Reader*. Associate editors were Cecil Brown, and Al Young, the talented novelist and poet who wrote *Dancing* (1969), which was followed by *Snakes* (1970) and then *The Song Turning Back into Itself* (1971).

Of the four, "Broadway" Brown would have the longest relationship with Pryor, would write for him and publish in 1983 the novel *Days Without Weather* with a Pryor-like character. All were black, deeply black, beyond color or statement; they were committed to producing true portrayals of black life. (Reed and Young—though Young was not part of this "running" group—are still involved in publishing ethnic literature out of Oakland.) They fought editors, publishers, street dudes, superfeminists, book reviewers, white liberals, bad writing, all the establishments, and still found time to write. Most of all, they had a collective sense of humor, irony and satire that often surpassed Pryor's—which sometimes made him feel insecure.

Joan Thornell, an observer and friend, said, "Richard thought about all these people who'd gone to college and written all those

---

* *Other members of the Umbra included Calvin Hernton, whose* Sex and Racism in America *(1965) and* White Papers for White Americans *(1966) created more storm than his poetry and fiction together; poet-playwright Tom Dent; writer-painter Joe Overstreet; poet Ron Snellings/Askia Touré; novelist-essayist Steve Cannon; poet Joe Johnson; and Henry Dumas, who was killed by a cop in New York in 1968 in a case of "mistaken identity." Much of his work has recently been reissued.*

books. He was awed by them, and they were overwhelmed by him. They were very kind to each other; there was no rancor or envy between them; none of that putting-down business. It just wasn't there, that I could see."

It was because a couple of them had been where Pryor said he'd been; they'd put it behind them, but Pryor used his past to try to shock them. Claude Brown had had to be sent away to Wiltwyck School in upstate New York; Reed, originally from Nashville, knew what Williams Street and environs were like in Buffalo, and knew New York City's East Village. The writers admired the member who was the comedian. They recognized what Pryor did not, and that was that in the fight against racism, everybody's skills were needed. They became a group. They probably heard about the incident where The Supremes walked out of the Latin Casino back in Cherry Hill, New Jersey, over a contract dispute. (Pryor recorded *Is It Something I Said?* there in 1975.) Claude Brown joined the group after Broadway Brown called him at three o'clock one morning to tell him that someone wanted to meet him.

Pryor came on the phone and said "Heeey, motherfucker. Is all that shit [in *Manchild*] true?"

Brown said, "Who the fuck is this?"

"You may have heard of me, man," Pryor said. "People think I'm funny, but that shit ain't true. I'm a serious motherfucker."

Pryor went into a routine over the phone and then asked Brown if he could come over. Brown told him no; he had to get some sleep.

They made a crackling group, Big Brown (Cecil) and Little Brown (Claude), Pryor, Reed, and on rare occasions, Henderson, sometimes Young. Cecil, Claude, Ishmael and Pryor constantly tried to out-funny each other; they seemed to affect each other.

Even in Berkeley, where there are so many strange sights, Pryor stood out. Some people out of that past classified him as an "unkempt person," and he often slogged up and down the streets in platformed zoris, a soiled kimono, and a cone-shaped hat. Sometimes he wore an oversized coat. He was working here and there, at Mandrake's, Basin Street West, The Showcase, and The Player's Club for what Claude Brown called "chump change."

On a night before the first show at Basin Street West, Brown and Pryor were in a restaurant preparing to order dinner. "The waitress came over," Brown said. "She was fine, too, man. She leaned over to clean the table and Richie put his hand on her ass just so. I said to myself, uh-oh! This crazy cat's done it now. Get ready to start swinging from the trees, 'cause I know we're in some shit now. The bitch can't believe it. *This nigger's got his hand on her ass!* And ain't moved it! Richard's cool. She turns and looks at him. She still can't believe it. Richard says, 'You drop this?' Nigger got a fifty-dollar bill in his hand. He still don't move his other hand. Bitch just snatched it, man. Leaned back. Guess she wanted to see if she'd dropped another one. Richard just went on after she left like nothin' happened. Said, 'What you want to eat, man?' 'Nothin,' I told him. I just lost my appetite, and I was gettin' the hell out of there."

Whether he was working for chump change or not, Pryor was not hurting for money. It may have been that he needed to be away from the club circuit, that in a way not understood by any of his friends, he was grieving over the deaths of his father and stepmother. He had not, however, brought his natural mother Gertrude out west to live with him. Whatever was riding him—and there seems to have been complete agreement on this—it was leading him to complete self-annihilation. Pryor swung between being completely strung out and going through periods of shimmering sanity. It was Claude Brown's opinion that Pryor was not intentionally funny. "That's just the way he is. And he always looked for somebody to follow."

He followed some of the group into some pretty heavy discussions, and one night in a Berkeley apartment, they were listening to a young black teacher who was working to achieve community control of the schools in the system where she worked. "We're not ever going to progress as a people," she said, "unless we garner our strength, and education is still the place where we have to do it to prepare our young people—" She broke off crying in frustration, and Pryor spoke up. "I promise you that when I make all these movies and get all this money, I'm going to give you what you need to build your own school."

"Richard," she answered, "you're a lying dog. You aren't going to do shit. Like everyone else, you're going to make a little money and run off with these [white] women and we'll never hear from you again."

But Pryor must have remembered this promise, because he made generous contributions over the years to Juliette Whittaker's school, The Learning Tree. "I guess I saw the best of Richard," she said. "And he's always been a man of his word with me." So that evening in Berkeley was not a total bust; in the long run, in the mysterious ways things often happen, it was quite a success.

When he talked of making movies and money, Pryor during this period usually spoke of Cosby. He was going down to L.A. because Cos was going to help him. People looked at each other. Was this another Pryor hyperbole? Had he become like the punch-drunk fighter whose next match was going to make him a contender again? Pryor's friends were not sure all this was going to happen—because they only knew Pryor's version of what had happened at the Aladdin. He went back to L.A. with Cecil and Claude Brown, with Ishmael Reed, and Cos, the reports say, "was very supportive, extremely helpful." Cosby knew, as he said, that "certain places had to be made available to Richie, or else he would die out. You don't want a cat like that to die out." Cosby began working on things for the near future: "The Redd Foxx Club, get him here and there."

Joan Thornell analyzed the influence of Cosby on Pryor this way: "Richard realized that of all the blacks in Hollywood, Cos, whose comedy he *did* respect, was a person who had all his act together. Cos probably blew Richard's mind. He had a family, education, came from North Philly, made good, and still had the stuff all in place."

And Pryor didn't.

Before the Cosby connection started clicking, however, Pryor was turning Berkeley—even Berkeley—on its ear. One day, in his Oriental garb, he borrowed a dime from a friend as they were walking down the street. He was "agitated" that day, vibrating like a taut piano wire. He went to a newspaper rack, dropped in the dime and took out *all* the papers. He wheeled and rushed into the street, strewing papers in the roadway. Cars squealed to a stop around him; drivers cursed at him. But some recognized him and shouted, "Richard Pryor!" Pryor passed out the remaining papers to drivers who'd opened their windows to curse him. To these he announced, "Hi! I am Richard Pryor!"

(The scene—without the newspapers—was repeated in Washington, D.C., after a performance at the Cellar Door. Pryor suddenly veered away from the group he was walking with on the way to a party, and headed out into the middle of Wisconsin Avenue and M Street into the flow of traffic made heavier because it fed from Pennsylvania Avenue. Once again drivers swerved to avoid him, braked suddenly, horns blaring. But Pryor walked in and out of the lines of cars, speaking to the stunned drivers, sometimes pretending to wipe their windshields like a Bowery bum. This was just a year after Bill Little of the *Peoria Journal Star* had watched him abruptly leave the stage of the Playboy Club and start stalking through the audience. Perhaps this penchant for "quick-tripping" reached its pinnacle in Kenya in 1979 when, the comedian says, he got out of his car and approached a pride of lions.*⁾

The Washington and Berkeley "quick-trippings" were laid at the door of dope; Pryor was high. He never denied being high most of the time in Berkeley. He was so strung out that people didn't want him around their kids—and told him so. They often didn't want him to be around *them*, either. But, he came out of it now and again. People felt a great sense of relief when he became a disc jockey/talk-show host on KPFA, playing jazz and doing commentary on the events of the day— civil rights, the student movement, Vietnam. He often dedicated records to his friends.

On another night in another Berkeley apartment, with people sitting or lounging on the floor, Pryor eased into a story about his life which hushed the group and made everyone feel uneasy. The story seemed to explain in part his rush to self-destruct. When he was fifteen or sixteen, the story went, his father, LeRoy, gave him a "white ho" and told him to "work her." He didn't know what to do, Pryor said, and as a result he became the butt of many jokes among the members of his family. He told the story, it was said, with "utmost pain," and everyone present shared that pain. There was some minor skepticism, which Pryor countered by saying, "I'm gonna take you to Peoria where you can see some of this shit. You don't believe this shit."

The comedian said that he first had sex at nine. If you peek through the keyholes of bedrooms, as Pryor said he did, you are quite likely to gain some idea of what's going on. One could envision a damaged libido arising after an encounter with a prostitute if the subject was nine years old; that is possible, yes. And, of course, people have been aware that Pryor's relationships with women appear to be destructive. We are not quite sure, though, who is being destroyed— Pryor or the women. He said of this period that it cost him "$600 a day just to get my dick hard."

Claude Brown remembered that when he and Pryor hung out in the Bay Area, 'We both had a love affair with that 'girl,' and he had the best girl in town—that coke. I was sitting in his dressing room once, and the motherfucker came in wearing this big coat—in the *summer*! He's got the coat on 'cause he's pulling out—looked like a salami—had himself two kilos of coke! And pure! And he was going, 'Want some? Want some?' But I was thinking the shit must be sugar. There ain't that much coke in the whole world."

---

* *Perhaps anticipating the antics of a genius like Pryor, the Kenyans rarely allowed vehicles not driven by wardens to enter game preserves.*

Brown decided to check it out.

Pryor said, "No. Wait a minute. Try some of this first."

"He had some overproof rum, 155 proof or something. I told him no, that I didn't fuck with rum. He said, 'You're gonna *need* it!' I took it—just in case . . . I hit it [the coke] and went right up on the ceiling . . . These dudes used to bring the coke right off the boat, and he'd say, 'How much you got?' And they'd say, 'Why you snort so much, anyway?' And he'd just say again, 'How much you got? Just leave it. I'll see you tomorrow.' Man, I used to have to keep away from him to get some sleep. We'd be going, going, for two or three days."*

When not strung out, Pryor returned to what some people described as a "very, very basic commitment to black people." With Cecil and Claude Brown, and Ishmael Reed, he went down to Santa Barbara to do a benefit on behalf of a victim in a police brutality case. Claude Brown suggested that Pryor *not* do his "Dracula" monologue because the well-tanned, rich and powerful white ladies of the town would not contribute if they were turned off. As Brown put it, "They had oogobs a money. So much that they can tell the oil companies to get that shit [rigs] out [of] the harbor. Conservative." Brown advised Pryor to do his light stuff, but Pryor protested: "You shoulda told me that before. You know I only do one thing, and that's my thing."

He did, before a sell-out crowd. A number of the rich ladies started to go when he hit his stride in "Dracula," but then they stopped, returned to their seats, laughed heartily, and contributed heavily.

Perhaps the most dependable member of the group was Ishmael Reed. Big, broad and often ferocious-looking, he knew more than most where the feces lay. He had energy in abundance and the intelligence to go with it. When he fell out with someone, the sound was heard from coast to coast. Reed had got some Hollywood nibbles on his novel *Yellow Back Radio Broke-Down*, but nothing solid; a lot of sound, but no substance. (To this day there is reported to be a letter of intent to purchase the novel floating around Los Angeles.) When Pryor had worn out or disgusted everyone else, it was Reed who "put himself out for Richard at a time Richard was really on the edge. He did make calls on his behalf, try to set up meetings for him, traveled with him. He recognized Pryor's genius, I think," said a friend, "and did whatever he could to help."

Something happened to that relationship. Today when Reed speaks of Pryor it is with a certain reserve. Reed does not discuss the convoluted meanderings of *Yellow Back*, whose major ideas went

---

*It is now common knowledge that overproof rum figured prominently in Pryor's 1980 burning.

through a series of grinders to become screenplays variously called *Tex-X*, *Black Bart*, and finally *The Black Stranger* (which was a script Pryor wrote for an independent producer), which bears a strong resemblance to Mel Brooks's *Blazing Saddles*. (*Black Bart* was also the name of a 1948 Western starring Dan Duryea.) The connection between Reed and his novel, Hollywood, Pryor as one of the *Saddles* writers, and Brooks & Company, has rarely been made. But one must wonder if the film would have been made had there not first been Reed's novel, which his publishers called "the first American Hoo-Doo Western." In the novel the black cowboy, Loop Garoo Kid, has all the magic (Hoo-Doo); in *Saddles*, it is all transferred to the white cowboy. In *Yellow Back*, the black cowboy is clearly the hero; in *Saddles* he is merely a sidekick and buffoon.

"Mel Brooks," said the late actor D'Urville Martin, "had problems with the script [of Blazing Saddles] and hired Pryor as the last writer to save the film. Max Julien (costar with Pryor in the 1973 film, The Mack) was also involved with the script."

Reed knew that America most located itself in the macho, "manifest destiny" syndrome of the Old West, where the enemy was indisputably red Indian or brown Mexican, as they saw it, with whites on the other side pushing, shoving and killing to get all that available land that rolled and humped onward to the Pacific Ocean. America still does not recognize the presence of black people in the Old West, people like Pointe du Sable, York, Beckwourth, Deadwood Dick, Cherokee Bill, Isam Dart. Or the Ninth and Tenth Cavalry and Twenty-fourth and Twenty-fifth Infantry, which rode or marched to the rescue more times than Hollywood has ever shown, or ever will show. Reed knew that the Old West was not America's crucible—the Civil War was, and the issues surrounding it. White fought white in that war. Not good. The Old West was simpler to deal with and therefore, the moral questions aside, as always, it became the sign-post of American maturity. In Reed's hands these perceptions became dancing, gallivanting satires. In other people's hands they became turnabout and farce and in a sly way, exercises in sexism and racism.

Claude Brown eased out to become a Regents' Lecturer at U.C. Santa Barbara; Reed and Cecil Brown were Visiting Writers on a number of campuses, but both settled in at U.C. Berkeley. Al Young also took a teaching post; later, he would have a more direct encounter with Pryor over the film *Bustin' Loose* (1981). Pryor made another film, *The Phynx* (1970) and another record *Craps: After Hours*. A film made in 1968,

You've Got to Walk It Like You Talk It or You'll Lose That Beat was released in 1971.

The New York Times said of that film, a satire about a young loser, that it "projects lots of walking and talking but precious little heartfelt beat, despite its willing cast and a plethora of sight gags and surface philosophies." Pryor and Zalman King, however, came in for special mentions. Pryor was already gearing up, apparently, to become the scene-swiper of the 1970s.

All his life, the stories said, Pryor wanted to be a movie star. He'd gone to movies and watched television the way most people breathe, and he'd learned that every film, no matter how bad, began with an idea that had to be set down in writing. He had written; had learned more about writing in Berkeley, had stolen away to write. That he understood the importance of writing is indisputable—most of his material is fronted by: "Material [usually all] written by Richard Pryor."

The writing was crucial, but writers seem to have been held in contempt in Hollywood. Or they were feared or even envied. Out there, as most writers learned when they ventured west, it was form, not content, that mattered most, although sometimes, given the happy pairing of director and writer, content occasionally shone through. This, however, was not to be the case with Pryor.

Eight

A couple of "senior" comedians, who felt some obligation to help nurse Pryor and his career, had determined that he was most comfortable in the smaller clubs and thus with smaller, more select audiences composed of super-hip admirers. They didn't think that the middle class, black or white, was ready for him. But Pryor, younger, perhaps more in tune with the times currently beating about the country, thought otherwise. There *were* people who were not "radical," who *were* middle class, who *were* both black and white—though he knew his base was black, not white—out there who *were* more than ready for him.

True, he was doing more writing—scripts for film and, soon, skits for Flip Wilson and Lily Tomlin. Profit-taking was less than expected for Hollywood, generally, but it was gearing up to fall back on the black exploitation movies that would be scored by the hip music of Isaac Hayes, Curtis Mayfield and other musicians. The major studios didn't seem to know how to handle "serious" scripts and therefore did *not* handle them, even through black exploitation, when they dealt with black people.

Pryor booked back east, passing through Peoria where he went out drinking one night. With childhood friend, Jesse Russell, a cab driver, they settled in at a bar for some serious drinking. They were interrupted by the bartender, who wanted to be paid for what they already had consumed. He didn't believe all he'd heard about Pryor's success, and was looking not to be stiffed.

"We ain't through drinkin' yet," Pryor protested.

"Just pay up, man," the bartender said.

Pryor shrugged. "Okay. You got change for a one-hundred-dollar bill?"

"Uh—no," the bartender said.

Pryor got up and stalked out. "Now," Russell said, "I don't know if he slipped back and paid him the next day or not. Probably. He was like that."

Pryor hit the urban centers where the black population was still belligerent, still looking for heroes to replace Medgar Evers, Malcolm X, Martin Luther King, Fred Hampton; they were still looking for spokesmen, *bad* new voices. The decision to promote Richard Pryor in major cities was certainly no mistake on the part of the comedian's agents. Pryor's "nurses" were dead wrong. The black middle class *had* rediscovered (if indeed it had ever lost) its relationship with the black masses. The members of The Black Academy of Arts and Letters, tuxedos shining, champagne flowing, remarked frequently that the relationship needed immediate tightening. They voted George Jackson a posthumous award for his book, *Soledad Brother*, and at its 1971 annual banquet, several speakers interspersed prepared remarks with fiery condemnations of the way the New York State Police put down the rebellion at Attica State Prison. The Academy was at that time seeking to establish headquarters in the house where the late Langston Hughes had lived for much of his life, on 126th Street in Harlem.

Another expression of the times was Pryor's treatment of Richard Nixon as a comic subject. The President, in Pryor's hands, became everything from the devil for sure to "fresh meat" going to jail where all the black inmates were waiting to gang-bang him, or in Pryor's words, "get the booty!"* After what had occurred in the 1960s, Nixon's reign served to underscore, for most black people at least (despite apparent support from such figures as Sammy Davis, Jr., Duke Ellington, and Wilt Chamberlain), that the government continued to be their adversary.

Therefore, an irreverent, bad-mouthed, apparently half-mad man, shrieking "motherfucker this, motherfucker that," or "nigger this, nigger that," or (in the face of militant feminism) "bitch this, bitch that"—a penis-holding, gyrating, staggering, dope-stiffened, ambling street apparition, certainly was no more obscene than what was going on in Washington, or in the news from Southeast Asia still flickering on the TV every night at 7 P.M. And Pryor did voice, sometimes in the crudest imaginable manner, like a Doré drawing of hell, precisely what

---

* *Some writers have waxed intellectual about this word. Some editors as well, not knowing what it really means, have displayed it in quotation marks. Basically, for black people, its meaning is sexual. In ordinary language it means seized or stolen goods, prize, award or gain.*

people were thinking and feeling about their country, themselves and others. The ancient gods Min and Dionysus had a proud modern counterpart in this comedian from Peoria.

Pryor had been writing in Berkeley, and had been worrying about scripts, ideas, forms. He did an original script for a black Hollywood producer "about a black cowboy who dabbles in the occult." It may have been that because of this he became one of the writers on the *Blazing Saddles* film. It is now universally known that he was angry when he didn't get the role of the black cowboy in the movie, because, it is said, Warner Bros. thought him to be unreliable. But the ball always seemed to bounce right for the comedian; he didn't need to appear in the film, because a year earlier he had been cast in another—*Lady Sings the Blues*, which proved to be far more beneficial to his career than *Blazing Saddles* would be for Clevon Little.

Motown Records, having topped most of the charts its performers appeared on since 1956, when the company was founded, decided to expand into films and moved to Hollywood. In the summer of 1969, Motown attorney George Schiffer visited New York and, among other tasks, explored the possibility of buying the film rights to *The Man Who Cried I Am*, published two years earlier, for its first film. According to Schiffer, Motown wanted the film to be a vehicle for its star, Marvin Gaye. But with problems developing between Gaye and Motown president Berry Gordy, that idea was scrapped. In its place, Diana Ross would do *Lady*, a film based on the William Duffy biography of the famous singer who had died in 1959. (Hollywood, being piggyback land, saw Twentieth Century-Fox briefly consider making a film of the Chris Albertson biography of Bessie Smith, *Bessie*, the same year *Lady* was released, but Fox dropped the project.)

Lady Sings the Blues, as Donald Bogle put it in his book, *Brown Sugar*, "was a lush, romantic melodrama dressed up with some political rhetoric and social trappings to alleviate any guilt feelings audiences might have about enjoying an old-fashioned soap opera."

Behind the camera, however, Gordy had managed to tweak the usual Hollywood practices. The Holiday book had been written by a white journalist dealing with a black subject, yes. (That practice was standard and was always far more acceptable than blacks writing about blacks.) But Gordy had white *and* black screen-writers, and Gordy himself was executive producer, the film being bankrolled by Motown money.

IF I STOP

Pryor's playing of the role of Piano Man in *Lady Sings the Blues* impressed many people. He was just plain good, except for a few moments of nervous, frenetic movement (which would be seen ten years later in the early scenes of *Some Kind of Hero*). The role of friend and booster of the tormented singer was ideal for the comedian. Audiences could not only see but also feel that he got as much out of the role as possible; he had clearly drawn deeply from his own life. The chorus of agreement that Pryor's acting had been splendiferous, together with his ever-increasing popularity before large concert audiences as a pure comedian, signaled the end of what associates would later call the worst period in Pryor's life.

This time (1973) was, in fact, one of the best periods of his career. He gave Miss Whittaker the Emmy he received for writing "Lily" for Lily Tomlin; he won a Writers Guild Award and an American Academy of Humor Award; he was writing for and appearing on "The Flip Wilson Show," and he'd done a stint on "The Tonight Show," Bill Cosby hosting in Carson's absence. He also performed in four movies: *Wattstax*, which *The New York Times* said was "hilarious in the way [Pryor] wrings laughs from . . . shared frustration and humiliation. . . . His stories of everyday hassling, of being regularly rousted by the cops, are spun out in street jargon with a kind of furious cool. What makes the jokes sting is not the punch lines but lethal accuracy"; *The Mack*, in which Pryor was applauded by Vincent Canby as a "first-rate comedian" in what was a "noisy, very exploitable black film"; *Hit*, and *Some Call It Loving*. Pryor played the Felt Forum in New York with Roberta Flack, and it was she who saw that he could go even further. Obviously, anyone who sang "The Ballad of the Sad Young Men" (among dozens of other equally affecting songs) the way she did would have sympathy for Pryor from the git-go. She said, "I wanted him to have someone around who'd protect him. David [Franklin] was the one."

As it happened, David Franklin had already become something of a Pryor aficionado. A young special assistant for contract compliance in the Secretary of Labor's office in the late 1960s, he had caught one of Pryor's early Basin Street West shows on a San Francisco business trip. He had in fact gone to see Charles Wright and the Watts 103rd Street Rhythm Band, and to meet women; Franklin hated most black comics, found the slapstick shit and bugging eyes "degrading to black folks." Pryor he thought funny enough, having seen him on TV on the Sullivan show displaying "a sort of an innocence," though the eyes still bugged a bit too much for his taste. But in person, Pryor's evolving character comedy blew Franklin away in a blast or recognition. "Richard was incredible," he said later. "He was like the guys I knew. I had seen guys like that in high school." Franklin sat through three shows and later began to track Pryor in his business travels, to spots like Lenny's on the Turnpike in Boston, and the Cellar Door in D.C., where Franklin lived.

It was in D.C. that Franklin almost accidentally began laying the foundation for his career in entertainment law that would bring him to intersect with Pryor. Franklin would frequent happy hour in a spot on Connecticut Avenue near the old Shoreham Hotel, where the Rick Powell Trio featured a talented, overweight Howard student on piano. One of the few blacks in the after-work crowd, Franklin befriended the combo and offered to do their taxes for free in lieu of stuffing the piano tip jar.

One day when Franklin came in, the pianist, Donny Hathaway, was gone; he had dropped out of school to accept a $25,000-a-year offer from a prominent singer-songwriter. But for that sum, Donny was expected to do everything: write, arrange, even, as Hathaway joked later, take the trash out on the road. "It was like an advance against your life," recalled Franklin, who answered Hathaway's appeal to help him out of what he considered a miserable deal. Franklin simply called Hathaway's employer and threatened to go public with the fact that Donny, not he, had composed a couple of his songs. It worked. "Donny thought that was magic," Franklin said later. "I didn't go the traditional legal way."

Franklin then signed on to manage Hathaway, and Donny in turn brought him Roberta Flack, who was married to Rick Powell's bass player. By 1972, Donny and Roberta, individually and together, were storming the charts with hit singles and gold albums, and Franklin, not yet thirty, was forging an identity rarely if ever seen in the entertainment business: that of a black lawyer directly tending the careers of black stars. But his biggest catch was yet to come.

On her way back from a date in Japan in 1975, Roberta Flack called Franklin and asked him to meet her in Los Angeles. He did, and when they finished taking care of her business at the Beverly Wilshire, Flack dragged him to the Comedy Store, a black-walled temple on the Sunset Strip where aspiring comedians went to strut their stuff, and stars also appeared, sometimes scheduled, sometimes—to the delight of the out-of-towners—on impulse, to hone their craft. Richard Pryor was there that night, to the surprise of Franklin but not Flack, perfecting his "Mudbone" routine. "It was classic," said Franklin, "the funniest thing I ever heard." And so he was in a receptive mood when Pryor came over, shy and deferential to Flack, and invited them to his house in the Hollywood Hills.

Sitting in his darkened living room, with water and soft drinks, Pryor said almost nothing while Flack launched into a sales pitch, arguing that what Pryor needed in his career was Franklin's management. It had been her plan all along. [Another suitor for Pryor's business had called Flack, asking her to put in a good word for him. Instead, she had determined to use the opportunity to bring Pryor into the Franklin stable.]

Franklin himself, meanwhile, was stunned. For one thing, he never wanted to seem to be begging for business. He knew he was *bad*, and he thought an artist who wanted his services should come to him. Most of his clients had come by way of referral from those he already represented. Flack's pitch was a referral of sorts, though an unusually aggressive one, and indeed when he had asked his people what performers they respected, Pryor's name had often floated to the top. But there was something else. Franklin hated craziness, suspected that comedians, even when they were not degrading, were often among the strangest folk in show business, and he had heard enough about Pryor in particular to make him leery. The evidence, in fact, was right before his eyes. Though the comic seemed oddly serene as Flack, in effect, pronounced his career a mess, Franklin noticed a framed gold record on the wall for *That Nigger's Crazy*. The glass was missing, and the gold platter itself bore, unmistakably, a bullet hole. I heard this guy is crazy, Franklin thought to himself. *He shot the damn record!*

Still, Franklin thought he ought to leave Pryor with something, and he offered a piece of advice and a proposition. The advice, which was to take on greater meaning at the end of their relationship, was pointed. "No one has a right to ask someone, manager or lawyer or best friend or whoever, to take you more seriously than you take yourself." The proposition was, at first, a simple bit of professional courtesy. Franklin would review Pryor's current contracts and his last three years' tax returns to assess his situation—provided that Pryor could get the stuff together before Franklin left town. Even that Franklin considered unusual largesse; he normally required a potential client to fly to Atlanta, where he based his practice, as a first step. "My plan was to make him a recommendation as to where he was," Franklin said. "As a black person I thought I should help somebody, but that didn't mean I had to be involved." To his surprise, Pryor came through with the material and asked Franklin to help him. Satisfied that Pryor was taking both himself and the relationship seriously, Franklin consented.

One of his first moves on behalf of his new client was more legalistic but not much more traditional than what he had done for Hathaway. Stax, the record label that had put out *That Nigger's Crazy*, still owed Pryor money; that was why the comic, in a moment of frustration, had shot his gold record, and why, according to one rumor, he had gone so far as to hire an underworld goon to strong-arm those who owed him about $100,000. Franklin, having heard that Stax was about to go under, flew to the Memphis headquarters one step ahead of the creditors, prepared to deal on the spot. He agreed to waive Pryor's claim to royalties and right-to-sue in return for the master of the record, which he then whisked out of town and sold for half a million dollars to Warner Bros., who re-released it and saw it go gold a second time. Pryor was as impressed as Hathaway had been, and thus their unlikely union was consummated.

Historically, all the managers of black talent in and out of Hollywood have been white. Black managers are just gaining acceptance in the industry, but they don't belong to the clubs, don't attend the dinner parties, or share the same social track that white managers do, and subsequently they are left to scramble for themselves and their clients. Some of the most famous black actors have had, even in Hollywood terms, "the worst contracts the devil could imagine." The list of black talent that awoke one morning, peered out into their orange groves, and then got a call telling them that they had no money is practically endless. Some, like Bill Cosby, managed to walk away from the financial tangles of his early career and begin another and have it managed successfully. Pryor was badly in need of a man like David Franklin during the early 1970s, but the fact that the comedian had gone outside Hollywood for a manager did not endear either him or Franklin to that enclave. This was especially true since many people in Hollywood thought they were doing black people a favor by making essentially "black" films. No outsiders were needed.

But then the black exploitation fad began a fast fade back to white. The old star syndrome regained its place in the heavens. Hollywood looked around. It saw John Belushi, Goldie Hawn, Sly Stallone, and Richard Pryor, whose reputation as a writer now almost equaled his reputation as a comic. And he was versatile, trotting through film, television and the concert stage with equal flair. In addition, *Blazing Saddles* had uncovered an until-then only sparingly dug gold mine of black creativity, and this pointed Hollywood in a new direction. The man called the "Smiling Cobra," David McCoy Franklin, was there to help Pryor pan the gold.

Saddles was significant because it was a reminder that the blacks and whites, the half-moon cookies, had been successful bondings not only recently, but in the past, in and out of film and television. There had been the three-year run of "I Spy" (1965-1968), with Cosby and Robert Culp; the 1970 *Brian's Song*, with Billy Dee Williams and James Caan; "McCloud," with Dennis Weaver and Terry Carter, which began in 1970 and ran through the summer of 1977. These, of course, had been preceded by pairings like Mandrake the Magician and Lothar, and shading off a bit, The Lone Ranger and Tonto, and the Green Hornet and Cato. The tap root to these pairings ran to literature—James Fenimore Cooper's *Leather-Stocking Tales*, Mark Twain's *The Adventures of Huckleberry Finn*, several of Melville's works. The bonding of dark and light was immutably set in the American psyche.*

When there were no coloreds physically present, their auras were—in the sassy, downfront, sex-hinting behavior of Mae West, whose voice sometimes came close to simulating a "black accent," and in the cool, distracted, existential manner of W. C. Fields, who disdained everyday niceties and was an admirer of Bert Williams. (And one could hardly fail to notice that the longer Cosby and Culp worked together, the more Culp came to sound and move like him, or how so many comedians—Robin Williams, Robert Klein, George Carlin, and so on—affected a "black accent," always deep and somehow threatening, or how even Pryor, when he imitated Jim Brown, deepened *his* voice several octaves.)

In addition to Tonto and Cato there had been other shadings of the black-white bonding. Moviegoers had been titillated with dark-suggesting actors like Rudolph Valentino, Caesar Romero, Desi Arnaz, Fernando Lamas—basically Latin types. It was all old American stuff, occurring long before the "crossover" term came into use to designate white interest in black stars. "Crossover," which applied mainly to Pryor and the films he played in, naturally only applied to whites. Hollywood had never accepted the fact that black moviegoers had been "crossing over" to white films for as long as Hollywood had made them—and that they had learned perhaps more about white America

---

* *In her* Big Bad Wolves: Masculinity in the American Film, *Joan Mellen treats male bonding or the "buddy" theme extensively, but only as it applies to white males. Parker Tyler's* Screening the Sexes *does, however, touch upon black-white "buddying": "do you remember that young film hero who left his girl flat to go off with the black boy? And if David isn't just naturally magnetized to his Jonathan, they can be chained to one another as Tony Curtis and Sidney Poitier were in a movie called* The Defiant Ones *(1958)."*

through films (and later, television) than was ever taught them on any level of any school. Why hadn't Clevon Little become a star after the bonding with Gene Wilder in *Blazing Saddles*? The answer may lie in the fact that he was too good-looking. Pryor, on the other hand, while not *bad*-looking, was interesting-looking, indefinite-looking. Good-looking black male actors, like Billy Dee Williams, are, as Pryor said in 1983, "threatening."

The "crossover" business was coming on fast; it took root in the 1976 film, *Silver Streak*, the one that would make Pryor a star for all people. The movies previous to that, *Uptown Saturday Night* (1974), *Adios Amigo* (1975), and *Car Wash* (1976) provided Pryor with sparkling moments, but did not challenge his talents. *The Bingo Long Traveling All-Stars and Motor Kings* (1976) did provide challenges which Pryor bested with solid performances in cameo satires of a black ball player trying to make the big leagues as alternately a black man, a Native American and a Cuban. His notices were exceptionally rave.

By this time the comedian had signed with David Franklin. In Hollywood this was seen as an attempt to thwart the usual client-agent pattern; both were black.* In the recording industry Franklin had secured for Roberta Flack an unheard-of sum for a black performer— $5.5 million for ten albums with Atlantic, *plus* an extra $50,000 per album; for Peabo Bryson he got $2.5 million. The industry was not used to paying black artists that kind of money.

Lots of zeros were not new to Franklin. He had been a Congressional budget accountant; a viewer of the "bigger picture" as consultant-confidant of Julian Bond, Maynard Jackson and former Congressman, mayor, and UN Ambassador, Andy Young. The black middle class, solidly educated, had always been savvy in Atlanta, even able to escape the harshest effects of segregation within a defined circle. They knew the liberal white Atlantans, the Charles Morgans, the Ralph McGills, the Morris Abrams, could talk both shit and silver without missing a beat. Franklin was blunt:

"Ninety percent of the black artists are getting ripped off today," he said in 1977. "The best service I could give them would be to take a machine gun and wipe out all the people around them and start over."

Franklin and Pryor talked, Pryor said later, "about how black men should be able to have a deal with each other based on face value and their words, and that no matter what happened that we would always be brothers and everything would be all right, and it wasn't necessary to have something written down. If we didn't want to be together, then we wouldn't need any papers to keep us together. . . . He was probably the best—one of the most brilliant men that I have ever known, and I thought that he really had a great love for black people. . . .

JOHN A. WILLIAMS

The fact that this quote was used over and over in relation to Pryor indicated that Franklin was stepping on some pretty sensitive toes, but that didn't matter to him. "In the old days," he said, "black artists went with white managers because they felt they were the people with connections. . . . What really burns me is that these black artists have such *bad* white managers. I mean the guys are bad. . . . from 1900 to 1979 there has not been a black artist yet who has been able to retire who has been handled by a white manager. That should tell you something."

It was no wonder that Hollywood dubbed Franklin the "Smiling Cobra," or that David Felton wrote in 1980 that Franklin was the kind of man "you might not want to meet. . . . alone in a dark boardroom."

What made him even more intimidating was his control of the career of a man who was on the verge of becoming a superstar and therefore able to command and demand millions of dollars.

Before Pryor and Franklin tied the knot, however, there was a tax case. Charged with not filing income-tax returns from 1967 through 1970, the comedian pleaded guilty to one of the four counts: "not knowingly filing a tax return in 1967." The other "failing to file" counts were dropped during the plea bargaining. From the indictment to conviction—a matter of a couple of months—Pryor used two lawyers, Ronald Rosen and Joel Behr. They were effective, enabling Pryor to ease out of the situation with Judge Manuel Real fining him $2,500, placing him on three years' probation, and sentencing him to ten days in jail. Pryor's "life is his act," an observer wrote, and accordingly the ten days became material for a series of monologues and an album called *L.A. Jail* (1976).

Two things bothered Franklin. The first was Pryor's widely acknowledged use of dope; Franklin told him to knock it off, and Pryor promised that he would. The second was the three years' probation. For Pryor had left a paper trail through both civil and criminal courts. One toot, one drink too many; one flash of temper—almost one more anything—and the comedian's career was on the rocks. And not only Pryor's career would be lost in such a situation. Both Pryor and Franklin (as Bill Cosby was trying to do) could work together, through film contracts, to provide jobs and opportunities for black actors, cameramen, writers, all kinds of filmmakers; they could establish a beachhead on the pure white sands of Hollywood.*

*Franklin located Pryor in the Playboy building on Sunset Boulevard, and also got him an office at Universal. Pryor paid Franklin $92,000 of the over $885,000 he made in 1975. Although Franklin bought a home in Encino, not far from Northridge, he did not have an office in California. He maintained his firm in Atlanta. This would prove to be the source of future difficulties.

Nineteen seventy-five was a good year for Franklin and Pryor to team up. The "Peoria Stroker" (stroking in *and* out of the pool hall), the "Booty Man" (*not* having to do with gold or other material prizes) had done the ten days in the Los Angeles County Jail standing on his head. Anyway, Hollywood was titillated by eccentricity. Professionally, the comedian had come bounding off a couple of years with a solid reputation as a writer for Flip, Lily, and Redd Foxx, and David Felton's 1974 *Rolling Stone* piece, "Jive Times," hadn't hurt either.

Then there were the profiles in *The Washington Post,* followed in 1975 by a big spread in the *National Observer* and the James Alan McPherson *New York Times Magazine* piece, "The New Comic Style of Richard Pryor." In addition, there were two major albums, *That Nigger's Crazy* (1974), which won a Grammy Award, and *Is It Something I Said* (1975), as well as the artistically disappointing *Down 'n' Dirty* (1975) with Redd Foxx.

And club owners were calling Pryor "The black Lenny Bruce."

Between his many appearances that year, Pryor stopped in Peoria to pick up his son Richard to bring him to Hollywood for a visit. After visiting relatives he stopped off to see Juliette Whittaker and her new private school, The Learning Tree. He climbed upon a high stool and looked through the one-way glass at the kids playing in the main room. "I wish we'd had something like this when I was a kid," he said wistfully. He turned to Miss Whittaker. "What do you need for this place? What would you like to have?"

"Richard," she said, "I've always dreamed of having a sliding board—but it's a special kind of sliding board. It's like a frontier post where the kids go up the ladder and they have the deck to walk around on. Then they can come down the stainless-steel slide or the firemen's pole." Miss Whittaker showed him the picture of the sliding board in a catalogue.

"When I get back to L.A. I'll send you a check for it," Pryor said. Two weeks later the check arrived, and at summer's end, when he returned with his son, it was Richard Pryor day in Peoria. He cut the ribbon on the new sliding board and did a show in the Shrine Mosque—upon whose marquee his name appeared—for the Y.W.C.A. Long after that day Miss Whittaker commented, "Very often when people rise they forget their roots. Richard has never forgotten. There is something about him that is exemplary and unusual."

A lot of people thought that, too, although not for the same reasons. With all he was doing, Pryor took the time—because Franklin believed that exposure certainly could not hurt—to do four films, all of which were released the following bicentennial year, 1976. Although Pryor was reported to have been embarrassed enough by Fred Williamson's Po' Boy production of *Adios Amigos* to apologize to his fans ("Tell them I needed some money"), the truth is that he had earned plenty. *Car Wash* found the comedian trapped in the preacher's role he'd created on records, and *The Bingo Long Traveling All-Stars and Motor Kings* was not the vehicle that would carry him to stardom, though it certainly was a major stop along the route. No all-black or mostly-black film has ever catapulted a black actor to the top; the Hollywood scenarios simply are not written that way. It took the bonding of Gene Wilder and Pryor in the Twentieth Century-Fox production of *Silver Streak* (with which the studio had dawdled for a while) to make Pryor a star among stars, a person who, almost without anyone noticing it, broke down Hollywood's artificial barrier between black and white to become what the town hailed as a "crossover" star.

Nine

The "crossing-over" was not planned.

Marjorie Green, discoverer of the first *Star Wars* script and story assistant to Alan Ladd, Jr., who was then Fox's president in charge of production and responsible for the film), said Pryor "originally had a smaller part... but the producers kept adding material because they recognized the natural talent the actor had, and Pryor rode that train all the way to Chicago."

They bonded well, Wilder and Pryor, *very* well in box-office terms, for when the film was released, it ultimately grossed over $30 million—one of only fifty movies in film history up to the mid-1970s to earn that kind of money. It was all quite by accident that Twentieth-Century-Fox stumbled into the gold mine that was at the core of the American mind, the togetherness of black and white in any great adventure. Accident because, if intended, Pryor would have been in the opening scenes of the film. As the movie was constructed, however, he did not appear until the picture was a bit more than a third over (page 61 of a 177-page screenplay).

Comparing the shooting script to many of the lines Pryor speaks in *Silver Streak* is intriguing, because what he does is not to ad-lib as much as to alter existing lines. He'd had problems with his lengthy ad-libbing in *Adios Amigo,* sending Fred Williamson (who'd counted on Pryor to ad-lib entire scenes) racing back to the typewriter to produce copy the comedian could work with.

The Colin Higgins script indicates that it went through at least one complete revision and four partials. Pryor as Grover Muldoone, a

JOHN A. WILLIAMS

small-time thief, first appears in the backseat of the sheriff's car that Wilder, as the innocent George Caldwell, a businessman, has just escaped in. Ultimately, with Pryor driving, they elude a road block and arrive at a used-car lot, where they prepare to steal a Porsche. It is about here where Pryor's subtle but effective alterations of Higgins' lines begin, as he takes what would be stilted dialogue and turns it into the language of real life, changing Grover's original line, "This Porsche is a pussy" into the more Pryoresque "This Porsche is pure pussy!"

The alteration draws a closer relationship between man and car as a sexual object. The Higgins version implies that "pussy" is a short-ened form of "pussy cat," a synonym for weakness or an inference that the car is easy to steal. Pryor changed the meaning so that it is no longer ambiguous. The street alliteration enhances the sexual imagery his alteration suggests.

There are places in the script when it is apparent that Higgins is not quite sure how to handle all of the exchanges between the black Grover Muldoone and the white George Caldwell. How, the script seems to ask, would a black man conduct himself in some of the less farcical scenes in the film? That uncertainty is not present when the script deals with the other black actors in roles where they are normal-ly found. Ralston, the porter, for example, played by Scatman Crothers, is a completely predictable character. But, nowhere is this awkward-ness more prominent than in the scenes in the Kansas City station. Pryor and Wilder are scheming to get back on the train past the cops guarding the entrance to it.

In the men's room Grover begins buying as George pays for items of disguise from the Old Black Guy, played by Nick Stewart. The script calls for Grover, glancing at the shoe shine man's beret, to tell the man that he likes the hat, ask him where he got it, and offer him money. Pryor's alteration is sharp, condensed and streetwise: "Hey man," he says, "that's a bad hat you got on."

In street parlance, "to dig" is to like, to understand. "Bad" is a superlative, or it can mean, in a "white" sense, what it has always meant. It may be that Ladd had a greater understanding of the lan-guage Pryor used than Higgins was capable of writing for him. Of course, no script reveals where lines were blown and had to be shot again. There are places in any script where that is likely to happen; it would be unusual if it didn't. The lines that Pryor altered make him more believable as a black character than the ones Higgins gave him, in most cases. In the scripted version of the Kansas City station scene, moreover, there is the nagging sense that Pryor is father to Wilder's wide-eyed son. Pryor's alterations recast the relationship between his character and Wilder's in less sentimental terms, reflecting an edge of resentment.

In the men's room, the shoe-shine man has whipped off his beret for the five dollars, and George is blackened up with the shoe polish they purchased. As he stares in the mirror, he announces ruefully that they are never going to get away with it. The original script called for Grover, busy with shoe polish, to suggest that George think of this as "instant suntan." Instead of delivering this line, Pryor plays with the racial tension, taunting Wilder's character with the rhetorical question, "What, you afraid it won't come off?"

"That's a good joke; that's humorous," Wilder responds, and for just a moment, Wilder steps outside the film with Pryor, and responds sarcastically to Pryor's alteration which itself is sarcastic. That director Arthur Hiller left in the exchange indicates that, even if he wasn't sure what was going on, it played damned well and on levels above the script. Wilder's line above is not in the script.

The script then called for Grover to provide instruction in how to apply the shoe polish, which causes him to make an allusion to Al Jolson, and note how he once mistakenly believed that the entertainer was black. The line Pryor ultimately delivers trades innocent ignorance for a harder cynicism: "Al Jolson made a million bucks lookin' like that."

The alteration goes to the heart of a lot of black bitterness at show business, resounding as it does with irony for anyone who knows the history of the entertainment industry. The line also turns upon the picture in which it is spoken and emphasizes the continuity of the "borrowing" tradition.

The script in this section is loaded with some of the worst pseudo-"black" language ever set down; it is white man's black, not black man's black dialogue. Now, as Grover and George leave the men's room, past the gawking shoe-shine man ("Lord, now I seen everything"), Grover instructs "Mr. Bojangles" to get going, as if this were a natural reference that Pryor's character would use to refer to a typical black man. The line Pryor eventually delivered was not only more believable, but much more funny. "We'll make it past the cops," Grover says, "I just hope we don't see no Black Muslims."

Back on the train, there follows an exchange between Grover and the smooth villain Roger Devereau, played by Patrick McGoohan that culminates with Grover "accidently" pouring coffee into Devereau's lap. Devereau still has not realized that Grover has replaced the original steward, and calls Grover a "blundering fool," and culminates his outburst by calling him an "ignorant nigger."

The shooting script has Grover responding by taking out a gun and angrily threatening to whip his ass. Pryor's alterations keep this anger, show it to be motivated by a foundation of self-respect rather than insecurity.

GROVER: Hey, man, who you callin' nigger, huh? (Whips out a gun) You don't know me well enough to call me no nigger. I'll slap the taste out your mouth. You don't even know my name. I'll whip your ass. Beat the white off your ass.

Both the script and the action here reiterate, undoubtedly without intending to, the classic invisible man theme. Devereau *never* realizes that Grover has taken the steward's place. And neither does George's girlfriend Hilly until made aware of it. Both Grover and the steward, and by extension all black males in white jackets (or not) are automatically interchanged with the next. Pryor's alterations make the men's room and roomette scenes work. The script itself imparts (by direction and dialogue) to Grover a crudeness of character when he meets Hilly. Pryor's lines reject this in favor of street praise, street sensuality, which, incidentally, reflects favorably on George for having such good taste. The difference between the written and spoken word is of course a matter of black perception.

This is most evident when Grover is called *that* name by Devereau. The script calls for unfocused nonsense. There is in it no real response to the racial insult. It is as if Higgins could not bring himself to write an adequate response. Pryor's altered lines resonate once again beyond the script and the film. The response he provides is much to the point and even echoes James Baldwin's *Nobody Knows My Name*; Ralph Ellison's *Invisible Man* is implicit in the action. Eliminating Grover's lines about having a high school diploma, which seems a ploy to reinforce both Devereau's suave, educated sophistication *and* the villain's lines about Grover's ignorance, leaves a fine edge to the exchange which otherwise might have been lost.

Pryor claimed that when he took the role of Grover Muldoone, he "was looking to hustle," but instead "got hustled." This may be true on the financial level, but artistically he turned a would-be flop into a money-making film, and that more or less insured that other good roles would come his way. Although most reviewers of *Silver Streak* said it was slow, tiring and uninspiring, Pryor easily walked away with the best notices even though he played in less than half the picture. (Canby of *The New York Times* said that he "turns up in the last third of the film") And nearly all the reviewers mentioned the men's room scene. Pryor responded to one interviewer, saying "Gene does a scene in black face, and they felt that having a real black actor in the movie would sort of make it all right. So I'm the token black, a modern Willie Best. It was a career move, and I'm not sorry I did it."

It was "crossover" time—or imminently so—and what Cosby had said years earlier was now true. "I don't think Hollywood is playing games with black people, because first of all, Hollywood doesn't *need* black people, but if it comes to money, if you get a blockbuster, they'll show anything, zankety, zankety, zankety."

Guided by David Franklin, Pryor would make another nine movies, seeking with only moderate success to mix comedy with drama in order to escape Hollywood's black-comic straitjacket. *Greased Lightning* (1977) and *Blue Collar* (1978) were the most obvious attempts, the first a too-solemn depiction of black racing-car driver Wendell Scott, the second a gritty morality play of labor and big business that may have been Pryor's finest dramatic hour. But it was another kind of conscious mixing, that of Pryor's stand-up and film careers, that produced his first unqualified success after *Streak*.

David Franklin had always been wary of the nightclub scene, with its often sleazy milieu and vestiges of mobsterism. (The mob didn't so much threaten people, he believed, as control them by loaning them money.) Besides, he knew his man was big enough to thrive mainly by doing concerts, and in big-time houses at that. "White people wanted to see him, but they didn't want to take their lives in their hands," Franklin theorized. "He thought if he played first-class venues his audience wouldn't come. I said they want to applaud you for making it." And realizing that Pryor the stand-up comic was also Pryor the actor at his best, he determined to capture the real thing on film.

The studios weren't interested. No one, they thought, would sit still for an hour an a half of a man on stage doing comedy. Even with independent backing, Pryor and Franklin were forced to hedge their bets; the tour included singer Patti Labelle, who was paid $20,000 for film rights. (Pryor also bought her a car when it turned out they didn't need her in the movie.) The result, *Richard Pryor—Live in Concert* (1979) was both landmark and masterpiece. It was also a brilliant stroke of marketing. A comedy double-album was released before the film, and those who had heard the brushfire word of mouth about the new routines, and even those who had caught the show at auditoriums like New York's culture-bound City Center, on West 55th Street, snapped it up. That in turn apparently only whetted the popular desire to see Pryor on film act out the lines they'd already memorized. Adding in the later videocassette rentals and sales that were not part of the original equation, many Pryorphiles (perhaps *because* they were so frustrated with the pale version they'd been seeing in other movies) ended up paying four different times to experience the same performance. Yet what mattered most at the moment was that the concert film made a lot of money and displayed Pryor at the peak of his form. The material was all his—and he romped wildly with it. Hollywood had not, at least not yet, made him lose his stroke.

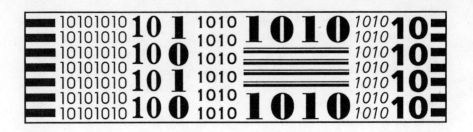

Ten

Curiously, most of Pryor's white fans discovered him in the mid-1970s, when he was pounding out film after film, and his concerts and club dates grew to monstrous sizes and numbers. It was bicentennial time, that period of reflection and celebration of two hundred years of American-style democracy, which Pryor marked with his album, *Bicentennial Nigger.* In the final monologue the comedian recounts the travails of Afro-Americans and concludes the list of wrongs with: "I ain't never gonna forget," lending an overtly political note to the album (which won him another Grammy) and perhaps even acknowledging his awareness of his own political influence.

Pablo Guzmán of *The Village Voice* wrote that "the heart of Richard's appeal is that he is a *political* force.

"That's right: politics, not mere entertainment, is what Pryor's always been about. The politics of being an Everyday African Male in America. . . . After all, Richard's comedy has always been both subversive and revelatory."

Silver Streak not only helped to make Pryor the "crossover" star—it helped to make him, unofficially, of course, but nevertheless palpably, a leader.

At no time during their bleak and circuitous sojourn in the American wilderness have black people been without a voice urging them to keep on keeping on. Sometimes there were several; sometimes they argued about the direction to take and how, but there was always a voice, and there was always laughter. The laughter was dark and removed. Those white people who had designed the wilderness knew that if the situation was reversed, they would not have been able to live, let alone laugh.

Even so, if a voice was to be heard, it was to be the preacher's voice; preachers most readily spoke the language the trail wardens understood—meekness and piety. The voices that were not raised purely and completely to God, but were instead leveled at the wardens, were ignored or silenced. Still, from out of the dark, the voices kept sounding and not the least among them were the voices of the funny men and women who made people laugh in the Saturday sessions at the barbershop or hairdressing parlor, in the mean bars and meaner street corners, in church basements where choirs gathered before marching upstairs to services, or out in the sharecropped fields.

The black funnymen like Bert Williams and George Walker were first heard loudly, speaking through their own voices, during the 1920s, when W. E. B. Du Bois edited *The Crisis* and Marcus Garvey had run afoul of both the government and the elements of the black population that did not like him or his Back-to-Africa movement.

In the 1960s and early 1970s there existed side by side black militancy, black piety, black academic rationalism, black political realism and black humor—and all were converging on the system in flank and frontal assaults. It did seem that way, and later, in some of the high places after things had been whipped back to near normal, it was learned by many of those in the several movements that the overcoming had been closer than any of them had ever realized, that the voices had not only been heard, but feared as well; the murders indicated that—whether they occurred in Mississippi or Soledad Prison, at Kent State or Jackson State, in Newark or Watts or Detroit. The Nixon administration's "Garden Plot" contingency plan for rounding up dissidents was the proof.

And Richard Pryor's voice stabbed the ferment with sardonic I-am-reaching-into-my-pocket-for-my-license-'cause-I-don't-wanna-be-no-motherfuckin-accident!" hysteria, and let every cop know that black (and some white) people understood precisely what was going on. "If," Bill Cosby said, "Richard isn't doing anything more than just letting black people have a hero in the monologue, a hero who kicks the white cop's ass, for that release, then Richie's a bad cat. And he makes them all bad cats. He's not trying to draw people out; he's just telling them what's in his mind."

What had been on Pryor's mind, though, was fame, how to become famous doing what he did best. He would say in 1976, "I want people to be able to recognize me by just looking at a caricature of me that has no name on it. I want to be great, and you can recognize great people like Muhammad Ali and Bob Hope by just looking at a name-less caricature and say, 'That's him, that's Richard Pryor!' Then I'll be great."

It seemed he always knew that shocking people would attract their attention, and in the early 1970s there were many things to distract people's attention away from Richard Pryor, who was moving briskly along the trail upward, becoming ever more prominent. The events surrounding his rise at this time included the recognition by many white Americans that the term "nigger" was demeaning. Crackers who beat up Freedom Riders and burned their buses used it; the men who murdered James Chaney, Andrew Goodman and Michael Schwerner used it. In the film *To Kill a Mockingbird* (1962) we *knew* Gregory Peck was a good guy because he *didn't* use the term while defending Brock Peters on a bogus rape charge in the Deep South. Of all the pieces of luggage in the racist baggage car, this term was the easiest to unload. To do so cost nothing. The times demanded that the term be stamped DO NOT APPLY IN PUBLIC. Private, in-house use was another matter, of course. One did have to be more careful. When force or control is present, one does not employ derogatory ethnic designations to those who have the force or control. Not wise.

Black use of the term has been consigned to the psychological shelf labeled "self-hate." The location may be apt, but the first step to eliminate that and to control one's destiny is to determine the name by which you shall be called. No one else can really do that. (The experience is not confined to Afro-Americans alone; all over the world people and places have been named by adventurers who came from someplace else. The word, Egypt, for example, is not 'Egyptian" but Greek.) Dick Gregory's book, *Nigger* (1962), purported to take the sting out of the term.

Pryor's use of the word in concert with others that were bio-logically *not* related to race brought a familiar shock to black people. It made some of them uneasy. Some complained, others had reservations about the comedian and his lack of "black pride." It was like hearing a language that might be spoken only at home being shouted through the streets. "Oh, he's dis*gus*ting," people said. But they watched and listened without missing a beat, equally fascinated and repelled because there were so many things to work through to get to where the comedian himself assumed it was all right to call people by something other than their rightful name. Was this the return the black middle class was getting for its investment in a Richard Pryor vogue? Why were the

JOHN A. WILLIAMS

white folks as delighted with him as they were? Sure, he spoke golden truth—but did he have to say *nigger* so much?

James Alan McPherson wrote: [Pryor's] scenes are sprinkled liberally with this gem, so much in fact that some black people have complained he is damaging the image of the group by moving the word from the pool halls and barbershops back into public usage. The word 'nigger,' however, has never gone out of style. The movie industry and some whites opposed to busing have done far more than Pryor to keep the word alive."

Whatever uneasiness some black people were feeling, there were some white writers like Mark Jacobson who were of the opinion that "Using the word 'nigger' was the masterstroke. It aced him [Pryor] out of the mainstream, plus it made it quite clear where his racial allegiance lay. Everyone knows white people are not allowed to say that word."

And *Time* joined the chorus that seemed to be all white when it agreed that it was a nifty word, cleverly used by Pryor to mean something other than what it had always meant:

"When Pryor says it, it means something different from what it did through too much of America's history. Depending on his inflection or even the tilt of his mouth, it can mean simply black. Or it can mean a hip black, wise in the ways of the street. Occasionally nigger can even mean white in Pryor's reverse English lexicon. However he defines it, Pryor is certain of one thing. He is proudly, assertively a nigger, the first comedian to speak in the raw, brutal, but wildly hilarious language of the street."

"Nigger" is a word, a term, that concretizes an idea, a concept, a historical entity, a designation of the caste and class to which black people have been assigned. It did not matter that when Pryor used it, it became like punctuation. At other times when he uttered it, the word dripped with contempt. It was the bear trap of history, with six razor-sharp teeth: n-i-g-g-e-r. Maybe Pryor was asking people to work their way through the pain, the memories, to conclude that this word was only a word.

Black publications, however, did not excuse its use; their writers did not attempt to rationalize or psychoanalyze it; for them the word was what it was, and that was precisely why so many white people stopped using it publicly. They didn't have to. For there was a voice "re-zounding" in larger and larger clubs to bigger and bigger audiences in the 1970s, and it pronounced "nigger" like a machine gun. It was Richard Pryor's voice. White people had found a black man who could call other black people "niggers" for them. *Richard Pryor is funny*! Funny, yes, and he always called white people white people or white folks.

There were many times, however, when Pryor while using the term deftly switched from his own persona to another—a white authoritarian person (a stock voice-character in his repertoire). His audiences learned that he was then speaking (and acting) in a way that was perceived by blacks to be accurate; that he then projected a collective white mind-set in regard to blacks. The classic example of this change in projection is the skit "The New Niggers" (*Is It Something I Said?*, 1974):

> "...Got all the Vietnamese in the Army camps an' shit takin' tests an' stuff, learnin' how to say nigger [*laughter*] so they can become good citizens. [*laughter*] But they got classes—you know—they have—[*authoritarian voice*] "All right, let's try it again, troops."
> "Nigguh! Nigguh! Nigguh!...Nigguh! Nigguh! Nigguh! Nigguh!"
> "Eh, that's close. If you get your ass kicked, you know you made it." [*wild cheers, loud, long applause*]

(A dispute between Korean grocers and black customers erupted in New York City in early summer 1990, when one of the grocers was accused of beating a black woman. The Koreans said she had been shoplifting. She denied the charge. The New York media pounded its drums; pickets and anti-pickets appeared in the street before the Korean shop. In the end, the woman said she did not remember which of the Koreans had attacked her, and witnesses appeared for the cameras in support of the grocers. The dispute probably is reflected a hundred times a week between Asian-Americans and African-Americans in those cities where the Asians have established businesses in the black communities.)

"His [Pryor's] vocabulary," wrote Janet Maslin in *The New York Times* eight years after "The New Niggers," "noticeably lacks the word 'nigger,' which was formerly one of its great staples." It was, indeed, and when the wisdom came, after the 1980 fire, few whites were using the term publicly. Before this time, with his multitude of voices Pryor *did* expose the word, pried open its nuances as used between black husband and black wife, between white and black (male, female), and between black and black (male). But one black college professor, who loved all the Dionysian displays, found that Pryor's use of the word still rankled.

He said, "When I was young I went to see Jean-Paul Sartre's *The Respectful Prostitute*. That was the first time I'd ever heard 'nigger' spoken out in a very public place. I was angry that I'd paid my money to go and hear that, and I am still angered when I hear Pryor—I am also puzzled that he seems to get such a positive response whenever he uses the word in those things he does."

The voices of leaders should show some constraint, but that depends on the kind of leader people need at a particular time; sometimes they need all they can get their hands on at the same precise time. We know that Dick Gregory all but gave up his career, not to be a leader but to serve. That, however, almost automatically makes one a leader, in the black community, anyway, if a person gives up a highly lucrative career in order to work with the people. Cosby is a role model for many black people. Neither Gregory nor Cosby flayed their audiences with "nigger."

It is possible that, during his Berkeley stint with "Broadway" Brown and the other writers, it occurred to Pryor that here was Cecil Brown, following the lead of Gregory, actually using the word on the cover of a book! Indeed, Pryor once introduced Brown to his audience, called him—not a writer—but a novelist, and mentioned the title of his novel, *The Life and Loves of Mr. Jiveass Nigger*.

In *Richard Pryor—Live In Concert*, the comedian introduced a former leader, Huey Newton of the Black Panthers, and in *Live on the Sunset Strip*, the camera rested momentarily on the Reverend Jesse Jackson. Pryor's politics have always reflected an awareness of racial injustice. This made it all the more difficult to understand why he used "nigger" for so long, unless it was to shock; certainly it cannot have been to make white fans smug. And "greed," too, must be eliminated as a reason, for he was fast approaching the point where he would have "enough money for a black man to live on forever."

In time he would say that it was his trip to Africa that made him realize that the word should no longer occupy a place in his public vocabulary—and that would be a good show-business rap. Fans responded to the announcement with whistles, cheers and applause, because they understood, however dimly, the political ramifications of the statement.

It was not that his fans always misunderstood the manner in which Pryor employed the term; the use was always two-leveled: black people using it against (the preposition is apt) each other, *perhaps* as a reflection of a long, ingrained self-hatred, cast onto a fellow, that had been taught by the American experience in subtle and not so subtle ays. Using it made you—maybe—feel just a little bit better about yourself, as in the stunning skit of "the Wino and the Junkie" (which has a couple of levels itself.)

The second level, obviously far more political, had to do with Pryor's crawling into the white psyche (or the ones that dominate society) and using "nigger" the way they do. And even if they did not, in Pryor's view, *speak* the word, they thought it, and Pryor gave those thoughts the voice all black people heard.

Still, it was the public shock that gnawed at so many black fans, together with a lingering sense of betrayal. It was like having a brother on the Civil Rights Commission who was supposed to do you some good, only the brother turned out to be Brutus' best teacher. Most people did not care about the levels of use of the term; they only knew what they heard and what it had always meant. For Pryor, the easy, frequent use of the word may have started at home.

In the skit "Have Your Ass Home by Eleven" (*That Nigger's Crazy*), the comedian relates a "conversation" with his father about going out at night, with the deadline for return at eleven. The father addresses his son as "nigger!" just about every five words. On the same album, the description of the commonplace ritual of sitting down and eating dinner is laced with the word. If, once again, Pryor's life is his act, what he brought from home was—some people think—peculiar baggage. A generation of black people concluded during the 1960s and early 1970s that the name *could* hurt, but it seemed to have taken Pryor far longer to understand its devastating effect on Afro-Americans.

Pryor told *Ebony*'s senior editor Lerone Bennett in 1982 that he went to Africa and discovered there were no "niggers" there. Bennett reminded Pryor that the comedian once said "that using the word took the sting out of it."

Pryor responded: "Yeah, I told myself all those lies. . . . It can't make you feel good, because when the white man calls us that, it hurts, no matter how strong we try to be about it. There's pain [in that word]. . . . I feel funny when I see black men and black women in positions of power use it."

So he had, by the time of *Live on the Sunset Strip*, "grown" (one of his favorite terms) enough to publicly announce that he would no longer use the word "nigger."

However, he made no such vow to give up the Black English he'd used so effectively in his monologues. The appearance of Black

English on the national scene coincided with the international emergence of the French-speaking Caribbean and African writers' philosophy of Negritude—which owed its beginnings to Langston Hughes and the Harlem Renaissance. Negritude was the philosophy of extraordinary pride in all aspects of black culture wherever in the world it might be found, but particularly Africa. In the 1960s, black writers—especially poets—often went back to the streets for inspiration and reaffirmation of the validity and vibrancy of black life. Black college professors, newly hired on at prestigious universities, often would finish a class on the British Romantic Writers, or American Literature to the Twentieth Century, then retreat with a black colleague and begin "talkin' the talk."

The double negative flourished in writing as well as in speech, an example of which is Pryor's "I don't wanna be no accident!" The intransitive verb, *be*—to exist not only in actuality, but also in a specific place and time—became the hippest way to use the verb *am*. "I be walking" was more powerful—and picturesque—than "I am walking." Two or three words were converted to one: "What is happening?" yielded "What's happening?"—which was finally rendered as "Zappening?"

Professor Geneva Smitherman of Wayne State University, through her talks and writings, became one of many defenders of the use of Black English, but there were many educators who opposed it. White teachers who favored the use of Black English as a way of getting ghetto kids to express themselves were looked upon with great suspicion, because everyone *knew* you had to speak White English to get any kind of a job, and maybe some white educators were running a game on the students. This battle was raging long before James Baldwin observed in 1979 that "People evolve a language . . . to describe and thus control their circumstances, or in order not to be submerged by a reality they cannot articulate."

Richard Pryor articulated extremely well in Black English, his voice rising and falling, his body flailing about as he acted out what it was he was saying. "Richard Pryor," Cosby had said in 1970, "is perhaps the only comedian that I know of today who has captured the total character of the ghetto."

In the 1970s, Black English became "Talking Black," the hip way to communicate, and Richard Pryor helped promote and legitimize it. His boyhood mentor, Miss Whittaker, approved, observing: "If he is portraying a man in the street, then he's got to do what a person like that does and says."

The question for Pryor in the mid-1970s was whether he was going to be a movie star or a comedian. Despite the attractions of movie money, there would be fewer chances in film for him to be the force he was in performance, because the script would not always be his. Most people knew by this time that the Richard Pryor on the screen was not the person they knew on stage.

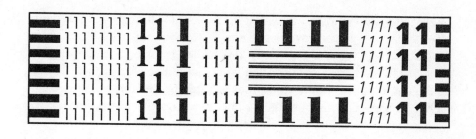

Eleven

On stage, Pryor might have been to his contemporary audiences what Charlie Chaplin was to moviegoers over a half century ago. Hannah Arendt noted that Chaplin "could not fail to arouse the sympathy of the common people who recognized in him the image of what society had done to them." Pryor did some Chaplin-like skits.

Many of the "common people" who empathized with Chaplin's portrayals have themselves become oppressors, but they raised, for one reason or another, a generation whose sensitivities seem to have been, in the 1960s and 1970s, alert to political and economic inequities based on race, and Pryor, therefore, may have been a contemporary version of the Chaplin figure in the way Reggie Jackson updated Babe Ruth.

As the underdog, Chaplin usually managed to achieve the small, timorous revenges of the common man, but these were tacit recognitions that the powers could grind him into dust if only endowed with his luck and cleverness. There is no victory for Pryor's characters, even Mudbones. Steve Allen recognized that "What almost all of them [Pryor's characters] have in common is a pathetic tendency to try to disguise or manipulate the facts of their own experience by pure talk, what the Irish would call blarney. . . . In bringing such men and women to the attention of his audiences, Pryor is much closer to literature than to traditional nightclub or concert comedy."

Whether literature or concert comedy, Pryor's characters were aggressively black, even if they were victims. And we recognized the characters, just as we recognized Chaplin's. Pryor's characters also were often pompously black, hot-air balloons wafting about in capricious winds trying to avoid the needle that would prick them, blow them apart. Pryor is as black as Woody Allen is Jewish—and as cynical.

In his best comedy, Allen laughs at himself, at his mostly ineffectual attempts to best a world that has stereotyped him as a schlemiel. That he sometimes triumphs is the classic rags-to-riches plot. On the other hand, Pryor played to the knowledge that one must conceal weakness, camouflage vulnerability with bravado, as in "We bad, we bad." The sham is immediately recognized. Fans of all kinds understand where power resides and the ways in which it can be exercised.

Aristotle said comedy was built on ridicule; one attacked some "defect or ugliness" within a system as well as within a person, within the self, within one's people and one's society. Such was the function of Pryor's scathing ridicule. He laughed at himself, his people, his country. He pinioned the black preacher to a bulls-eye of a target when he mounted what was his most horrifyingly hilarious skit in his "Bicentennial Prayer" from his album *Bicentennial Nigger,* in which the preacher alternately soothes his congregation and then rages at it:

> I'd like to say to the crippled peoples that come here—can't you find another church to go to? [*laughter, oooos*] Goddamn, come in knockin' shit down [*laughter*] 'n' breakin' up furniture 'n' shit.... [*laughter*] Learn how to crawl!! Shitttt. [*laughter, oooos*] An' you deaf and dumb motherfuckers, you motherfuckers that can't talk, we don't need ya here! [*laughter*] All that whoo-whoo shit, kiss my ass! [*laughter*] They got schools for ya to go to. [*laughter*] Go learn how to speak, goddamn it! [*laughter*] Shittt.

Chaplin, of course, did not and could not use such comedy—to trip up a pursuer with his cane seemed to have been enough, given the time when Chaplin performed. To pose defects against religion (or more accurately, some purveyors of it) is a loaded double-barreled shotgun. Pryor's skit did not shock us as much as scatter all our fine sensibilities to the wind. And yet we laugh, and Aristotle is again proved right, as Richard Pryor demonstrates once more his stated theme that "those cats in church were jive."

If Chaplin and Woody Allen are understated, and Bill Cosby is supercool, and Redd Foxx blasé, Pryor took an entirely different approach; hyperbole was his thing, exaggerating for understandings other than credence. The monologue above was a hyperbolic romp: We know that even the most unsavory preacher is not likely to conduct himself in this manner in the pulpit.

It is the nature of black comedy to be hyperbolic, for expressions are needed that will more precisely highlight black life in the United States. Sometimes the hyperbole is sexual, at the root of things that are so bad they almost defy description from a white point of view. The hyperbole of the language in the two-voiced skit "The Wino and the Junkie" offers two statements that give the term new meaning.

The Wino has told the Junkie that he knows nothing about women, and the Junkie responds that he does indeed and that he had a woman: "Bitch was so fine I wanted to suck her *daddy*'s dick! Izzat fine enough for your ass?" When he has a tough time at the employment office, the Junkie reflects on the female clerk there and says, "Ugly bitch—I seen better faces on a iodine bottle." This last, of course, deals with concrete "ugliness," yet, an unattractive person can no more do anything about the way she looks than can a person who is black. Thus, the tradition of hyperbole, older than Stagolee and Shine, was continued by Pryor in the presentation of American comedy.

The United States has attracted or had brought to it a greater variety of peoples than any other nation since Rome. Each incoming group brought its humor and its comedy, and employed them as it underwent ridicule from groups that had preceded it. No group was more vilified for the ugliness and defectiveness assigned to it by its oppressors than the Africans. Laughing at the powerless was easy and habit-forming. Thus in the United States we have had the redskin joke, the nigger joke, the greaser joke, the spick joke, the Mick joke, the Kraut joke, the chink joke, the kike joke, the dago joke, the Jap joke, the Polack joke, and so on. However, the laughter at the undergroup did not alter, did not lessen, the victimization by the more powerful.

Why then should a black comedian like Pryor be immune to the tradition that has washed over, indeed inundated, almost every American? He wasn't. He simply took that tradition to its basest level, and in discussing the "New Niggers" reaped the laughter, from deep within the belly, that always seems to ride with our fears upon which we so easily place stereotypical concepts:

> An' if you ain't done it, be careful if you get some Vietnamese pussy, Jack. Right? Cause they got a VD scare the shit outa penicillin. It be up there waitin' for penicillin, Jack. 'C'mon up in here, peni—yeah, we got sumpin' for your ass, c'mon up in here. Git a big knot on your dick. . . .

DENNIS A. WILLIAMS   101

This monologue (like a few others) not only elicited wild laughter, it produced uneasy silences, rising crescendos of "oooo-oooooooooooooos," as if to say, "Boy, you ought to be ashamed of yourself," but, in the end, it was the laughter that rocked the club or concert hall.

It is not that sex has ever been far from the collective American mind. It was always there, partially concealed in innuendo. Another generation found it in the endless round of traveling salesmen jokes. In the black community (upon which many whites fixed much sexuality anyway), discussions and considerations of sex were always more overt than among whites. And black preachers in these tales and discussions and jokes (along with icemen and coalmen and milkmen) were a favorite target—which is to say, given American history, that black leadership from the pulpit was accepted with a grain of salt. Pryor exposed the relationship, and his audiences agreed with him—otherwise they would not have been falling out with laughter. There was that recognition.

By the same token, white churches and their leaders were viewed by Pryor as pretty pallid stuff, some evangelists being as much charlatans as the black preachers. Much of Pryor's work, in any case, consisted of drawing comparisons between the two groups in sex, manners and politics; in addition, there were the "private" skits that dealt with his family and himself. ("Who is Richard gonna talk about *tonight?*"). More as with Chaplin than with Allen, Pryor's figures were universal; Allen's are definitely New York or Hollywood chic, not much in between. Perhaps Pryor's comedy would not have been so successful without the range and variety of his intonations, which he matches up with not only the character of the moment, but the mood of the moment.

There were times during a monologue, as in the classic "The Wino and the Junkie," when audience hilarity stopped cold and Pryor's voice sank, bringing his audience with him. Winding down into self-pity, the Junkie says, "I'm sick, Pops. Boy, can y' help me? My mind's thinkin' about shit I don' wanna think about . . . I can't stop the motherfucker, baby [*sighs of sympathy*] . . . " The Wino's response picks up the monologue, moves it back into high humor. But Pryor had the audience, his eyes glistening momentarily with tears that did not brim over, as he trod the edge of things most comedians—even the black ones—have not dared to.

"Acting out" has always been an integral part of black comedy; the straight stand-up could be stifling; the genes cry out not only for movement, but for other characters, other voices, for black consciousness is a collective experience. Perhaps the touchstone for the "other voice" was Cosby's "Noah." Doing a dialogue—two characters building a skit—of course takes skill and some knowledge of how to use the mike, and the body. At this Pryor's mastery was clear in skits like "Dracula," the "Faith Healer," "Eulogy," Mudbones in "Little Feets," and other dialogues.

All this is a far, far cry from the days when Pryor did "poop the ship" jokes, or one-liners that began with: "Did you hear the one about . . . ?" Or told hecklers that he was being paid to make a fool of himself, what was their excuse? There were times when he reached so deeply into the psyche of his black audiences that he *did* become that charlatan preacher. The response then was as if a giant awoke; it was more a roar than applause. And there were those times that hark solidly back to the ancient call-and-response which plays over the comedy like a durable backdrop:*

"Mudbones was born in Mississippi. Tougaloo."
From out of the audience a female voice calls, "Where is that?"
Pryor responds: "Tougaloo? It's near Woomaloo."
The roar comes again. There is no "Woomaloo" but Pryor met the challenge, and the roar is praise for his quick thinking. If he asked for an amen, he got it, the roof trembling on its moorings. In the 1970s and 1980s, many in his audience, black and white, thought themselves victims on some level. And Pryor displayed the victim, complete with hip language and bravado, along with something else—the probability that, when people became aware of their common victimization, they might do something about it.

Sex, genitalia, body functions and human smells were Pryor's major metaphors for just about everything—including politics. Sigmund Freud would have been interested in the comedian because of the extent of his sexual references, which evoke the gods Min and Dionysus. Preceding them, as evidenced by the 15,000-year-old Venus of Willendorf statuette (as well as other finds), sex and genitalia in ancient cultures were highlighted. The Willendorf Venus is all buttocks (*steatopygia*), hips, belly and monstrous breasts, like the Pryor character, Miss Rudolph. Erect phalli on small replicas of ancient Egyptians, and

---

* Perhaps an even more vivid example is in Bicentennial Nigger, *through the Preacher character: We're celebrating two hundred years of—of white folks kickin' ass [applause, roars, cheers] . . . How-elsn-ever, we offer this prayer, and the prayer is: How long will this bullshit go on? [applause, roars, cheers] HOW LONG?*

the wall reliefs and friezes in India that display an astounding variety of sexual gymnastics of thousands of years ago, attest to the natural public place of sex and genitalia in everyday culture. This changed when the Europeans invaded the southern latitudes, bringing along their missionaries to "save the savages." Sex of all kinds was herded into the closet and remained there until relatively recently when, having forced its way out—at least partially—it was excused because society had become "more permissive."

Whether by instinct or design, Richard Pryor arrived at precisely the proper moment to project what is truly the human comedy, and the fact that it has been widely accepted must surely mean something. "I've never seen anyone walk out on his act," Cosby said. Maybe Pryor's fans understand better than most how commonplace sex is in their lives; that it is nothing special, that it just has its place.

"You can't talk about fucking in America, right?" Pryor told an audience. "People say you dirty. But if you talk about killin' somebody, that's cool. I don't understand it [*from the audience: Amen!*] myself. I'd rather come. I've had money and never felt as good as I felt when I come, when you're gettin' the nut—especially if it's a girl." [*Audience howls*]

For Pryor, the most pathetic man was the one who couldn't have an orgasm—the miserable role he once assigned to Richard Nixon. And a revolting spectacle was evoked when he later conjured up Ronald Reagan as "a penis in a suit." On the other hand, an erect penis was hyperbole in Pryor's terms, an image reflecting the highest admiration, as in the way Sugar Ray Robinson used to fight. ("That Sugar fight so good, make y'dick hard. Sugar *git* in a motherfucker's ass. Ask Jake LaMotta.") Pryor worked sodomy in metaphor: When he was sentenced to his ten-day term, he told his audience in a monologue that his pants were down around his knees and that he asked the judge "not to stick it in too far." Why, he wondered, do cops, when they arrest you, demand that you "spread your cheeks?" He suggested that in jail you ran the risk of having to "give up the booty," or being sodomized. "Didn't nobody fuck me no place," he boasted, because he kept everyone laughing "to keep their minds off the booty." On it goes: "the air that gits in there" when you're making love, the failure to get an erection and how you react. He had found a common denominator that people seemed to understand, because they laughed, howled, screamed—and didn't walk out.

There was a lot about fighting in Pryor's material, some of it between men and women. But in many of his stories, he affirmed, as in the cliché, that after fighting, making love was groovy. Being in love, however, was condensed to a metaphor wherein a man does not want his woman to have sex with another man once he has found one (pussy) "that fits!" A stranger would "stretch it outa shape." The comedian's women were "bitches," for the most part, females without names, but curiously, his sexist terminology was overshadowed by the fact, repeated in several monologues, that his women invariably triumphed in their encounters with men, like the wife who leaves her husband, declaring that had his penis been two inches longer, things might have worked out. Another character, Big Irma, was bad, tolerating no foolishness; as was the Playboy Bunny who had Pryor the narrator talking like a child before she gave it up. And when Pryor did skits built around his family, the mother gave quite as good as she got. In portraying marriage, the husband trying to psyche out his splitting wife was finally reduced to angry tears and threats to get her to stay. In Pryor's comedy, women put out their cigarettes on him as he stood at the elevator of a women's hotel waiting to get picked up. A fantastic-looking woman, who was into body-building, bedded down with him, and he discovered that no sex was involved, only "cosmic communication." Women were usually the winners in intersexual conflict.

Chaplin's characters were shy; Allen's usually stumble onto a good thing, Pryor's males made the hip moves; they were cool and bombastic by turn, but down deep they were losers in relationships with women. If they were unable to make love, then they had to fight them. And if they didn't have to fight, they were cuckolded, like Mudbones, who came home from work to find the toilet seat *up* that he had carefully nailed *down*, in order to trap his woman in an infidelity. "Ain't no bitch in the world piss with the toilet seat up," Mudbones says.

Pryor's exploration of the basic extended to additional cloacal analyses. Bad smells intrigued him—of feces, urine, vomit, unwhiskeyed bad breath, perspiration, whiskeyed bad breath, flatus. But good ones did too; one woman character, a friend of Mudbones, did have "breath as sweet as Carnation milk." Watching and listening to a Pryor performance, in many ways—especially in the use of language that described bodily functions—must have been the way it was sitting through a play by Aristophanes. None of the "bad" words the comedian used derives from the Greek. Indeed, very few even possess Latin origins, unless one uses the polite forms (urinate, defecate). Most of the words are from the Middle English (fuck, ass, bitch, piss, shit) and one of his favorites comes out of Swedish/Icelandic: pussy (the vulva of a mare). This is the language America speaks, not on television (except for cable channels like HBO), but increasingly in film; not in church, but more and more in other public places. It was always there and sometimes we use it. But not like Pryor. Lenny Bruce had used profanity to shock, but Pryor had woven this language so thoroughly into his work that it seemed peculiar when he did not use it. (As when he did a monologue on "The Tonight Show" that omitted the language he would insert in the same monologue on the concert stage.) For people who still had reservations about certain words, Pryor was the bad boy for them; they lived uncomfortably through his language and exploits that were detailed in his monologues.

English the language may be, but black people tend to carry the African aptitude for tonality to it, so that one intonation can mean one thing, while another can mean quite something else. Pryor did this exceptionally well and thus provided a learning experience for those who thought that "bitch," for example, had only one meaning.

The character Mudbones, like Gleason's "the Poor Soul," or Sid Caesar's young man at a dance, or Chaplin's underdog, or Allen's schlemiel, was enduring because it reflected the experience of a life of small tragedies. He was Pryor's greatest achievement in characterization. Probably based on his Grampa Tommy, Mudbones in many ways was also Pryor himself. Everyone tolerates an old man who mixes bombast with shreds of wisdom and also tells immensely funny stories. The character not only was a vehicle but a shield from behind which Pryor could attack anything, anybody; Mudbones could be the left hook; Pryor himself the right-hand cross. But a comedian once explained that "If you've got yourself a character and you're working through him and the routine bombs, you can always tell yourself, 'Well, *I* didn't bomb. The character did.' Helps protect the ego."

In Mudbones, Pryor arrived at a father figure, a man who had done nearly everything and survived, the character who reminded the comedian that "You don't git to be old bein' no fool, see. A lotta young wise men, they deader'n a motherfucker, ain't they?"

In one monologue from *Live on the Sunset Strip*, Pryor even split his persona, having Mudbones go to work on Richard Pryor himself. "I knowed that boy . . . see. He fucked up. See, that fire got on his ass and it fucked him up upstairs. Fried up what little brains he had. . . . 'Cause I 'member the motherfucker—he could make a motherfucker laugh at a funeral on Sunday Christmas Day. But, y'know what happened? He got some money—that's what happened to 'im—he got some money."

106   IF I STOP

There was more money to be made in the movies, but the movies would not allow Pryor to be as great a movie star as he was a comedian. No way. The movies made Charlie Chaplin, and they extended Woody Allen's talents, but they would almost certainly do nothing like that for Pryor. Yet he always wanted to be a movie star— a term which was correctly jabbed into place with Peter O'Toole's line in *My Favorite Year* ("I'm not an actor, I'm a movie star"). Yet, Pryor continued to expend just as much energy working on his comedy and preparing for concert tours. Why? Probably because he knew that in his own comedy he had full artistic control. He wrote the material or oversaw what was written; he approved staff, the technicians—he had, we assume, the final word. He could set his own pace, which appeared to be murderous, or he could quit before the end of a tour.

All these he couldn't do in filmmaking or television production, where control is firmly in the hands of others. *They* said "yes" or "no"; "jump" or "stay." From 1976 to 1980, when he again teamed up with Wilder, Pryor appeared in nine movies, none of which showcased him to great advantage. He made money, got good reviews, and starred in two of those films, *Greased Lightning* (1977) and *Which Way Is Up?* (1977), neither of which did more than to say for his career that he "needed the money."

In the United States (and probably elsewhere), being in the movies (or on television, the poor man's silver screen) has always symbolized success, whatever one's previous career, or however well-known an artist has been in other media. Sometimes the change in careers works out. But handling two careers at once is a problem, and Richard Pryor had a problem.

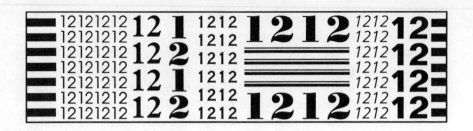

Twelve

Between 1975 and 1980, it was obvious that David Franklin was guiding Richard Pryor more into the movies and that this was what Pryor wanted. Although the black exploitation fad had passed, *Greased Lightning* and *Which Way Is Up?* could have been placed in that category without too much difficulty (and probably were by many people)—although neither thematically reflected the melodrama of the black hero against the white villains. This theme was de-emphasized, and the focus placed on a story centering on attainment of success in the white world.

Greased Lightning is based on the life of the late Wendell Scott, the first black national stock car racing champion. (A better vehicle might have been the life of Jack Ray Joe, a black racing car driver in California during the 1920s).

Of the two, *Which Way Is Up?* was the more interesting for its attempted reach beyond the ordinary black and white travail. *Which Way Is Up?* united Pryor and Cecil ("Broadway") Brown in their first major production; it also involved Michael Schultz, who had previously directed *Car Wash*.* Based on Lina Wertmuller's *The Seduction of Mimi* (a fact that caused a lot of cynical smiles in Hollywood), *Which Way* depicts conflict between farm workers and agribusiness management. The film was Pryor's first starring role, but it didn't have much to offer, other than two great cameos by the comedian as the grandfather and as Reverend Thomas. His primary role as Leroy Jones did not engage us.

---

* *Pryor had done what amounted to a cameo to goose the box-office of* Car Wash *as a favor to Schultz.*

At the end of the picture, after regaining the integrity he has lost running between two wives and being co-opted by the agribusiness firm, Leroy strides down the street, happy at last—and we don't care. What the film tried to say, it didn't say very well. film critic Judith Crist thought the scriptwriters had failed, and she had a point. Cecil Brown said that producer Steve Krantz changed his script and ruined it in the process. Krantz himself said that the concept "changed substantially during the time of production." Perhaps there were two few pots and too many cooks. Screenwriting credits also went to Carl Gottlieb —about whom no one talked. Krantz also said Pryor "contributed much of the material which eventualized in the screenplay but . . . that material was dictated as opposed to having been handwritten."* In 1976, before Brown was asked to do the writing, Pryor was to have written the first and second drafts and to apply whatever polish was needed. He did not. When Brown completed the script, applied with changes and polish, he returned to Berkeley to await a retyped copy that never came. When filming began he returned to Hollywood and in Pryor's dressing room read the script. He "found it interesting," he wrote in *Mother Jones*, "that the kind of changes made in my script all had to do with making black characters into caricatures."** The film grossed only $9 million.

The year before, in *Bicentennial Nigger*, Pryor had said, "I don't like movies when they don't have no niggers in 'em. I went to see *Logan's Run*, right? They had a movie of the future called *Logan's Run* . . . ain't had no niggers in it. I say, 'Well, white folks ain't plannin' for us to be here. That's why *we* gotta make movies."

Right from the beginning, there were people who saw that motion pictures had unlimited potential for making an impact on culture. Black filmmakers, like all filmmakers, wanted the money, prestige and respect that white filmmakers were accruing with unprecedented speed by their association with the magic of film. But Hollywood control was always white.

When a producer-writer-director-public relations person like Oscar Micheaux began to make films with all-black casts in the 1930s,

---

* *According to Krantz, he submitted Pryor's name as co-screenwriter, but the Writer's Guild of America approves such credit only if the material is handwritten or typed.*

** *Continuing with his analysis of Hollywood racism in the same* Mother Jones *piece, Brown suggested that there were black accomplices. He pointed out that Bill Cosby had put down Stepin Fetchit, only to "appear in* California Suite *(1978) clowning as pointlessly and inartistically as had Stepin Fetchit in his films." What Brown neglected to add was that Cosby's clowning was with Richard Pryor.*

DENNIS A. WILLIAMS

there was little chance of his establishing a black foothold in Hollywood. First of all, black movie fans preferred the Hollywood films to those made on shoestrings, because, very often, the shoestring budgets resulted in schlocky, one-take operations on chintzy sets with bad lighting. (The advent of the black exploitation films was simply a rearrangement of black audiences from the communities where they lived to theaters "downtown.")

Historically unemployed—even in the present—for reasons too obvious and too often cited to be repeated here, black people who had the money—ten cents, twenty-five cents, seventy-five cents, or a dollar or two—could kill what was left in a day of job-seeking by going to the movies. In the old days they could see the feature, the B-movie, cartoons, coming attractions, a newsreel, and if they were lucky, some vaudeville acts as well. The movies have always been an escape from reality.

Second, Hollywood had the household names, the familiar faces in familiar roles.

Third, black films invariably were poor imitations of what Hollywood was already producing: cowboys and Indians, cops and robbers, debonair men and sophisticated ladies, villains and heroes. "Black themes" were not found in the story lines of black-produced movies; the only difference then was in the presentation of black characters. This is not to say that there were no available black dramatists; there were. But their dramatic themes centered on the theme of bigotry, and besides, people like Micheaux wouldn't have wanted to pay them much, anyway.

Fourth, Hollywood had a million-mile lead in studios, distributorships, financing and technology.

Fifth, Hollywood had all the power image-makers can ever hope to possess. It sent its blazonry and bombs all over the world, influencing people in ways that have even today not been completely assessed; America flickered in the most distant villages. Those who could, joined the movie steamroller, became somehow part of it; black people were not invited before nor behind the cameras.

It is this long, bitter, cynical history of Hollywood—and not the fan—which determined what the fan should see; it asked whether the love affair with Richard Pryor, begun in earnest in 1976, was the beachhead so long awaited by all kinds of people for the emergence of another kind of Hollywood.

In a curious twist, during the five-year period when Pryor was with Franklin, he was more "black" off-camera than he had ever been in a starring role in film, where, in the logical sequence of Hollywood, black actors move from one stereotypical level to another, from "Buck/Coon" to "Mr.

Dark-But-Clean," to "Super-Spade/Honky Ass-Kicker," with hardly anything between. A lot of people who have been caught in this situation never protested, but Pryor had some pungent things to say about the movies and TV, and he was not the first. His statements, sprinkled with the dust of stardom, built around him an aura that now begged for the successful resolution of black expectations in and about filmmaking.

Inherent in that resolution is the goal that (as Sidney Poitier wrote in his book, *This Life*) in every film with or about black people and minorities in general, audiences be able to find "a certain nourishment, a certain substance, a certain complement of self . . . a loving comment. . . . "

Early in the 1970s, Clarence Avant, a record company executive, was urged by some studio officials to buy the rights to books by black authors and to commission original screenplays by black writers. As a result, he optioned the novel *Sons of Darkness, Sons of Light* that had been published in 1969. The option included the first draft of a screenplay from the book by the novelist. Avant also optioned the George Davis novel *Coming Home*, published in 1971. What would have been Michael Schultz's first directing assignment was *Simmons from Chicago*, written for Avant by Matt Robinson (who played Gordon on *Sesame Street*). According to Avant, Pryor had closely monitored the script, and was himself then writing *The Black Stranger*. But none of Avant's projects got off the ground; the studios that had urged him to get into film lost interest, perhaps because none of Avant's properties adhered to the formulas of films like *Watermelon Man* (1970), *Cotton Comes to Harlem* (1970), or *Shaft* (1971).

Still in the record business and close to the entertainment world, Avant remains by choice involved with, but not in, the movie industry. He recognized that blacks in Hollywood "must be willing to gamble," as he did, and that should they come into any kind of power, such as that reflected by stardom and a topflight manager, they should "dictate their own production deals," a fact that David McCoy Franklin seemed to understand very well when he hooked up with Pryor. Furthermore, Avant added, "the new [film] technology makes [black] control of a film a must."

While Franklin and Pryor were still on paths that would cross, and Avant was struggling with deals that would never be consummated, actress Ellen Holly was writing: "One of the penalties of being black and having limited money is that we seldom control our own image. We seldom appear in the media as who we say we are, rather, as who whites say we are. . . . The visible tip of the iceberg, the actors whose images flash on the screen, have been black, but they have been no more than hired hands. . . . shills employed as window dressing. . . . Below the waterline, hidden from public view, lies the other seven-eighths of the iceberg, the writers who create the material, the directors who shape it, and the producers. . . . who put up the money, specify and control content and pocket the profits."

Pryor understood this, and in both his public and performance voices spoke out. His sentiments were recorded in the media, which was not all that receptive to the same charges being made over and over again by other black show-business people. *Their* charges were aired in the *black* media.

In order to circumvent some of the barriers, most black actors wrote their own scripts, just as Pryor did. (For him, being listed as a writer was almost as important as being the star.) It is rare to find a black actor who has not written a screenplay with himself/herself cast as the star. They know that white writers will *not* have them in mind, and even if they should, past experience has demonstrated that there will be something not accurate about the black character. Ishmael Reed noted with resignation that "They [black actors in Hollywood] all got pretensions about being writers."

Obviously, though, coming up with a good screenplay is a lot cheaper than coming up with $20 million, which is the crux of the problem insofar as black actors are concerned. A good, even a great script, generally speaking, will not automatically attract backing if blacks are in it, so the black actor is back on square one holding a script—which is not much better than being on square one without it. The clear answer is to become so big, so important, that you don't need to trundle scripts around with you; they come flying at you in pursuit, neck and neck with the moguls with the money—a position only one black actor enjoyed at the middle of the 1970s, and that was Pryor, thanks mainly to *Silver Streak*.

Before him, Cosby managed to crack the behind-the-camera aspect of Hollywood, using sometimes as many as "twenty-two cats," including "directors who never directed before, black actors who never acted before."* But he ran into trouble with the unions, a not unusual

---

* *In 1982, the film and television industry posted a horrendus minus 5 percent average in the use of black and Hispanic actors, when there were 1,817 minority roles available. In 1928, there had been more than 10,000 non-white roles, hardly any of them dignified. Five studios were involved in the 1982 study: MGM, blacks, 8.5%, Hispanics 4.2%; Twentieth Century-Fox, blacks, 7%, Hispanics 2.1%; Columbia, blacks, 7%, Hispanics 3.33%; Warner Bros., blacks, 5.4%, Hispanics 2.1%; Paramount, blacks, 5.1%, Hispanics 1.7%.*

problem all over the country; Hollywood is not the place where brotherhood is encouraged on a regular basis, even though the possibilities of creating additional markets could be a result. It has had some tentative experience in depicting a degree of brotherhood, despite the fluff that usually attends such efforts. *Home of the Brave* (1949), *Guess Who's Coming to Dinner* (1967), *In The Heat of the Night* (1967), *One Potato, Two Potato* (1964), and *Nothing But a Man* (1964)—the last two made by independents—demonstrate but a few of the efforts.

Hollywood understands so well its power to create images for good or bad that it is hardly worth discussion. What Darryl Zanuck said years ago remains even more true today: "God, man, the movies are the greatest political factor in the world today. For propaganda, I mean." Propaganda, yes, into which is built the strategy for moneymaking, and when the movies are tied into television (which has become more of a farm club for talent than the stage), with its 100 million sets, that power is magnified. When upward of 58 million of those sets are equipped with video cassette recorders, the propaganda potential goes through the roof.

W. E. B. Du Bois recognized the connection between art and propaganda in 1926, fifteen years before the birth of television, and one year before the advent of sound film. He said, "All Art is propaganda and ever must be, despite the wailing of the purists. I do not care a damn for any Art that is not used for propaganda. But I do care when propaganda is confined to one side while the other is stripped and silent . . . . White artists themselves suffer from this narrowing of their field. They cry for freedom in dealing with Negroes because they have so little freedom in dealing with whites."

Du Bois meant that white artists often don't even recreate the truth about white people but feel uninhibited about recreating "truth" for blacks. Of course the obvious problem here is that if they can't tell it about whites, it is unlikely that they could tell the truth about blacks. To some extent, Pryor seemed to have understood the need to offer an alternative to white filmmaking when he told a San Francisco reporter that he liked "to make movies that are excellent and, if you'll pardon the expression, kick ass across the board. I think that's what filmmaking is all about—to reach as large an audience as possible." And with the truth, Richard.

To propagandize and commercialize through film and television in our time is a single endeavor, for you can sell a President as well as a product, rolling one directly into the other. To reach the largest possible share of a moviegoing audience that is 72 percent white and 28 percent black, Hollywood considers, but seldom satisfies, the audience of millions of black fans who spend about $40 million dollars a year going to the movies. Even considering population growth, these figures are probably proportionally the same for the era of black exploitation films. Why then were these films discontinued?

The reason given for the demise of black films was that they stopped producing profits. But this makes curious the stardom of Richard Pryor and more recently Eddie Murphy. (Curious if we set aside the movie formula of black-white male bonding.) Lack of profit may not in fact have been the reason behind the death of black films. Rather, we have to look at the messages of the black films that were being made. True, many of them frantically reversed the stereotypical black image on film. Most were different, stark departures from the traditional Hollywood concepts of blacks, even if they were produced by whites. They were in ways threatening, perhaps even revolutionary. If they were violent, that violence was not always black-to-black. Hollywood understands violence, and in its creations much of it down through the years has been directed against black characters, from *Birth of a Nation* to *Taxi Driver* to *White Dog*. Images celebrating the arrival of the "New Negro" (*Guess Who's Coming to Dinner*), crook (*Superfly*) or cop (*Shaft*), pimp or President (*The Man*), were not the norm. And they had to go. Hollywood remembered what Zanuck had said.

Richard Roundtree, whose portrayal of Shaft most typified the tough, swaggering, new blackness of the early 1970s, and whose huge photo used to hang alongside other stars' in the cafeteria of Universal Studios, believed the market never dried up. "You can't tell me [blacks] don't want to see each other on film."

Pryor, beginning with *Car Wash*, made seven films for Universal and, in a real sense, replaced Roundtree as the starring black, not in ethnic exploitation but as a "crossover phenomenon." The consideration remained, however, that if people like Clarence Avant felt that recasting the black image truthfully is of greater importance than making money, then surely some of those who had created the false and accepted images in the first place would be equally motivated to maintain them. The adulation of Richard Pryor, however, appeared to indicate that things were changing.

Pryor's comedy was electrifying and enthusiastically received. Cosby ranked him number one, before Jonathan Winters and Redd Foxx. There was no discernible conflict between it and the comedian's film career, as far as he was concerned. David Franklin was handling everything.

If Pryor was offered X number of dollars for a project, Franklin jetted in from Atlanta and asked for Y and Z, too. Most times he got them. When Franklin arrived, said Pryor, "We would sit down and decide who we wanted to be in the movies that we were doing, and what type of scripts would be best to do. He'd tell me about offers he received and advise me that this would be good or that movie would not be such a good idea, or we would plan a concert [comedy] tour."

One deal Franklin put together was a four-year, multimillion-dollar package at Universal, with the studio keeping "first right of refusal" on Pryor's "creative ideas" for several motion pictures. The comedian also got a share of profits, and freedom to appear in films at other studios. Pryor's response to the contract was characteristically pungent: "Well, I guess that means if these movies don't make money, a whole lot of niggers gonna be in trouble."

Pryor's financial well-being was all but guaranteed, through Richard Pryor Enterprises, a corporation Franklin had set up, which brought in money not only from concerts and acting roles but from writing as well. *Which Way Is Up?*, for example, carried a stipulation that Pryor was to be paid an additional $13,000 a month for working on the script—and given Writers Guild credit. A day's work on *Car Wash* brought $10,000, *In God We Trust* (1980) would bring him $50,000 for two days' work, and *Stir Crazy*, $1 million plus a percentage of the take.

But there were problems here and there. Dissatisfied with his affiliation with Laff Records, Pryor attempted to break the contract in order to return to Warner Bros./Reprise. Laff responded by suing Pryor for a couple of million dollars, but through lawyers Michael Ashburne and Howard Moore, acting in concert with Franklin, the matter was resolved so that both Laff, using previous material, and Warner Bros., using new material, could represent him.

Between 1975 and 1980 there were as many projects conceived and abandoned as movies Pryor made. Among them were *Macho Man*, which was to have been scripted by Neil Simon; *A Day in the Life of* (Richard Pryor), to have been produced by Franklin; *Gordon Entertaining Nightly*, *Cyrano*, Orwell's *Animal Farm*, *The Charlie Parker Story*, a project simply called *Lily Tomlin Idea*, and Cecil Brown's script, *Nobody*. The latter was a story about Bert Williams, the black comic of vaudeville in the 1920s; it was then and still remains one of those stories that when told would do much to improve white understanding of black life. Pryor recalled that Universal didn't like the script. Of course the difference between a script and an idea is immense. Since the idea was never rerouted through another script, it is plain that it was the idea that was rejected and not just the script. This should have been a signal to Pryor that his stardom was very much contingent upon his making films that "are not about Negroes at all," as Ralph Ellison said of earlier films like *Home of the Brave, Intruder in the Dust, Lost Boundaries* and *Pinky*, but "about what whites think and feel about Negroes."

Several years later in *Days Without Weather*, Brown wrote: "Nobody ever gets the film he wants to do. It's a myth."

What was no myth when Franklin and Pryor were together was that the comedian was working extremely hard fulfilling a schedule that would have killed anyone else. Yes, the money was good, but he worked five times as hard as a white star would have for the same amount. But Pryor kept on moving, racing ever onward, to what he was not always sure himself.

Thirteen

The year after *Silver Streak* raced to success was yet another crucial period for Pryor and his career. He had bought a $50,000 home for his grandmother, Marie, in Bartonville, a suburb of Peoria; a home for his son Richard and his mother valued at $60,000; a home for Maxine and Elizabeth Ann in Los Angeles worth $155,000. There's little doubt that he did as much for his other children and their mothers.

He gathered all the kids and took them on a trip to Europe—Renee, Richard, Elizabeth Ann, and Rain; it was a trip he found utterly exhausting. In the meantime, David Franklin was dealing with NBC and Burt Sugarman, and a team of writers was being assembled in preparation for the new "Richard Pryor Show," due to air September 13, 1977. NBC, it is said, offered Pryor $2 million for the exclusive rights to his services over five years—and it didn't matter if he appeared or not—as long as he produced at least two hour-long specials a year.

Pryor had only barely left behind *Silver Streak*, *Which Way Is Up?* and *Greased Lightning*, and already he was rushing to locations for *Blue Collar*, *The Wiz*, and *California Suite*, which was, at least, being shot locally. Pryor made Sammy Glick look frozen in place. (Later it would appear that this torrid pace was not completely to Pryor's liking. He seldom even had time to lower his car window, as he sometimes did, and shriek in exultation that he had made it—the skinny, screwy stroker from Peoria had made it!)

The best thing that seemed to be happening to the comedian was a relationship with one Deboragh McGuire, a young model and actress who was not a name in anyone's household. The relationship resulted in a well-publicized marriage on September 22. Earlier, Pryor had asked her to come with him on a trip to Peoria, and he presented her to Miss Whittaker, who said, "He introduced me to her and said he was going to marry her. I asked why. He said, 'Because she's young.' I said, 'Oh,' and left it at that." Pryor was 37 at the time, but clearly, he felt much older. Miss Whittaker was not the only person to express some degree of surprise. For some, the surprise was that McGuire was black. Some speculated that the comedian had caught up with the new black solidarity, and others theorized that the not infrequent attacks and slashing innuendos directed against him for what many perceived as a preference for white women had beat him back into the fold.

Four days before the marriage, Pryor had appeared at the Hollywood Bowl for a "Star-Spangled Night for Rights." That was the night that the comedian exercised his right to tell an audience to "Kiss my happy, rich black ass!"

There were 17,000 people there, gathered to demonstrate the concern of the entertainment industry for human rights in response to well-publicized attacks against gays, such as those by singer Anita Bryant. The event was backed by the gay community and the American Civil Liberties Union. Participating were Olivia Newton-John, David Steinberg, Lily Tomlin, Valerie Harper, Paul Newman, Bette Midler, the rock group War, the dance group The Lockers, and others. It didn't take people long to sense during the first half of the show that the emphasis was going to be on gay rights.

Backstage, Pryor noticed that The Lockers, the black dance troupe, were being shabbily treated, while some white ballet dancers were being given the red carpet. Afterward, the film director Michael Schultz said, "The manager, the guy who was running the whole thing—somebody connected with Bette Midler—was definitely giving the black group second-class treatment and talking offensively to them. It really flipped Richard out. There he was, willing to go out on the line for people who were being discriminated against, and, backstage, he was witnessing . . . racial discrimination."

There is agreement that the comedian had been drinking fulsomely. When he came on, he complained that everyone had ooo-ed and aaahhh-ed over the white dance group; that the staff had painstakingly arranged the spotlights for them, and that the audience had applauded wildly. But, he accused, nobody "did shit for The Lockers." The statement was almost a repeat of the second part of his monologue about the way (white) people "don't give a nigger a break. . . . Jackson Five be singin' they ass off, they [white people] be talking' 'bout the Osmond Brothers . . . mother*fuck* a Osmond Brothers!"

Feeling no pain, Pryor lashed out at some of the stars, too. He accused some in the audience of being out cruising while Watts was burning, of not really being out of the closet at all. He told them he was the only one of the stars who stood up there and told them he'd once indulged in a homosexual act. He raged for fifteen minutes during the second half of the show, his comedy as cutting as a razor. Finding it not sharp enough, he went directly after his audience. It responded mostly by booing him. "This is an evening about human rights," he said, "and I am a human being. And I just wanted to see where you were really at." He kept talking between the boos. "I wanted to test you to your soul. I'm doing this for nothing—they ain't paying me no money." He banged the mike back into place after delivering his closing line and sauntered off. When Bette Midler came on a little later, she said, "Well, who wants to kiss this rich white ass?" She got a standing ovation.

The event raised an estimated $350,000 from the audience of mostly white males; it was to go to the Save Our Human Rights Foundation. In response to the Lee Grant newspaper account of the affair, the *Los Angeles Times* excerpted several letters from people who thought Grant's story much too kind to Pryor. The letters called the comedian "vulgar," "racist," "crude," "bitter," "a bigot," "hostile," "disgusting," and "filthy." And by direct statement and inference, they said that Pryor owed his success not to his own efforts but to the support of many of those in the audience: "We made him [Pryor], we gave him stardom in the movies, we allow ourselves to buy the products to pay for his television shows . . . . "

Pryor had committed the sin, often fatal, of offending one of the most powerful groups in entertainment and the arts. However, one black gay wrote that "the California homosexual is the most extreme of all bigots. He hates blacks, women and himself most of all. Pryor's actions were crude, but sadly, true. If one refuses to believe, let a person who is fat, black, ugly or female try going to a gay club alone."

Pryor married Deboragh in a white suit, fed his bride a piece of wedding cake, and then drove into Hollywood to tape one of his NBC shows.

NBC ran the first of Pryor's network specials (they did not label it a test) on May 5, calling it "The Richard Pryor Special?" NBC executive reaction was astoundingly good. The network then went ahead with planning for "The Richard Pryor Show." The best two skits in that spring special were derived from his concert routines. There was the rascally preacher, this time the Divine James L. White, TV spiritualist, in a shirt cut down close to his navel and wearing a whopping Afro. The Divine One complained that "We're not getting the crossover buck—the white folks' money, the Billy Graham dollars."

The Idi Amin skit was a bomb.

The wino bit with writer Maya Angelou was taken from the comedian's routine, "Nigger with a Seizure," but was extended beyond the comedy into a subtle and moving discourse by Angelou as the wife, on what so often happened to black men and why. *The New York Times* television critic, John J. O'Connor, noted that "Mr. Pryor . . . is complex. He creates characters that go beyond calculated outrageousness to being genuinely disturbing . . . . The Pryor talent is special beyond the limitations of this special." O'Connor was equally approving (though with reservations), as he was of the first show which was run again in September.

The opening had been censored. It had been taped with Pryor wearing a body suit so that he looked naked, while he spoke words to the effect that he had not given up anything to do the series for NBC. There were three solid skits, and the rest of the show was fragments, short takes, and jibes at tradition. In the first skit he played a dour, snappish waiter in a bar peopled by characters out of *Star Wars*, whom he treated with commonplace cool. He talked baseball, angrily reminded the patrons that there was no dancing, and told one of the creatures that he looked like a neighbor from Detroit.

The second major skit displayed Pryor as the President, declaring that the neutron bomb is a neo-pacifist weapon—hooking neatly upon the double-talk politicians swamp us with. The press conference (for that was the setting) then went racial. The President admitted that yes, he had considered Huey Newton (formerly a leader of the Black Panther Party) for director of the FBI. A "reporter" asked if it was true that the President would keep on seeing white women, and Pryor as President responded, "As long as I can. Why do you think they call it the White House?" In the ensuing scramble to ask questions, the President ignored white reporters and got into a soul bag with black reporters.

The third skit was poignant, poignancy being as much a Pryor trademark as his wildest comedy. A soldier returns home at the end of World War II to find his "girl next door" performing in a Harlem nightclub. Of course, he had all the prejudices other people had about nightclub singers. Paula Kelley and Pryor played understated parts that moved the situation from "a re-creation," O'Connor wrote, "of a period that is quintessentially black" into the realm of the universality of experience. "If there are any problems about the content," the critic wrote, "the time slot should go but Mr. Pryor should definitely stay. Television can use his originality."

However, Pryor quickly attacked the censorship of the opening, after the show was aired, declaring that it was "a violation of an artist's right . . . an offense to our mentality." He admitted that the network did have control over what was aired, but added, "that's why they're number 3."

He also said that "A lot of the people who control the television medium are fascists. They have one-track minds when it comes to creative thinking." In addition, he admitted, he hadn't wanted to do television, but they'd offered him so much money that he couldn't refuse. He was, he said, "greedy," a term he used over and over to justify the many projects in which he was involved. Perhaps closer to the truth was that he was not as greedy as he was (maybe appropriately) fearful of losing all he had gained. So he kept moving. Fear is as much a spur as fame, and sometimes they are so tightly intertwined as to make it impossible to detect which is which.

There were two landmark skits in the second show. The first had Pryor eating alone in a swanky little restaurant. Sitting across the room, also alone, is Marsha Warfield. Both are eating neatly and daintily. The skit was all mimed except for one word. Pryor and Warfield happen to glance up at each other, and the camera, alternating between medium-and not-so-tight shots, reveals in the eyes of both an instant's small conflagration. Suggestively using the manner in which they eat—while eyeing each other—they move slowly and sensuously through their meals. They alternatingly eat—with exquisite sensuality—spaghetti, cherries, corn on the cob, oranges, grapes, each bite accompanied by optic suggestion, a sense of making love. Pryor, in frustration, smears first the pasta over his face; he has not the patience to eat the grapes one by one, so these, too, he smears in sexual frustration across his face. They stare at each other expectantly. They blow out the candles on their tables and then Pryor leaps up and bounds for her table. They embrace hungrily, dive to the floor as the other patrons watch, and kiss and pull and tug at each other in frenzy. The headwaiter calmly signals and a fire hose is brought in and turned on them, bringing them to their senses. They rise, slip and slide sheepishly back to their tables, wet and food-smeared. Then Pryor's date arrives. Warfield's date also arrives, and the skit ends. Eating food so sensuously that it led to total sexual abandon had been displayed for the first time on television. Parts of the skit, the exchange of glances, were very much like the final scene in Charlie Chaplin's *Limelight*.

The second skit featured a clown, who can only be seen by kids, in a ghetto junkyard. He tames a tiger and makes it jump through a hoop. The animal is never seen, but is distinctly heard. Then the clown walks a high-wire with a chair, carefully and slowly, but of course, he hasn't really moved off the ground. Flowers and candy appear as if by magic. The children are called home by their mothers offstage. Of course, the mothers do not believe such a clown exists. One kid returns to the junkyard and there finds the clown's derby on the ground.

Pryor's writers for the show included David Banks, who had met the comedian in Berkeley in 1966, and who produced some of Pryor's albums, as well as Jeffrey Barron, Booker Bradshaw, Paul Mooney, Arthur Sellers, Jeremy Stevens, Tom Moore, and Rocco Urbisci, who was also the producer.

Some of the material for the other shows obviously was adapted from Pryor's records, like the "Wino and Jekyll and Hyde" skit, which is much like the "Wino and Dracula" monologue. Another skit, about the sinking of the *Titanic*, was based on the black epic poem "Shine." Still another, where Pryor as an archeologist finds the oldest tomb in the world and in it are the mummified remains of a black man, indicated that the comedian, or someone on his staff, was extremely knowledgeable about black prehistory and the debates raging around it. That all this was boiled down to a three-minute comedy skit represented for TV (though TV didn't know it), a breathtaking airing of a long-simmering controversy. For, like all people, archeologists tend to view their discoveries with an ethnocentric bias.

It was probably a break for Pryor that he and NBC came to a parting of the ways. Schooled in the classroom of "Saturday Night Live" back in 1975, with people like John Belushi, Dan Aykroyd, Chevy Chase and others, Pryor got his dissertation doing his own show. He also planted seeds for the future. In 1990, Keenen Ivory Wayans' "In Living Color," a hip-hop collection of wicked black satire, debuted on the upstart Fox network and captured an Emmy Award. Critics ritually likened the show to "SNL," but Wayans was quick to acknowledge his debt to Pryor, whose NBC series, he said, was "the granddaddy" of his own.

Marie Carter Pryor Bryant had her seventy-eighth birthday on October 31, 1977, eleven days after the last of the four "Richard Pryor Shows" aired on NBC. Pryor arrived in Peoria to help her celebrate on November 9 and almost immediately began to complain about chest pains. He was taken to the Methodist Medical Center's intensive care unit; it was feared he was having a heart attack.

The hospital officials did not confirm or deny that Pryor's pains were the result of a heart attack, though his grandmother said, "He's doing as well as can be expected considering he's had a heart attack." Pryor's condition was listed as "satisfactory," and then characterized as "stable and good condition."

The hospital registered over five hundred phone calls from people wishing him well, among whom were Aretha Franklin, Sammy Davis, Jr., Olivia Newton-John, Diana Ross and Natalie Cole. Because so many Peorians claimed to know Pryor, a security guard was stationed at the door to his room to keep them from barging in. One Pryor investigator discovered there was almost no one in Peoria's black community who had not grown up with the comedian or who had not gone swimming with him in Illinois Lake. The problem with the latter claim was that, even though Pryor later had a swimming pool, he could not swim.

Deboragh did not accompany Pryor on the 1977 trip to Peoria where he was said to have had the heart attack. His grandmother, Mrs. Bryant, made all the official statements. Hospital spokesmen, throughout the four days Pryor spent in the hospital, declined to disclose what had actually been wrong with him. When he was released and had flown back to California, he told the press, "I had chest pains and I went to the hospital. They decided that I was tired and should rest a while, and they took some tests involving my kidney functions. . . . I feel great. I'm just relaxing now and catching some fish."

The incident made national news. In many ways, considering the schedule he maintained, Pryor had every right to have had a heart attack. Since, as Deboragh would say, "his life is his act," the "heart attack" would eventually surface in his comedy, in the 1979 film *Richard Pryor in Concert*. The situation, all in all, seemed to be a sign of Pryor's need for help. He was on a treadmill, moving with reckless speed, and he could not get off without injuring himself—if he wanted to get off. There may have been times when it was intensely exhilarating, but even exhilaration can kill.

In the fall of 1980, he told *Ebony* managing editor Charles Sanders that he had not had a heart attack, but a "murmur." "But it's no longer there," he said, "it reversed itself."

Sanders asked how the reversal had taken place, and Pryor answered, "That's another mystery. Just like when I was in the hospital and one night my kidneys just went out and they thought I was going to die. They were O.K. the next day. Same thing with my heart; the murmur just went away."

Because of the monologue, however, most people *do* believe the comedian suffered a heart attack on November 9, 1977. And five years later, Pryor told a lawyer that he had indeed had a heart attack.

LAWYER: You do a comedy routine and you talk about your heart attack. Is that not the case?
PRYOR: Yes, sir.
LAWYER: . . . Is that a real event or is that just a thing you do in an act?
PRYOR: No, that was a real event.
LAWYER: Do you remember what year that was?
PRYOR: No.
LAWYER: Did you in fact have a heart attack?
PRYOR: Yes.
LAWYER: Isn't it true that the doctors told you that you didn't have a heart attack?
PRYOR: No, the doctor told me I had a heart attack.

No one could watch the skit and not explode with laughter; both fact and fancy melted before the onslaught of the comedian's artistry which, perhaps, could only be achieved by blurring the line between the two, by not being willing to concede where the stage ends and real life commences. Anyone who knows actors or entertainers must realize that in this, Pryor is not by any means a singular exception.

Fourteen

Sunday morning, January 1, 1978, literally began with a bang in the Pryor home in Northridge. Actually, there were about ten bangs.

Scrambling out of the house, dashing around some of the fruit trees the comedian was so proud of, were his wife, Deboragh, and two of her friends, Beverly Clayton of Los Angeles and Edna Solomon of Washington State. In the gray, misting daylight, they raced for a Buick in which to escape Pryor who, in a blinding fury, was unleashing round after round from a .357 magnum pistol in their general direction.*
Earlier, conflicting reports said the comedian first fired a shotgun and then the pistol. The gun empty, Pryor jumped into his Mercedes-Benz and, in a frenzy that would do credit to a championship demolition derby, rammed it into the Buick again and again. And again. The three women managed to get away, but the shots and the sounds of smacking cars attracted the neighbors, who called the cops. Police cars were soon streaking for Parthenia Street. It was eight in the morning, and Deboragh and Pryor had been married about four months. And it was, of course, New Year's Day.

Before this circumstance, all had been inside, talking and partying in the New Year. The mood changed. Pryor got angry, called one of the women a name, suggested they all leave at once. Perhaps they didn't leave fast enough. Pryor was booked on a charge of assault with a deadly weapon, and/or assault with force likely to do great bodily harm, and malicious mischief. He was released on $5,000 bail. The

---

* *The* Los Angeles Times *of Tuesday, January 3, 1978, reported the following: "According to the police report, Pryor fired several shots at his wife and her friends outside the house, then chased the visitors in his Mercedes-Benz when they left in their own car."*

charges were processed early the following evening, a Monday, and Pryor was represented not by David Franklin, but a local lawyer, Leo Branton. The complaint had been signed by Clayton and Solomon, according to reports. There was speculation that Pryor needed time to contact Franklin, and that Franklin had arranged representation through Branton. The assault with a deadly weapon charge was dismissed in February when a municipal court judge ruled there was "insufficient evidence to sustain it."

One aspect of the case was resolved in September with Pryor being fined $500 and given the chance to do ten benefit performances instead of four months in jail. He was also ordered to get rid of his collection of guns—a collection Pryor-writers usually mentioned, as if suggesting that he was a hard-core menace because of them. Pryor's attorney this time was Jack Tenner, who asked the judge if the $100,000 Pryor had given to Jerry Lewis Muscular Dystrophy Telethon could count toward the public service part of the sentence. Pryor, however, said, "That was for charity. I didn't do it on account of this case, and I don't want it to count as a part of my sentence."

The apparent failure of Franklin to be present for some of the court proceedings undoubtedly caused Pryor to have some second thoughts about their relationship. These did not surface, though, for another couple of years. In the meantime, the Pryors were legally separated on January 26, with the divorce to become final in July. Pryor was enjoined from threatening or molesting her. Court records show that he was to pay her $62,000; $32,000 before July 1, $15,000 on or before November 1, and $15,000 before March 1, 1979.

In *Richard Pryor—Live in Concert*, filmed almost on the anniversary of the shooting/ramming escapade, the comedian predictably included his version of the incident:

> And I am really, personally happy to see *any*body see me, right, specially as much as I done fucked up this [past] year. [*applause*] I don't never wanna see no more police in my life—at my house. Takin' my ass to jail. [Actually, he turned himself in to the police about twenty-six hours after the incident.] For killin' my car. [*applause*] And it seemed fair to kill my car to me, right, 'cause my wife was goin' to leave my ass, and I say, Not in this motherfucker you ain't. [*laughter*] If you leave, you be drivin' those hush-puppies y'got. [*laughter*] 'cause I'm gone kill this motherfucker here. [*laughter*] And I had one o' them big ole magnums—you know how

much noise they make, you shoot sumpin'? I shot a tire, I say WHOOOM! Tire say, aaaaaaaaaaaa. It got good to me. I shot another one, BWOOOM! aaaaaaaaaaaa, and that vodka I was drinkin' say Go 'head. Shoot sumpin' else. I shot the motor. The motor fell out, motor say fuck it! Then the police came . . . I went in the *house*. Cause they got magnums too, and they don't kill cars—they kill nigg-aws.

This monologue was early in the show, and from that point on, the routine was awash with laughter that was loud, long and belly-crunching. Obviously, Pryor's version was funnier than the real thing.

The year 1979 was off to a romping start, picking up where 1978 had left off. First was the release of *The Wiz*, which dived. *Blue Collar* also came off the board and went almost straight down, but won the grand prize at the Paris International Film Festival. For the first time in the festival's history, films were judged by fans instead of the Paris film critics—who disagreed with the choice. *California Suite* didn't do such great business, either. The opportunity to do something special with Cosby and Pryor apparently never crossed the minds of Ray Stark and Herbert Ross. They only provided what must be considered comic relief—although the Walter Matthau/Elaine May skit was more to the point of comedy; what Pryor and Cosby did was slapstick.*

But *Richard Pryor—Live in Concert*, released early in the year through Special Event Entertainment and Universal, was Pryor again at the summit of his talent. Using his life as a part of his act, he also went into the heart attack routine, playing on the publicity his hospitalization garnered back in November 1977. It was David Franklin's idea to film the final two performances of the concert in Long Beach at the Circle Star Theater, and whatever Pryor was to feel in the future about Franklin, this film above all others made him THE name in Hollywood. It not only brought him even more fame—it also bought him more time, since the only other movie he was in that year was *The Muppet Movie*.

But, as true to form as anything else in Pryor's life, some of the gold was mixed with lead, which had found its way into his life in 1978. It was his exhausting schedule that was responsible for all the things that had happened to him when he told his audience at the Circle Star that he had "fucked up."

---

* *Pryor, who remained hot despite the disappointing grosses on most of his pictures, was offered twice as much to appear in* Suite *as Cosby. Honoring the help Cosby had given him earlier in his career, Pryor insisted they split the difference. Later, when Cosby approached Pryor about another film project, the no-nonsense Franklin cautioned that it would be every man for himself this time: "We're not going to go through life as twins."*

Maxine Silverman went back to court in October 1978, still listed as a legal secretary with a monthly income of $1,418. However, her expenses were $2,330.50 a month, including $250 for entertainment. She needed the money, she said through her attorney Gloria Allred, because Pryor was making in excess of $1 million a year, and her expenses were mounting. She was now asking for $1,200 a month, plus medical expenses and tuition and other costs for Elizabeth Ann's private school.

Represented by Michael Ashbourne, Pryor said a month later that he was making $41,000 a month (or $492,000 a year) and had over $20,000 in expenses, which included $3,318.41 in car payments, $297 for his grandmother's car and $432 for her home, $1,021 for Maxine's home he'd bought a year earlier, and almost $350 for his son's home. These were all monthly payments (totaling approximately $64,884—which exceeded his stated income monthly by $23,884). And he had his own home, valued roughly at about $500,000, and part ownership with Franklin and others in the Courtyard Shopping Center in Atlanta, worth, he said, $800,000, as well as in the Peyton Heights Apartments in Franklin's hometown, estimated to be worth $607,500. Mortgages accounted for 85 percent of the value of the listed property, the comedian said.

The court ruled that he pay to Silverman $800 a month, and bear the cost of medical needs and private school. He could visit Elizabeth Ann the first and third weeks of every month, and she could spend eight weeks with him during the summer.

All in all, this may not have been a hard pill to swallow financially, for it was clear, if not to the court, that Pryor was now, at least on paper, a millionaire.

In December, in what was perhaps a mixed blessing, Marie Carter Pryor Bryant died, and the last tough vine of women who had set direction in his life was gone. She had been a hard and determined woman, the central stabilizing figure around which so much of Pryor's often unstable early life revolved. She outlived two sons, one sister and nineteen brothers. In sessions with his therapist, Dr. Alfred Cannon at Drew Medical Center,* the comedian must have examined his relationships with his mother(s), grandmother, the mothers of his children, and other women as well for, surely a relationship of mighty proportions did exist. (A skit in Richard Pryor—Live in Concert concerns a beating with a switch from a tree that is administered by his grandmother. The mon-

---

* In 1982 Pryor claimed that a check for $50,000, a donation to Drew Medical Center, was "voided" by David Franklin.

strous, roaring laughter that accompanied the skit attests to the recognition, at least by black men.) Those relationships would have included Miss Whittaker, the surrogate mother who let Pryor as a child know there were alternatives to the life he knew in Peoria—a fact recognized by Mrs. Bryant since she seemed not to have opposed in the least her grandson's activities at Carver Community Center.

In the strange way of circles quietly closing, Pryor's attachment to his grandmother ended just days after his thirty-eighth birthday. This was the second family death in his birth month; the first was his stepmother's, Viola Anna Hurst Pryor. So he journeyed once again to Peoria in the winter, perhaps at last free of the need to dominate women, who may have represented the strength he could not best in Mrs. Bryant. In his concert film, done not long after her death, he did a monologue on the Macho Man, whose only power seems to come from his genitals—and often not much power at that. Here then was a switch from the usual monologue where men lose to women because the women are sharper and faster; in Macho Man the character loses because of his selfishness.

Nineteen seventy-eight and 1979 may have been good times for Pryor, but they were disasters for other black actors. *Ebony* magazine related that "Very few of the stars bother to wear sunglasses or other disguises. They are out of work. . . . Things are so bad for many black actors and actresses that some have taken jobs as bartenders and cocktail waitresses. . . . " Fred Williamson summed up the situation briefly and to the point, the way he used to play when pass receivers rushed into his area of the Kansas City Chief's defenses: "Things here in Hollywood stink! They just stink!"

It always happened—periods of seeming prosperity, then the decline. With black film people, actors mostly, there never was a constant; fluctuation was more the rule than the exception than it was for white film folk. The next period of the black highroller was ten years later, and not too many of the old faces were visible. They were replaced by actors Danny Glover, Whoopi Goldberg, Eddie Murphy, Denzel Washington, Arsenio Hall and Morgan Freeman, to cite a few, directors Michael Schultz, Gordon Parks and Sidney Poitier were joined by Robert Townsend, Spike Lee, Keenen Ivory Wayans, Wendell B. Harris, Charles Burnett, and Reginald and Warrington Hudlin (who characterized the resurgence as being "The best time in history to be a black filmmaker"). The reason was the sudden, unanticipated success in the late 1980s of several independent black film projects by Lee and others. Yet the status of black films, as always, remained precarious as far as Hollywood was concerned. One black entrepreneur was told by an agency: "As soon as there's one dud, it's probably going to close up the whole shop."

In the late 1970s there were the usual beginnings (and the ultimate endings) of black film companies dedicated to the utilization of black talent in front of and behind the cameras. Jim Brown and Spencer Jourdain teamed up to form Independent Film Ventures, which was bankrolled in part by federal and matching funds; Richard Pryor Enterprises, formed in 1975, was similarly committed (David Franklin and Barbara Wilson were also listed as officers of the company). Fred Williamson's Po' Boy Productions for a time seemed about to break through, because the ex-football star concentrated on securing European backers and markets.

None of these ventures were long-term successes, and, as *Ebony* noted, Hollywood remained "a gloomy place for all but the superstars—Sidney Poitier, Bill Cosby, Richard Pryor and a few others who are so rich that they have no immediate worries; or have careers and business investments; or have 'crossover' appeal to whites." It was only with *Bustin' Loose* that Pryor, as coproducer, publicly influenced what happened before and behind the camera. The informal record indicated, however, that when he wanted to be the proverbial 800-pound gorilla, he got what he wanted.

Things were equally bad for black people on television, of course. Both the Annenberg School of Communications and the U.S. Civil Rights Commission noted that there were extremely limited opportunities for minorities and women to appear in serious roles. A producer of the television show, "Benson" (starring Robert Guillaume, who later became a producer when the series ended), Paul Junger Witt, said "The white viewing public might be more comfortable with blacks in comedies, not necessarily of the 1930s, '40s or '50s stereotypes, but comedies nevertheless."

Steven Bochco, whose productions achieved prime-time prominence with "Hill Street Blues," "L.A. Law," and other shows, offered an explanation. One of the things that made "Benson" pleasant was that he was "a black man in the *right* place. He's a servant. Whites don't have to deal with the black man who is territorially threatening."

In fact, they don't even have to deal with Dr. Cliff Huxtable or his wife, a lawyer, or their kids, because "The Cosby Show" is not a reflection of life as most people know it. More likely to be accepted as certifiably realistic were the black cops and detectives (and criminals) seen on so many shows. "The Oprah Winfrey Show" was deemed more suited to television than her short-lived dramatic series "Brewster Place." Comedy continued to be the format within which black performers survived on television in shows like the recent "Amen," "227," "A Different World," "Family Matters," and "The Fresh Prince of Bel Air." Ironically, it was the phenomenal success of "The Cosby Show" that saved situation comedy on television at a moment when many believed the genre had run its course. And by proving that whites would accept certain kinds of shows about blacks, it may have helped condemn them—at least in the perverse thinking of Hollywood—to a comedic ghetto.

There was also the matter of dollars. Shifting demographics and a decline in overall network viewership due to the explosion of cable and video forced the networks at the close of the 1980s to cater to any identifiable subgroup it could get to watch its wares. African-Americans were just another such group. But even though they were generally understood to be undercounted by the Nielsen ratings, the conventional, if unstated, wisdom was that it was unusual if not impossible to have a successful television show without a black audience.

Of course there was no reason to expect the film industry to be any more responsive than television. Certainly in the late 1970s, the black film audience was not considered crucial, and actors, directors and writers stood at the mercy of studios.

Pamela Douglas, for three years an executive in feature film development at Universal Studios, and the first black woman ever voted to the board of directors of the Writers Guild of America, was close to it all. One of her adventures at Universal, where Pryor later had a superstar deal, involved recommending to a highly placed executive a script that she had found "true" and "beautiful." The executive yelled at her, "Don't give me that crap! How much is it gonna make? If you can't show me more than $20 million, get outta here. And if you don't quit with that 'beauty' and 'truth' shit, you better get out of the business."

Even as Douglas was being subjected to such treatment (and she was not alone), producers were slinking around to secure black writers who could make the few black parts or black scripts done by whites "black." And they always found them without having to offer screen or Guild credit; nothing except the kind of money white writers would not even consider. It was like dealing with The Hollywood 10, those blacklisted white writers of the 1950s who either wrote under phony names or no names at all, and got peanuts for their efforts.

Not since *Buck and the Preacher* (1972), *Uptown Saturday Night* (1974), *Let's Do It Again* (1975) (all directed by Sidney Poitier), and the TV min-series "Roots" (1977) had so many black actors and technicians (except for "Roots") secured any notable, however brief, amount of work. Hard times continued through the end of the 1970s into the 1980s, so it was natural that all eyes turned to the hottest cat in town, whose pronouncements ("The time for being white is over!" "If you want to do anything—if you're black and still here in America—get a gun and go to South Africa and kill some white people!") were still reverberating in Hollywood.

Pryor seemed a contradictory figure. He was the *Great* Brother, the ass-kicking, stone-solid-as-chitlens-were-good brother. Yet, could journalist Bill Brashler have been right in his assessment of Pryor that "His life vacillates between sweet appeasement of the people he knows he must deal with in order to make it—producers, studio heads, writers, fans—and the opposite, the point at which he begins to feel that he has become the nigger clown for all of them?"

Thus Pryor's trip to Africa in the spring of 1979 with his friend, Jennifer Lee, was paradoxical. Why did it take a trip like this to tell him what should have been obvious? Other black American actors had visited the continent, among them Canada Lee, Eartha Kitt, Juano Hernandez, Sidney Poitier, and Bill Cosby (who had made some investments in coffee in the 1960s in Kenya). Ossie Davis and Ruby Dee had also made the pilgrimage, as well as thousands of other black Americans. All naturally had opinions; few came away as changed as Pryor. But Pryor had one of the loudest voices. He announced that he had found no "niggers" in Africa, that it was the "motherland." If it seemed odd to many people that he had to travel to Africa in order to be convinced that he did not have to use "nigger" in his routines, they did not often say so; the important thing was that *some* experience had made him stop using the word. Like many of Pryor's experiences, his first trip to Africa, to Kenya, became a part of his act. He was impressed by what he saw just outside the Nairobi Hilton Hotel. In answer to a question that a "voice within him" put, "Do you see any 'niggers?'" he answered "No." But the little park just across the street from the Hilton teems with people looking for handouts, and for foreigners they can hustle. From there all the photo safaris begin. The hotel is like a great horn of plenty in the midst of a shimmeringly modern capital which only barely conceals the past degradation of extensive colonialism. Kenya had already entered the American camp that stands guard over the Indian Ocean. Editors like Hillary Ngweno were being harassed by the government of Daniel Arap Moi; great writers like Nugi wa Thiong'o had had to flee the country. Down on the coast, Mombasa, a city in whose streets one expects to encounter Sydney Greenstreet or Peter Lorre, belonged to the Kenyan government by day, but at night it became one big red-light district dominated by the American sailors and marines and the local bar girls. Government officials could not then use their chits; they had to pay cash like everyone else. But Mombasa, unlike Nairobi, remained more African than European. Nairobi, at 9,000 feet high, has a climate that attracts many of the world's African correspondents to base offices there.

Nevertheless, Pryor said in an interview that in Kenya he "had had an understanding" of himself. "Now you are a man, you're dangerous now. You are a man, you're dangerous. . . . Now no one can put words on you . . . back here in your subconscious . . . you are awake. When you are awake, you are dangerous." During this trip, he realized he wouldn't say "nigger" anymore. Could it be that at that time he finally realized the power of his voice, his power to do good or evil, because of his position?

Sammy Davis, Jr., confided to *Ebony* editor Lerone Bennett that when Davis realized that money and power had created chaos in his life, he tried to commit suicide. A comparison of the reactions of Pryor and Davis to the responsibilities of their political influence is instructive; Pryor was actually talking about power (which he equated with danger) and was circling this discovery with some caution; Davis had already decided that it was something he didn't want to handle— but ultimately, of course, did. Back in Hollywood, a lot of people were waiting for Pryor to return and to exercise some of that "dangerous power" on their behalf.

This first Africa trip considerably extended Pryor's anthropomorphic routines at which he excelled, endowing animals with human qualities. His African animals became "black" in speech and act with an intensity of which he may have been only vaguely aware. Even if he was to some degree "politically naive" on his first junket to the "motherland," the trips widened the vision of the comedian.

For Africa is not just a continent gravely imperiled by its colonial past and its present acceptance of systems that had subjugated it, it is also run by black people in many countries. Where there is not black domination there is the fear that this may at some time come about, and not through ballots, but bullets. And the United States, ostensibly not much involved in this issue, is more deeply a component of it than most Americans dare to realize.

Africa also has a special if unrecognized place in world history and civilization. Pryor made reference to the discoveries of the late Dr. L. S. B. Leakey, his wife, Mary, and son, Richard, who helped locate the oldest remains of man in Africa. (Pryor overlooked the discoveries of Dr. Johanson of the Cleveland Museum, which pushed the age of man back even further.)

Undoubtedly, the comedian got a sweeping sense of time and his place in it—the place he shared with his people. In subsequent trips to Zimbabwe, where he helped to finance hospitals for women and children, the relationship between himself and the "motherland" grew stronger, and in a very real and political sense he *did* become "dangerous" because of that kind of support in the face of many different foreign-policy winds which preferred that Zimbabwe, as well as other black African nations, return to a degenerating civil war.

In the concert film *Richard Pryor Here and Now*, the comedian talked briefly about Zimbabwe, but the focus of his African junkets had always been on the animals. And he was right. In the game parks and reserves they are entirely different than they are in even the freest zoo. Pryor described their activities with great relish. An observer watching this routine could easily get the sense that he too wished to be free, responsible to no one except the members of his pride of lions, perhaps. In contrast, the images of leonine freedom reflected the reality that he is almost in a zoo, being watched and laughed at, held in by commitments made by his keepers, his agents, managers, lawyers, studio heads, etc., though the "Smiling Cobra"—apt in the context of Africa—*was* his agent, manager and lawyer.

Fifteen

Frank Wells, vice chairman of the board of Warner Bros., would later say that, as a part of the deal Pryor had with the studio, David Franklin was assured of the position of executive producer of any film in which Pryor appeared (the comedian had done *Which Way Is Up?* and *Greased Lightning* for Warners). In 1977, Franklin also wanted for this service "an annual payment of $50,000" that would be added to "a provision for $1,000 a week," some of this money to be paid in advance. Warner Bros. agreed to this "as an accommodation."* The entire deal was scrapped later the same year, because Pryor "had been unable to submit a script"; Wells said, speaking for the studio, "[we] really felt we had to tidy up our arrangement." Even so, Warner Bros. felt Pryor owed something and was angered that his first filmed concert had been taken over by Bill Sargent/Special Event Entertainment and Universal in early 1979. The studio dropped what it considered a legal claim and, like other studios, tried to woo Pryor and Franklin back into a deal.

Melvin Sattler and Thom Mount of Universal also said that Franklin got hired for the film *Bustin' Loose* as an executive producer for a fee of $75,000. Such arrangements in any case are not unusual in Hollywood, where the executive producer's position is said to be a "brother-in-law's job," anyway. The dispute over this situation, however, was among the factors in the ultimate divorce of Pryor and Franklin, whose relationship, Pryor said in 1978, had "started to get a little strained, but . . . [was] never unfriendly."

---

* In the late 1940s when the novelist Chester Himes was hired by Warners as a writer, he was taken to Jack Warner for the final okay of his employment. Warner was startled and angry. "We don't want no niggers on this lot!" he screamed. Himes went back to writing novels.

By now, it was May 1979, and Barbara Walters was bringing ABC into Pryor's Northridge home. A careful viewer could have detected at once that a conflict was about to begin. There were shots taken inside the house, showing a closet filled with clothes and shoes, Pryor in headgear working out in his ring with a sparring partner ("We bad, we bad"), and Walters describing how Jennifer Lee and Pryor had met. (She was asked to decorate his house and they fell in love, Walters said.) There was a shot of Pryor and Lee kissing and then strolling arm in arm along a walk to the house. (The comedian definitely was intent on shocking a lot of people on Walters' time.)

Television is not like Las Vegas or publishing or the big-screen movie business; "cross" people in those industries and the blackballing is activated. But TV executives very often choose to forget, which is why so many of the same actors come back to do series not unlike the ones they were previously in. Pryor was always saying things about TV, none of them flattering. Of his brief sojourn with NBC, for example, he said:

> I was selling a lie to a lot of people that I would be success-
> ful and therefore there were no problems in the world, and
> not to deal with them because *I* was making it. And why
> should I complain about what happened to black people?
> That's not my business: I'm making money [so] I'm sup-
> posed to get on TV and say what a great nation this is. And
> I refused to do it.

"Success means he can buy whatever he wants, but not *do* whatever he wants," Walters said, by way of getting down to the interview, after the preliminaries dealing with his growing up in a red-light district and dropping out of school. "Much of his life has been a search for love," she said. "Awards and fame have come to him, in spite of brushes with the law, and his insistence on telling it like *he* feels it really is . . . [with] pride in his race and pent-up anger. . . . " So it began.

There was a clip from Pryor's "heart attack" monologue, followed by the "bold" question: "Are you totally off drugs?" The answer was no. He loved them. Then into violence, and Walters, with some intensive distraction from Pryor, tried to read what can only be described as an ABC-compiled rap sheet. The comedian went into the old North Washington Street days back in Peoria. Then there was Pryor's teasing as to whether biting a finger was violence or sex. Walters had to raise her voice several times, a thing she never had to do

JOHN A. WILLIAMS

when interviewing people like Fidel Castro or Anwar Sadat. Pryor spoke sincerely of his attitudes about love, lessons he had learned, and pain. Neither Walters nor Pryor could have guessed that, in just a little over a year, they would be back into another, more subdued interview.

In the meantime, Pryor was preoccupied with implementing David Franklin's strategy, which included developing two books, one for children and one about the characters the comedian used in his monologues. In addition, the plan was that Pryor would do a serious movie and a comedy film, go on a concert tour, wait for the movies to come out, and then do a record. "He said he was going to get me a deal with every studio in town," Pryor said in 1982, "and we had one, but we never did a movie, and it was looking bad for me. I kept asking him about it. I said, 'This is going to make me look like an ass, make me look stupid, that we have all these deals and we haven't done a movie yet.'"

But he did have three pre-Indigo films in 1980, *In God We Trust* with Marty Feldman and Andy Kaufman, *Wholly Moses!* with Dudley Moore, James Coco, Jack Gilford, Dom DeLuise and Madeline Kahn, and *Stir Crazy* with Gene Wilder. When they were released, the 1970s—that period when black stars discovered plastic surgery, had their lips "shaved" and the bridges of their noses made narrower—would be over.

Although Pryor got good notices for *Moses* and *Trust*, and would get even better notices for *Crazy*, there were, as usual, many off-the-set complications.

Family Dream/Bustin' Loose went into production before *Stir Crazy*, but *Crazy* was finished first. For this film, Pryor was a highly paid actor. He was also a co-producer, whose deal involved taking on Franklin as the executive producer for a fee of $75,000. This may have been done not only because of his association with Pryor, but because of the insistence of people close to Franklin that the idea for the film was originally given to Franklin by an acquaintance in Atlanta. Franklin then suggested it to Pryor, who is now credited with it (the film credit reads: "Based on an idea by Richard Pryor").

Michael S. Glick, Universal executive and coproducer, said he didn't know at the time the film was in development that Franklin was to be involved. Glick also said that Roger L. Simon was the "principal writer" on the film, even though Pryor had written a draft of the script.

Also contributing was "a man by the name of Lonne Elder*. . . and Oz Scott." In trying to determine the precise credit, Glick recalled the following: "There was a story outline, as I remember, from going through the files, but I don't recall who was the individual that originally had the story idea."

The question of who came up with what and got credited with what goes to the heart of the mechanistic workings of Hollywood, where, as Joan Didion has said, making deals is the newest Hollywood art form. In filmmaking obviously no deal can become a reality without a script or an idea for one. The more successful scripts a writer can produce, the more valued he becomes. At least a script is concrete; Hollywood pays for, and just as often borrows, ideas—which are not. Yet, it is plain that Hollywood, while valuing writing highly, also holds contempt for writers, as testified by too many—a considerable number famous—to be listed here. Perhaps Pryor's previous association with the Berkeley writers created in him a deeper appreciation of writing and ideas than his studio colleagues had. It happens, however, that when a person lives in a place long enough, he can become like the inhabitants.

Thus, late in February 1979, as praise was still rebounding around the country for his filmed concert, the poet-novelist Al Young was contacted by his agent, Dan Ostroff, at International Creative Management. Young and Pryor were about to be reunited. More or less.

It seemed that Universal had hired Roger L. Simon to do a screenplay based on an idea of Pryor's, but, "in the opinion of producer David Franklin and Universal executive Thom Mount, [it] was urgently in need of revision." Young said he requested and received two drafts of the screenplay by Simon. On the first of March, Young met with Franklin and Mount and offered suggestions to improve the script, "which were enthusiastically received," Young said, but the script had to be redone in a hurry because shooting was to begin in July. Another meeting was scheduled, and Pryor and Cicely Tyson, who was to costar, were to be present.

Young said he called Simon—who did not know why he'd been taken off the script—and they discussed the history of the earlier drafts. Young "shared some [of his] insights for prospective changes" with Simon. Neither Pryor nor Tyson appeared for the March 13 meeting at Universal, but Young discussed his changes with Mount, who then made the contractual arrangements. Young was to be paid

---

* Elder should have been better known to Glick. He is the author of the play, Ceremonies in Dark Old Men, and several film and TV scripts.

IF I STOP

$20,000 for the rewrite. The novelist wanted at least sixteen weeks to do the script; Universal wanted it in four, and they compromised at six.

In the meantime, Tyson, having learned of Young's involvement, called to urge him on because, she told him, she really could not work from Simon's script; it was "too white."

Young worked an average of eighteen hours a day, so hard that his best friend, Ishmael Reed, "was worried about his health." Young began work on March 26, and on the second day of May—the month of the Barbara Walters' interview—delivered the script to Universal. Thom Mount pronounced it "substantial," and said that the rewrite "clearly strengthened the film, particularly with respect to characterization, scene development and story resolution." Some trimming would be required, but that could easily be handled if Young spent a few days in Los Angeles going over the script with Pryor and Tyson. Young agreed.

On the morning of his departure from San Francisco, however, Mount called to tell Young the meeting was being put off because Pryor was in one of his moods, and Mount had to go to Northridge "to hold his hand," Young said.

Another meeting was later set up, but before leaving this time, Young decided to call Mount to see if it was still on. It wasn't. Mount would let him know when another would be arranged. Mount never called back and therefore the meeting never took place. Young described himself as having been put into "turnaround," from having easy access to people like Mount, to suddenly not being able to reach him and certainly not having his calls returned. It all reminded Young of the time a prominent black actor once asked an equally prominent black writer to hurry to Hollywood to discuss something of the utmost importance. When the writer arrived, the actor had forgotten what it was he'd wanted to discuss.

In the middle of July, Young called Simon, who told him that he, Simon, had been reassigned to the project and that Lonne Elder had been called in to polish Tyson's lines. Simon had not contacted Young as Young believed he should have, and as Young thought that Writers Guild rules required. Puzzled by the new alignment of writers, Young continued to make inquiries; he finally succeeded in getting Cecil Brown to ask Pryor what was going on. Brown reported back that Pryor "didn't want to deal directly with Al, because every time Al had problems, he always went to the white man." Pryor may have meant Thom Mount, but the comedian wasn't acknowledging that Franklin had also been present at the first meeting and that he himself had blown two previously scheduled meetings. Although he probably had no reason to care, there were at least two writers still in Berkeley, and Pryor's name was a very bad word indeed. From these writers there were snorts when an interview with the comedian was published bearing the subhead "I didn't cut nobody's throat to get where I am."

By November, Universal publicity blurbs were saying of the film, then on location near Seattle, that "It was written by Roger L. Simon and Lonne Elder III, based on an idea by Pryor." On the screen, though, Elder's name was gone. Young stated that he filed a protest with the Guild and in it cited specific instances where his material had been used, suggesting that there was some confusion about Simon's *two* first-draft versions, one of which was dated two months after Young delivered his draft to Mount. According to Young, the fourteen-page protest changed nothing.

Pryor may have made some California writers angry, but he was a hero in Peoria. David Franklin had contacted Miss Whittaker and asked her to conduct auditions to select several kids to play roles in *Bustin' Loose*. However, because of the distinct midwestern accents the kids had, only three were finally selected. The film called for the children to have come from Philadelphia. AREA BOYS LAND ROLES IN RICHARD PRYOR MOVIE, the *Peoria Journal Star* headlines read. Maynard Wade, ten; Joab Ortiz, ten; and Eric Alai, twelve, were the ones who made it through Miss Whittaker's tough auditions.*

Miss Whittaker accompanied the three to the Seattle suburb of Ellensburg, and was not shy about offering advice after watching the dailies. "One scene features Cicely Tyson near a closet. Since everything in the closet is brown and she is brown, she fades from view. I pointed out a key light would make her face more visible. . . . After working for years with stage lighting, you develop an eye for some of these details," she said. Miss Whittaker also did a cameo role in the film.

Privately, the tensions between Pryor and Franklin were growing. While in Seattle, for example, the comedian was wondering what was going on with $60,000 of his money that Franklin had invested in Excalibur, a company that manufactured shoelaces which wouldn't come untied. (Later, Pryor said he had not wished to invest, that the company was nonexistent. But others charged that Franklin first offered him a 3-percent share, and that later Pryor wanted another three.

---

* *Pryor gave them each $15 a day spending money, and their own dressing rooms off the set; all the crew knew that these kids could sit in his seat and ride the booms.*

JOHN A. WILLIAMS

When the location shooting was finished, with the picture still to be wrapped after an interruption while Pryor reported to Arizona for *Stir Crazy*, *Bustin' Loose* closed down. The rest would be shot at the studio.

Stir Crazy, re-uniting Wilder and Pryor, went into production in early March 1980, with a script done by Bruce Jay Friedman. Friedman's works included the novels *Stern* (1962) and *The Dick* (1970), and the play, *Scuba Duba* (1968) which starred Cleavon Little. In none of these works had minority characters appeared in a favorable light; his Jewish characters were schlemiels, his colored minority characters, cocksmen who were held in disdain because they carried more weight downstairs than up. The film has only one important character change. Pryor didn't get the girl. But he does get kissed at the end by a gay prisoner.

Personal problems delayed the completion of the film until May. There are always members of a cast and crew who know precisely what the problems are; sometimes they see them coming, but naturally they do not tell. They circulate the stories among themselves, with each telling embellished here or there. There have been so many such stories circulating in Hollywood involving Richard Pryor that the label "another Richard Pryor story" was sufficient to create a sense of anticipation. The number of Richard Pryor stories had multiplied since *Blue Collar*, when he was involved in punch-outs with costars Harvey Keitel and Yaphet Kotto. Once a picture gets underway, trouble is the last thing a producer or director wants to handle.

Late in 1979, Pryor had been unable to show up for his scheduled one-day's work on *Wholly Moses*. He told Franklin he had been doing drugs for two or three days and was badly strung out. Franklin reported that Pryor was sick and offered a 25-percent discount on the comedian's $100,000 fee. Pryor, after a recuperative trip to Hawaii, was able to live up to his commitment. But it was an ominous sign, not only for Pryor's ability to maintain his work schedule, but for his relationship with his manager.

Franklin was not answering Pryor's calls and the comedian was seething. Some $200,000 was supposed to be invested in a cable television company, but Pryor wanted to know more about the deal. Those who circled the Hollywood doings were certain that Franklin was trying to straighten Pryor out; not answering phone calls was a way for the lawyer to let the comedian know he was not pleased with his behavior, which, according to various reports and some of Pryor's own admissions, need straightening. Pryor called the Columbia studios and demanded that his $100,000 checks—there were ten of them—be sent directly to him in Arizona instead of being sent to Franklin or to his accountant, Irwin Pomerantz, whom Franklin had hired. Pryor got two of the checks and cashed them for safe keeping. He later deposited the cash in his own account. Earlier, the comedian had taken $700,000 out of a savings account so no one else could touch it. He had it converted into cashier's checks, which were kept in a steel lockbox under the bed of his Aunt Dee, who had moved in with him after Pryor's grandmother's death.

By spring the *Stir Crazy* set was embattled. Previously, Pryor had always gotten along well with his film crews; he knew that they could make him look good. But this time the crew was up in arms. Pryor was arriving on the set at noon, four hours late, and holding everything up. And he claimed that members of the crew were driving out to the house where he was staying, two hours away from the film's Arizona prison location, and shooting at him. One day, he said, a crew member dropped a watermelon from a ladder near him, and that was the last straw. He ordered tickets to Hawaii and packed to leave the set.

Franklin was frantic. Hollywood, he knew, would countenance any kind of personal perversion or erratic behavior, but for a star to walk off a picture would be the kiss of death. What made it worse was that this was Pryor's first million-dollar project, and he was also getting 10 percent of the gross, one of the biggest deals ever for a black star. Franklin rushed to Pryor's side and found him extremely agitated. "He said he was going to leave and he was not going to take that shit, and these people were racist dogs and they were dropping watermelons and they were shooting at his house, and he couldn't do it," Franklin recalled. "He was going to crack up." Franklin also learned from Pryor's bodyguard that he was freebasing nearly every night. That clearly disturbed Franklin, but first things first, he had to save the deal.

By that time the movie was nearly completed, and the budget had ballooned from $10 million to more like 15. Franklin's strategy was simple: he told Pryor they would make the studio pay for the indignities he had suffered; they would ask for a half a million more. While director Sidney Poitier shot around Pryor for a few days, Franklin went into a meeting with Columbia executives and announced that Pryor was prepared to walk. They threatened, predictably, that he would never make another picture; Franklin assured them that he knew that, but it wouldn't save their investment on this one. Standoff. "They knew I had them, and I knew I had them," Franklin said. Pryor got the extra half million contingent on finishing the picture, which he did with Franklin hanging around for a few days as a calming influence. But the episode left a toxic taste in the manager's mouth. "Making deals had always been a swashbuckling thing," he explained. "We felt like we were on the outside and we were taking them. But when I left that meeting I felt like I had put a black mask on. And I knew Richard would have me do it again," (i.e., attribute all the problems to racism).

It was generally agreed among people who have been close to Franklin that he does have the lamentable habit of not answering calls unless they are crucial, and he decides whether or not they are. But Pryor was a client and perhaps felt that people who worked for him— as Franklin most certainly did—should respond to his calls, any "punishment" aspect aside. Pryor never failed to give Franklin his due for obtaining all kinds of deals for him, but anxiety and resentment frequently soured their relationship. As Pryor said in one of his monologues, "Greed is a motherfucker, boy."

But there was something else yet to surface that summer in the wake of Pryor's holocaust, and it smacked of class-consciousness. Franklin held a press conference then, offered some speculation as to the source of the tensions that had occurred between them; including "because he formally has only a ninth-grade education, *he* [Pryor] believes he's not bright." It is the nature of people who have not been extensively and formally educated, yet who have done very well financially (which in American society—or any other—seems to count the most), to hold concealed (but not deeply) disdain for those who have been well- and formally educated yet who have not done anywhere near as well financially. But the latter quite often needs the former, like Quasimodo needed Esmeralda.

In addition, perhaps, things were not going all that well in his relationship with Jennifer Lee, a situation he summed up in his skit on freebasing (even though he used nearly the same line to describe his former wife Deboragh's departure from the Northridge estate): "My bitch left me and I went crazy."

Sixteen

"Who needs Hollywood?" asked a disembodied voice as the camera panned across New York City in the opening scenes of *Stir Crazy*. "I hear they're really nuts out there."

More scenes with the credits rolling over them, and Wilder sings, "I need a place where love is everywhere." This establishes his Skip Donahue character; he's a peace-maker, loves everyone, and is a part-time store detective as well as a part-time playwright.

Pryor plays a part-time butler and part-time actor named Harry Monroe. And in this film, for a change, he makes an early appearance, serving a swanky lunch in white jacket and black tie. He has been fired from his butler's job because some of his African grass is served by mistake in the food instead of oregano. Donahue is fired at approximately the same time when he mistakenly accuses a patron of the department store of being a shoplifter.

Awaiting his friend Donahue's arrival in their restaurant meeting place, Monroe lusts after a delicious Asian lady dancing to music on a record player. Donahue arrives and joins Monroe; the dancer heads for their table. Monroe looks up expectantly, but it is Donahue that she goes to and kisses. Square, lovable Skip Donahue will always get the girl; hip and down Harry Monroe will not. That is the tradition of being the darker sidekick.

However, once they are in prison, having been convicted of a trumped-up bank robbery charge, Monroe can have Rory, the gay hanger-on they meet there. "Hollywood, that's the place for you and me," Donahue had said back in New York, and so the two talentless creatures had gone west, reaching back into the fifty-year-old American dream that envisions Hollywood as the place where even the talentless will be revealed as people with magnificent abilities.

More so than in *Silver Streak*, in *Stir Crazy* Pryor/ Monroe was straight man to Wilder/Donahue, who lived in a world where things are expected to turn out well. And in the end they do. In the real world, of course, a man like Pryor/Monroe would have cut him loose long before the ending. Pryor's role was to be subservient to Wilder's, which was not the case in *Streak*. The best scene in the film is a remake of the "black walk" scene in *Streak*. They enter the prison, and in preparation for meeting with the hardened types, Pryor/Monroe starts "walkin' bad." Wilder/Donahue asks why, and the reply is, "If you ain't bad, you get fucked . . . if you bad, they don't mess with you." So Wilder tries "walkin' bad," but as in *Streak*, it is parody. The scene, however, is one where Friedman—or Poitier—caught the essence of Richard Pryor the comedian, which is the attempt to conceal total vulnerability under a veneer of bravado. Not unexpectedly, the film is cliché, slapstick and lightweight melodrama—but in its time it was one of the 10 all-time highest-grossing films in history.

In terms of acting, Pryor was asked to do nothing more than play second banana and be Richard Pryor; Rochester to Wilder's Jack Benny. That's what the script called for and that's what the fans got—with a little added titillation in Georg Stanford Brown's stereotypically gay Rory, who calls Pryor/Monroe "Sweetpants," and against the main action of the film is always trying to seduce Pryor, while Pryor fends him off. While the script of *Stir Crazy* dealt with prison homosexuality as a comic annoyance, Pryor's concert monologue about the making of the film reflected a harder-edged, more realistic (though still comic) perspective:

> It's really strange [in the Arizona state prison where he made *Stir Crazy*] because it's 80 percent black people in there, an' you say, Why is that strange? Because there are no black people *in* Arizona. I mean, they bus motherfuckers in! I talked to some of the brothers—thank God they got penitentiaries! An' Gene Wilder always like to jump in the middle—Hey guys, how y'doin'? I say, Gene, bring your ass outa there. What do you think they'd do to us, Rich? I say, Fuck us.

When the film was released late in 1980, Pryor said he and Wilder seemed to work well in the "combination and you couldn't have predicted, a white guy and a black guy comedy team—you couldn't have made it up." He didn't know then that this worked precisely because it wasn't new; it worked because it was so very old and so quintessentially American.

Columbia undoubtedly was pleased that the film was finally in the can. But Pryor's personal problems showed no signs of diminishing. Jennifer Lee had left him. There were other film commitments, short ones, to be sure, but nevertheless contracted for. And he was making money, but was in a position to make *more* of it than most other people.

"My greed," he said in a monologue, "does not exceed my self-respect. My greed is good, though. Greed is runnin' a close mother-fuckin' second. Greed is up there when I'm asleep. Greed is workin' on my self-respect." He continued:

> I do a lotta shit now that I never did when I didn't have money. I didn't have the problems that I have now, like watchin' motherfuckers count it. I must drive my accountant crazy, 'cause I wake up at three in the morning, go, Hey, man, what the fuck—how much is it?—Well, prove it, bring it over (But it's three in the morning.) Fuck that! I want to see it now!

The money, "*my* money," Pryor called it, correctly, and who was doing what with it and how often, had become the focal point of all Pryor's thoughts; people under great stress, in a last attempt to hold on to some kind of sanity, usually do focus on one issue that expands in their mind to the breaking point.

Just before noon on that Monday, June 9, Pryor stalked into the United California Bank at Sunset and Vine, where he had bank accounts. He told the vice president and manager that he was closing out his accounts at once because Franklin and Pryor's accountant were taking his money. The officials explained that because the comedian had several accounts, it would take time to prepare papers and new signature cards. If he could arrange to return after the lunch hour, everything would be ready. According to one source, Pryor did return, but did not sign the new forms. Still another source claimed that the comedian did sign the cards, but the bank officials decided to ignore them. That evening Pryor had his holocaust.

A neighbor along Hayvenhurst Avenue saw Pryor in a slow jog passing her house. "He was in sheer agony," she said. "He was loud, and I was unable to understand most of what he was saying." As Officers Helm and Zielinski closed in on him, Pryor screamed, "Auntie, help me!"

Lumbering up behind the cops and onlookers came Aunt Dee, crying out, "I'm trying!"

The police said they did not find any drugs in Pryor's home. Franklin flew out of Atlanta Tuesday morning, planning to hold a press conference on Wednesday to counter all the publicity about drugs that had already riddled the press. David Felton of *Rolling Stones* sat down with him for what would be the writer's third piece on Richard Pryor.

"I have found," Franklin told Felton, "that generally when Richard has 'gone off'—some big thing prominently reported in news of some type of social setting where there're people and they say, 'Oh my God, he's crazy, he's *gone off*—on 90 percent of those occasions, there was cause for him to go off. But as I told Richard, what he has to watch is where he takes it."

There was no way for Felton to know that, as far as Pryor was concerned, Franklin was not easing his problems, but creating them. In pain, even while the doctors were bombarding him with details of upcoming treatments, his statistical chances for survival—which were by no means anywhere near even—Pryor was clutching his friend Jim Brown the way a drowning man embraces a log in the middle of the ocean. (Brown, of course, is now also enshrined in a Pryor mono- logue—the one about freebasing.) There were heated discussions between Brown and members of Pryor's family while he was in the Sherman Oaks Hospital Burn Center. Perhaps their arguments had to do with who was going to control Pryor's power of attorney. Franklin did not have it, in spite of having operated as his manager, agent and attorney; all Franklin had was limited POA restricted to the use of preparing tax returns or preparing materials for an audit.

Pryor later said that in the hospital "Jim Brown and I signed a power of attorney . . . to protect me and to go to the banks and be able to say to them that David Franklin could not do any business with me." Pryor said he didn't trust Franklin because Franklin wanted power of attorney to handle his business while he was confined to the Burn Center.

It was Brown who "was going to make sure that nobody could sign checks at the bank" for Pryor, although Pryor was not sure that Brown was able to carry through with his wishes. The comedian claimed in the 1982 labor hearing that the power of attorney agreement he's signed with Brown wasn't any good. "I was told that. . . . so that nothing ever happened. He couldn't do anything with it."

That is what Pryor said the doctors at the hospital told him "within a couple of days" of Brown and Pryor signing their documents. Doctors didn't believe that, with the comedian being on medication at the time of the signing, the agreement would stand up to a legal challenge.

Jim Brown, however, told a different story in his book, *Out of Bounds*. The Pryor family, at the start of an "uncharacteristic" early morning visit to the hospital to see Pryor (Brown does not provide their names) rushed out as Brown entered. "They hardly looked at me" he wrote. "When I got to Pryor's room he was upset." Brown asked what was the matter, and Pryor answered, "Well . . . look . . . I don't think I really need you anymore. I think my family can take care of everything."

Brown said okay. Pryor said his family didn't really like Brown.

"The Bank," a Pryor monologue from *Live on the Sunset Strip*, suggests how much under the influence of drugs he was at this time: "I would be at the bank, cashin' a check, and the mother [bank official] say 'We have to certify—' n'mind. Fuck it. I go in the car, be [demonstrates smoking on pipe] and the pipe say, 'You know you right.'"]

While all the infighting was going on in the hospital, Jennifer Lee, Deboragh and Maxine in attendance, nearly everyone was wondering who had been with the comedian when the explosion occurred ("On the night I got burned, my partner and I were sitting in my bedroom drinking rum"). Pryor said he knocked over the bottle of rum. His buddy said he'd get a towel. Somehow a cigarette lighter was lit and the place exploded. The buddy ran—right into oblivion. Now, this is a curious thing for a buddy to do, especially if his partner has just caught on fire and desperately needs immediate help. In August, during the interview with Barbara Walters,* the buddy was not identified. Nobody—not the cops who picked up Pryor, or his Aunt Dee, or the neighbor who watched the cops handle Pryor so gently—reported a person other than Aunt Dee herself who emerged from the house in pursuit of Pryor. "The buddy" was chalked up to being just another mystery in Pryor's life.**

Although Franklin would continued to be Pryor's public voice for the next couple of months, they had for all practical purposes reached the end. For Franklin, the clincher came when he had to fly out to Los Angeles and "face twenty-four camera crews and ninety-five people" to explain the exploding rum bottle. "When I said that ridiculous crap, a reporter asked me if I believed that, and I said, 'Yes, I

---

* *The second Walters interview took place August 5, 1980. In this telling of the incident, Pryor stated that the partner did try to help quell the fire. Among the things that Pryor said was, "Everybody gets wise . . . a fool stays the same." He said he probably wouldn't even drink anything except beer. Walters said, "I always thought with you that part of you wanted to live and part of you wanted to die." Pryor agreed, but said ". . . the part that wanted to die, did."*

** *Nine years later in his book, Jim Brown seemed to deepen the mystery with his version of what happened: ". . . Richard told me he had tried to kill himself. He didn't say why, didn't have to. Trapped by the pipe, Richard saw one way out."*

do,'" Franklin recalled later. "I never watched TV that night. I didn't want to see myself lying." According to Franklin, he said it because Pryor was in the waning days of his probation for his car-shooting rampage and an admission of possession of contraband would have landed him in jail. He had told Pryor's maid—as if she needed telling—to cleanse the house of any incriminating evidence.

In the hospital, Franklin said, Pryor told him he loved him. But it was too late, and if Franklin knew that then, Pryor figured it out soon enough. The manager laid down some stiff new rules for Pryor to follow if they were to continue doing business. The comedian would have to take a year off—no work—to get his act together, swear off drugs, and enlist in group therapy. (Pryor had been seeing a black psychiatrist as a condition of his probation, but Franklin believed the actor, more convincing in life than on film, had conned the shrink.)

Strained relations between artists and their managers, of course, are as old as show business. Franklin, at least in retrospect, believed the problems to be almost inevitable. "The reason why they want you and love you and think highly of you is the same reason they dislike you and don't want you and sue you," he said. "You know how to make them money. Yet they begin to fear that, because you know more about how they make money than they do." Given an artist who was paranoid to begin with, and whose paranoia was magnified by cocaine, the real surprise may be that Pryor's resentment took so long to surface. Like one of his comic characters who gets at the heart of the matter by burrowing through the official bullshit, Pryor responded to Franklin's conditions by accusing him of "not backing his play." He had had enough, and passed his final judgment, as he often did, by making his experiences with lawyers—though he did not mention names—a part of his *Live on the Sunset Strip* performance, too.

> An' you know, I got lawyers an' shit, you know. Lawyers is some expensive motherfuckers. I got a lawyer, first week the motherfucker brought me a bill for forty thousand dollars. I say, Motherfucker, I just met you! Them motherfuckers will keep you outa the penitentiary and outa of the courts—but it's gonna cost a lot! I had a guy . . . I'm suin'. . . . it's a black attorney was my brother . . . right on . . . he was, it's true, a brother . . . motherfucker took me hook, line and sinker—on dry land.

(Franklin didn't sue Pryor for what he said in this monologue, but David Ashburne, one of the attorneys who represented Franklin in Los Angeles, did.)

In 1981, Pryor announced his filing of a suit against Franklin. Actually, there were five related lawsuits between that time and 1984:*

Pryor filed suit against Franklin in Georgia, February 1981; Pryor filed suit against Franklin in Los Angeles, August 1981, with the Labor Commission; Franklin appealed for a new trial when the commission ruled for Pryor in August 1982; and Pryor in February 1983, filed another suit against Franklin in Los Angeles Superior Court. And also in February, Pryor's Georgia lawyers filed to enforce the judgment of the California court which had also ruled in Pryor's favor.

The chief strategist for Franklin was Los Angeles attorney Thomasina Reed, a fixture in the Black Entertainment Lawyers Association. (Reed, a former Superior Court family judge and Beverly Hills judge, had also done a two-year stint at Columbia Pictures.)

The legal battles seemingly posed no impediment to Pryor's career. He plunged into work, completing *Bustin' Loose*, after which he went to Maui where he had a home and a Grumman plane (valued at $49,000) which undoubtedly cost more than he said it did. This combination of what people referred to as "his accident" and the release and financial success of *Stir Crazy* were intertwined. He had become a death-defying myth. Audiences panted for the release of *Bustin' Loose*.

Popular adulation had come to a man who said flat-out he was a junkie. Audiences were fascinated with this comedic high-wire artist, tiptoeing ever so slowly across an almost invisible wire, with wind-whipping death teasing beneath his feet. They read about his adventures, fully expecting imminent news of the most horrendous, even if mysterious death. It was what many people would like to do—court death, take her to bed, and walk away unscathed, boasting about just how good the encounter had been. Pryor had survived his catastrophe and turned the experience victoriously into art, as Donny Hathaway and Charlie Parker and Billie Holiday and John Belushi had not been able to. Only Pryor had boomed to both heaven and hell and back on cocaine craft. And if he crashed en route once, twice or three times, he had come back with pure Hollywood style, an actor who seemingly dies in one role, but then is alive and well in the next, cavorting like a god on the big screen once again.

When heroin was pouring into the black communities after World War II, the authorities didn't seem to mind too much. There

---

* *In all the proceedings, Franklin had black attorneys; Pryor white. In a March 1983 deposition, Pryor said he didn't believe that two African-American gentlemen should handle their dispute through the courts—but he later said he would spend all his money fighting Franklin in court.*

were arrests, of course, accompanied by extensive media coverage. Where motive of any crime was unknown, the police and the press expressed confidence that the crime was "drug-related."

If the police were slow to address the problems of drug use, Hollywood was a bit faster. In 1955 it produced a film based on Nelson Algren's *The Man with the Golden Arm*, starring Frank Sinatra, Eleanor Parker and Kim Novak, and in 1957, a film from the Michael Gazzo play, *A Hatful of Rain*, with Anthony Franciosa, Don Murray and Eva Marie Saint. In both instances the junkies were white, while the public was being force-fed the notion that heroin addiction was only colored black. While white drug users had appeared as characters in Hollywood movies, it was not until 1971, with *The French Connection*, that the public was presented with cinematic depictions of white people controlling the dope trade, though federal agents knew that whites had dominated this industry.

Paraphrasing the scene in *The Godfather*, when the dons gather to achieve peace instead of war between their families, one says, "Give the drugs to the dark people, the colored people . . . they're like animals and have no souls anyway." But Don Corleone responds, "If we go into drugs, everyone will be down on us. . . . " The contempt that this quote reveals is ironic because the town of Corleone, Sicily, was founded by the Moors around the ninth century. In Arabic, the town is spelled Qurlyun.

The cops, however, have never closed down the drug traffic. Drug addiction in some black communities has reached epidemic proportions. But drug use has continued to increase in white America, too. Pryor, in his concert film *Richard Pryor Here and Now*, noted that "They call it an epidemic now that white folks are doin' it."

Drug use and trafficking have been of concern to the federal government since the Drug Act of 1890, which imposed a tax on opium and morphine and on the manufacture of smoking opium. In short, you could use the stuff if you wished, but you had to pay to do so. This law appeared to racially target the drug commerce of another group of nonwhites, the Chinese on the West Coast. Forty years later, in 1930, the Federal Narcotics Bureau was organized. It, however, proved as ineffectual at curbing the growth of the gigantic drug industry as the current organization, the U.S. Drug Enforcement Agency, in President George Bush's "War on Drugs."

Perhaps the most publicized episode of the modern anti-drug era was Richard Pryor's holocaust. The media covered his burning with great dedication; it was as though if the story played long enough, the problem of drug use by whites—film stars or otherwise—could be minimized. If drug use could be focused on and screened through the agonies of a Richard Pryor, or the activities of LeRoy "Nicky" Barnes, labeled by the press as the New York City "Drug King," a diversionary illusion might be created; if the embarrassments and stupidities of Washington's exposed Mayor Marion Barry could be covered at length, that illusion could be deepened. The fact is, to a significant extent, cocaine is a white, middle- and upper-class narcotic. Crack or rock cocaine has become the form of drug most frequently associated with black communities, yet how could it not also be in demand as well as accessible in white neighborhoods, given the history of drug distribution and sale?

In the early 1980s there were an estimated 20 million coke users in the United States, twice the population of Greece. At that time, one of every three Americans between eighteen and twenty-five had tried cocaine. Entering the 1990s, the Senate Judiciary Committee estimated that one of every 100 Americans at all age levels, uses or has used cocaine. Of these, about five million are addicted to the drug. It may be for these reasons that nearly everyone has heard of a Cocaine Hotline, but never a Heroin Hotline. Americans continue to believe that the coke junkie is somehow more respectable than the heroin or skag junkie wallowing around at the foot of the social ladder.

During the last half of the 1980s, much criticism was laid at Hollywood's door for creating—intentionally or otherwise—the idea that snorting coke was hip and that, unlike heroin, it bore no social stigma. Pryor spelled out the terms of coke addiction in clear terms in his landmark skit in the concert film *Richard Pryor—Live on the Sunset Strip*.

The names of people linked to drugs through accusations reported in the media as using, selling, or consorting with users of coke or skag are legion and often quite familiar: politicians, athletes in football, baseball, basketball and tennis, coaches, actors, film producers, writers, airline pilots, train engineers, bus drivers and others.

How was it that Pryor escaped arrest, especially since he made no secret that his habit once cost him $600 a day? The comedian represented the most favorable image of an influential drug user that any advertising agency could ever have conceived. He talked about it, did great and often moving monologues about it, joked about it, warned against it. He told Barbara Walters on prime-time television that he loved drugs, loved to sit around with his friends and use drugs, the way other people sat with their friends and drank coffee or tea. Whatever disasters befell him, he always bounced back, the way all addicts believe they can. He was the epitome of the black junkie imbedded in the psyches of all too many white Americans. And he confirmed the image. He shot guns, punched out women and sometimes men, could be crude, rude and dangerous, some said, to himself and to others. Pryor stood up front with his dope and sometimes was belligerent with others about it. It was his life, his business. And everybody knew where he lived and who came and who went, but no one ever laid a glove on him when he became a star. Maybe it was because in Hollywood, as a *New York Times* reporter noted in 1980, where "In some circles, cocaine replaced the after-dinner drink four years ago," the Hollywood folk were used to such behavior, though in other instances the town worked diligently to prevent news of it from getting out.

A more realistic assessment, however, would be that Pryor escaped because he was making money for a lot of people in Hollywood —and inadvertently shilling for the drug trade which, by then, was three times bigger than the movie and recording industries combined.

In 1983 coke use and traffic was a $25-billion off-the-books industry. The cost to the economy in lost productivity, medical expenses and crime, *Newsweek* estimated, was another $25.8 billion.

Even a $50.8 billion business can use a little advertising, and Pryor for a time was its full-page, four-color ace. Major defense industry companies frequently advertise their products in popular magazines with the full knowledge that individuals will never buy them; government is the only consumer. The ads are public relations.

By 1990, the drug industry was valued at $150 billion and going strong, in spite of the "War on Drugs." The Medellín cartel of Colombia thrived, characterized by President-elect César Gaviria Trujillo as the "richest criminal enterprise in world history." Money laundering banks around the world did a booming business; drug smuggling was pronounced stopped at Avenue A, but continued untouched at all other avenues. Gaviria said the United States and Europe were not behind the drug war. In fact, trade pacts between Colombia and the United States, particularly as they affect coffee, were being cut back. The inference here was that Colombian farmers would be forced even more than they already were into raising coca plants in order to subsist. If this was to be the case, it would not be unlike what the British did to China in the late nineteenth century, forcing the Chinese to use opium against their will. This led to two wars and the eventual settlement of the British (and other powers) in Shanghai to profit from unobstructed trade.

A 1990 interview in the German magazine *Die Tageszeitung* with former Rand Corporation consultant Daniel ("Pentagon Papers")

Ellsberg provided a window on the drug situation and why the "war" doesn't really exist at all. Ellsberg voiced the theory of Peter Dale Scott of the University of California at Berkeley that our political system, relying on huge donations "to finance election campaigns, is already dependent on sources involved in the drug trade." Ellsberg continued, "It was certainly not by chance that our covert operations in Southeast Asia were accompanied by an epidemic of heroin consumption, and that our covert operations in Central America were accompanied by a domestic epidemic of cocaine consumption."

Relating Scott's theory, Ellsberg also said that many U.S. banks, because of their policy loans, "depend on the economic survival of certain Latin American countries and can't afford the luxury of one of their main sources of income, i.e., drug money laundered in the United States, drying up. According to this theory, an interruption of the drug trade would lead first to a moratorium in the debtor countries and then to a collapse of the U.S. banks."

Ellsberg believed the theory held some validity "because otherwise you can't explain the refusal to expose those links between the Reagan administration's covert operations and the drug flow into the United States." When the savings and loan scandal first broke, there were reports—which swiftly dropped out of the news—of clandestine CIA and mob connections, suggesting a drug link to the vanished money. And by the summer of 1990, a number of commercial banks were sending out an information notice from the Federal Deposit Insurance Corporation—the outfit that insures bank deposits up to $100,000. New rules were going into effect to strengthen commercial banks, which were considered to be at financial risky because of the S&L scandals.

After his holocaust, Pryor said he repented and went off drugs, but it seemed clear that they still held an immense attraction for him, perhaps because they affected his art and his self-image, became a part of it. One could see this in his fascination with Charlie Parker's life and his desire to do a film on the life of the legendary alto saxophonist. Never mind that Dick Gregory had already done a "Bird" film; Greg wasn't a junkie; Pryor had been. He understood the junkie's life.*

* Spike Lee's Mo' Better Blues, with Denzel Washington, captured some of the life of a jazz musician who is not a dependent junkie or a drunk, as black musicians are portrayed in Clint Eastwood's Bird (1988), or Bertrand Tavernier's 'Round Midnight (1986). Like Charlotte Zwerin's documentary on Thelonius Monk, Straight, No Chaser (1990), Lee's film focuses on the musician's discipline and the music that it produces. Mo' Better Blues was released within months of the publication of Frederic Dannen's powerful exposé of the recording industry, Hit Men: Power Brokers and Fast Money Inside the Music Business.

As with other musicians who have been junkies, Parker's life was alternately wretched and funny—and ultimately pathetic. Many jazz musicians were hounded by narcotics officials at local, state and federal levels. In some cities their cabaret cards—licenses to perform—were taken away, leaving them with no way to earn a living. Although the music of those stars forms the foundation of post-World War II jazz and still influences young musicians, many of them died early and broke. Only their music dignifies their deaths, but for countless jazz artists, music was almost literally all they had. Richard Pryor revered this image.

Pryor studied the sax, and word went around about his doing the Parker film. There were brief clips of him with a horn on his children's television show. Then quite suddenly, the word was that Clint Eastwood was going to make the film. He did, and it was released in 1988 as *Bird*, starring Forest Whitaker. Pryor's failure to make the film remains a puzzle—and to some a great disappointment, for it was believed that by playing Parker, Pryor at last could have come into his own as a serious actor.

Performers like Parker, Holiday and Monk together did not earn during their lifetimes what Pryor said he spent on coke in a single year (about $250,000). Maybe this is what he meant when he said his life was a cosmic joke. He made so much money that, as one wit said, "If Pryor really got busted, ten thousand cats would be out of work." Even after his burning, Pryor wasn't charged; nothing incriminating was found. Surely he must have asked himself many times just how much he was worth to other people to have escaped the consequences of his acts. Pryor might have been foolhardy, but he was far too intelligent not to understand that he had managed to elude the punishments others could not. You don't have to come from Peoria to know that money talks and bullshit walks.

A black man who is rich, a public figure who is often devastatingly critical of his society, may be "dangerous," as Pryor told an interviewer, but he is also *in* danger. It is not that white America wanted to "get" him for his multileveled success; it was that American society was not constructed to comfortably house such a person. The few black millionaires that are around, including those in show business, tend to maintain low, careful profiles for fear of disturbing a slumbering dragon that is predisposed not to understand how such millionaires came to be in the first place. Richard Pryor was the exception; he flirted with danger as if it were a "fine bitch."

By his own admission—several times over—Pryor was a junkie. Every junkie has a story of how his or her addiction began, but we can never be sure of the story. Yet we are as suspicious of no explanation as we are of one that seems overly thorough, one which may be peppered with psychiatric jargon. This, however, does not necessarily indicate truthlessness. Pryor kept returning to Peoria, he said, for one thing: "acceptance" from the people who had turned away from him, those who thought he was not worth their time. These may have included members of his family. Then, still rejected, he believed he could win them over "by offering them money, because that's what they really wanted. The didn't understand nothing about me. . . . Only cash related. It seemed they liked me for that only. . . . I felt that I didn't have anyone that I could just pick up the phone and talk to in the middle of the night unless I was calling to say I was sending some money." (One of the comedian's monologues had him returning home to be greeted by a "friend" who told him scornfully, "You used to do that sorry old shit around here. Wasn't nothin'. Gimmee a dollar.")

"See," Pryor continued in the 1980 interview with *Ebony* managing editor Charles L. Sanders,* "you're lonely . . . rejected by your own people . . . you get real low . . . looking for someone to love you. You run into some guy or some lady and they say 'Here, take this. Go ahead. Try it.'"

He tried it. He believed he was feeling better, feeling okay. He believed he'd found "good friends" and observed that "such people make you feel better, so they must love you." He explained the dynamics of becoming addicted: "It builds and builds. But it's a life that's hard to get away from once you're in it. I tried. Many times." Whenever he tried, he said, people thought something was wrong with him— so did he—and he continued snorting.

That yearning for acceptance, and the need to have others prove their devotion to him, led Pryor—under the influence of cocaine —to oddly contradictory behavior. Cocaine-enhanced insecurity also demanded a measure of secrecy, perhaps as a form of denial. David Franklin, for example, knew about Pryor's problem, but tolerated it as long as it didn't interfere too much with the work—and as long as he didn't have to deal with it personally. Pryor obliged by never doing drugs around Franklin. One day, as they were riding in a limousine to a reception for an African dignitary at the Century Plaza Hotel in Los Angeles, Pryor stopped at a house to pick up something. He wouldn't

---

* *One white writer suggested that Pryor has given* Ebony *and its writers more interviews than he's given* Playboy *because he "wanted to help the sales of* Ebony," *which was but one of several ill-advised statements that writer made. Richard Pryor needed* Ebony *as much or more than it needed him. It has the largest black circulation in the world, and it was through this publication that Pryor could speak directly to his fans.*

let Franklin out of the car. "He wanted to shield me from that part of his life," Franklin said later. "He treated me like a virgin." Franklin never attended a party at his client's house in the evening, and the only time he got close to catching Pryor in the act was when he walked into a trailer on a movie set and saw "some stuff" there. Richard looked shocked" at being seen by Franklin, he recalled.

Partly as a result of Pryor's self-consciousness, Franklin believed himself able to control his star. He considered theirs almost like a big brother/little brother relationship (with Franklin cast as the big brother, though he was three years younger), and he was sometimes asked by a producer to linger on a set to make sure Richard stayed cool.

Freebasing changed all that. Pryor had assured Franklin he would continue to take his powder the old-fashioned way, because he had seen people rendered helplessly immobile by the pipe. But basing, in Franklin's words, went through Hollywood in the late 1970s "like a hot knife through butter," and it cut deeply into his meal ticket as well. "It began to eat at his core," Franklin said later. "And it increases the paranoia. You can never trust anyone so you only start trusting strangers, because you figure that the stranger doesn't know you well enough to hurt you. So your friends become strangers."

Pryor's freebasing skit in 1982's *Live on the Sunset Strip*, with its platoon of voices, real and psychological, places his addiction in sharper focus, even as humor rides hard alongside the misery:

> I freebased about eight months straight. My bitch left me and I went crazy. But I fell in love with this pipe. This pipe controlled my very being. This m'fucker says: "Don't answer the phone. We have some smoking to do." . . . And I don't give a fuck—when you a junkie you—will—not—admit — it. You will find excuses to smoke, shoot up or somethin'; you be—Hey look—"Rich, you gotta go to work." Hey, I don't like the way you said that. Fuck it, I ain't goin' a motherfucker, an' you go in a room and you lay down 'n' say [to the pipe] "You understand, doncha?"

The low-fat milk cookie explosion ends the monologue.

Pryor has a number of drug-oriented monologues: "Cocaine," "God Was a Junkie," "Wino and Junkie," "I Feel," "Acid," "Gettin' High," and the junkie skit he does in the film of his 1983 concert *Here and Now*, which is a mime, without sound effects, of a junkie shooting up and nodding off.

Pryor provoked hilarity with these bits, and maybe at the time he was doing them, he too was laughing—at himself. The image of the flawed hero, divinely created to be ripped apart and put back together, like Zagreus, had not hurt the comedian's career. Pryor has himself said that he doesn't think he was as funny (as before the fire). His instincts told him that while most of us applaud the fact that he said he was off drugs, we really wanted him back on the high wire, tiptoeing across, as high in his head as an acrobat in the air. We awaited his next drug-inspired stunt, perhaps because we wanted a reason to celebrate yet another tragedy that had befallen the mighty.

"He got there on drugs, he'll leave there on drugs," an actor said.

Maybe. Maybe not.

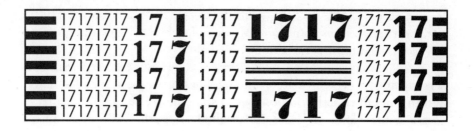

Seventeen

By the time Pryor was ready to complete shooting for *Bustin'
Loose*, Franklin was literally out of the picture. Ultimately he would
bring suit against Universal, presumably for breach of contract. All
reports indicated that the comedian was a changed man when he
returned to the set. He had lost weight and had to be padded up to
match the earlier scenes.

Perhaps more important than the film, which in 1981 earned
$16 million (overall, $43 million), was the fact that it was the first one
over which Pryor had some degree of control. But it turned out to be a
slushy mix of comedy and romance, which critics characterized as
being an inferior *African Queen*, with Pryor playing a small-time thief
assigned to escort a stern teacher (played by Cicely Tyson) and her
eight charges across the country.

More was expected of the film than was received. The fact that
the stars, director (Oz Scott), executive producer (Bill Greaves), and a
coproducer (Pryor) were black did not lift the film out of the ordinary;
nor did the fact that at least three of the four writers on (but mostly *off*)
the script were also black. Some claimed that the disappointments were
in the script, but one of the writers said that "writing for him [Pryor] is
sort of like writing jazz—bars and notes, and the rest is improvisation—
as opposed to the way it is with most actors. He's better on the first or
second take, but you don't come up with a balanced script."

Tyson defended Pryor's penchant to alter the lines when she
said, "He did write the script, and if he decided he wanted to change it,

he certainly had the prerogative to do so." If the basis for any film is the screenplay, then some sort of control, whether later modified or not, is marked out by the script.

There is, of course, a pronounced difference between writing a screenplay and writing concert monologues or single scenes for films. Writing an entire script for a movie is something else again, but that *is* where a film finds or loses its original strength. "We gotta make movies" is an idea far easier said than done, and sometimes the vanity of having credits for writing just a part of a screenplay is misplaced.

Whether or not Pryor's ego took control of the script, *Bustin' Loose* was not a "Sambo" picture. There was love, jealousy, fondness for kids, and a determination to overcome hardships. Black male/female relationships are rarely shown on TV or in film; that these traced a well-worn Hollywood path is not really a failing unique to this movie. It seemed that the film might turn out to be a practice run for something better.

Pryor's reaction to being alive and back working was super-expansive. He gave away money (not that he hadn't always done that), gave advice, cautioned about drug abuse, apologized to people who'd been victims of his drug-induced rages. He even offered to reveal his drug experiences to a Congressional committee, but later backed off—wisely, some people in Hollywood thought. As extensive as Pryor's connections must have been, he probably could have blown the lid off half the town, naming users and dealers he'd known before his holocaust. (Later, before the California Labor Commission, Pryor took the Fifth Amendment when asked if he had ever used nonprescribed drugs or alcohol.)

On August 16, 1981 he married Jennifer Lee, although he'd said he would never again marry a white woman. In many monologues, he talked about the differences between black and white women ("I've been married to both—yes I have"). That he married Miss Lee was not much of surprise to black women who had known Pryor and who swore that he did not "*like* black women." Pryor felt no need to justify his marriage. The comedian had always challenged his audiences and his interviewers to find fault with the life that was his and his alone. He could marry who the hell he wanted, didn't care what anybody thought. During his ordeal by fire, Jennifer had stood by his side when he "was in need." Pryor said, "She stood by me through a lot of pain as most people walked away from me." They married in Maui, and Pryor talked about having a family—something he discussed again and again, as though not having a family was one of the experiences he most missed.

Pryor had always done impressive work with the concept of race. He had made the empirical stance of Du Bois—that the problem of the twentieth century would be color—succinct and flat-out down-to-earth. He made Langston Hughes—whose best moments were when he, laughing, twitted the concept—roll over in his grave with laughter, probably, though Hughes was not given to excesses in language. Pryor made "race" both personal and universal, and if people were concerned with his crossing barriers to achieve what he felt he needed, he was prepared to say fuck it. So there were politics reflected in his work; there were *racial* politics. If people liked what he was doing or saw it as wedge to ease himself over to the other side, the white side—fuck it; he believed he was his own man. The problem was that in working in Hollywood, very few in reality were their own men or women; the screen and those who make what appears on it do seem to be capable of stealing the soul.

David Franklin had brought the original script of *Some Kind of Hero* to Pryor in 1979. "He suggested that I do the movie," Pryor said, "and tried to talk me into doing the movie. He said he could make me a good deal and probably get me an Academy Award." But there was a rape scene in the script that Pryor didn't like, and he decided he didn't want to do the film. However, after the fire, when he was on his way to New York to help promote *Stir Crazy*, he met paramount's David Simpson. He told him that while he liked the script, he found the rape scene in it extremely distasteful. Otherwise, he'd "like to do it." Simpson said Paramount would be happy to remove the scene, and Pryor responded by saying if they did, he'd consider making *Some Kind of Hero*.

Simpson, former head of production, had gone after "everyone from Robert Redford to Nick Nolte" to play the male starring role of Eddie Weller. After the contact with Pryor, at least a draft of another version was rewritten for the comedian.*

Michael Pressman, who directed *Some Kind of Hero*, said he believed that he had helped Pryor to reveal himself as a "bright, sensitive man, just the opposite of how he's appeared in other films." While it was acknowledged that the comedian was both bright and sensitive, these characteristics were not shown to any great advantage in the film, and this may have been because the script (based on the novel by

---

* *Curiously, Paramount had also planned to cast a white actor in the role of the drill sergeant in* An Officer and a Gentleman. *Four turned down the part. Black actor Lou Gossett, who had made his debut on Broadway in the 1950s in Louis Peterson's delicate* Take a Giant Step, *took the role and won an Oscar, bringing to the part a certain wry, recognizably "black menace."*

James Kirkwood) originally called for Eddie Weller to be white (that was obvious). Kirkwood and Robert Boris did the script, deleting in newer versions the rape scene Pryor did not like. There were other things, however, that Pryor should have been aware of as well.

Although the Weller character is black, there is only one word in the entire script that calls attention to this fact. (In Vietnam, Weller's cellmate, played by Ray Sharkey, calls him a "wonderful black fuck!" when Weller seems to have put one over on their North Vietnamese captors.) There is not a single acknowledgment by any character that Weller is black. This is a presumably well-intentioned if unreal attempt on the part of the director (Pressman) and producer (Howard W. Koch) to create an America in which racism does not exist. *Some* recognition of Weller's blackness would have added strength to the film. Pryor as Weller played an expatriated Vietnam prisoner of war who upon his return home finds himself somewhat of a hero. While a prisoner, he had made statements opposing the war in order to save his cellmate from torture and death. His buddy died anyway.

At home Weller finds that his wife, believing he died, has found someone else. A daughter has been born during his captivity, but he never sees her except in a photograph. Just once he hears her voice. The revelation by the wife (Lynne Moody) comes in a hotel room the first night of his return. They are about to make love, until she finds that she must tell him about the other man in her life.

The other person Weller is attached to is his mother. She is suffering from a stroke and cannot communicate with him. One of her friends tells him that the cost of her care is going up and that unless he can come up with the money, his mother will be kicked out of the hospital. This problem is compounded by the Army's refusal to give him his back pay until the matter of the statements he gave to the North Vietnamese is cleared up. Thus, Weller is cut adrift in a white world, without family or friends, and that world is not even curious about his presence there.

He meets Toni, the hooker (played by Margot Kidder), who doesn't seem to have any clients. She feels sorry for Weller. A one-night stand eventually turns into more. For the most part, reviewers only lightly emphasized the interracial "romance," which in many ways was *Hero*'s centerpiece. Kidder, of course, is best known as Lois Lane in the *Superman* films. Lois Lane, Superman's girl, appearing as Toni the hooker. . . . There was something almost sacrilegious about the transference.

Some Kind of Hero made $24.5 million in 1982, the first year of its release. One, if not the major, reason for its success was laid out by New York *Daily News* reviewer Lorenzo Carattera: "The added attraction of a sweaty windshield of an interracial romance should not do much harm to the movie's box-office take." And why not? Here was Superman's girl *doing it* with a black man. Never mind that he has no black roots in the movie, but moviegoers have eyes; they see what is on the screen. One can almost imagine the moguls anticipating a pretty good gross because *Hero* would perhaps be the first feature film to "actually" show a black man and a white woman doing it, graphically doing it. And maybe through that act, the black man gets one up on Superman, since he has copped his girl.

The script of *Hero* calls for Eddie to be "pumping into her" in at least four scenes, but in the released version there are only two, and they are back-to-back. In both —one is in a bedroom and the other in a bathtub—Eddie in a sense is not the fucker, but the fuckee, since director Pressman placed Toni on top. "Don't move," she says. "I'll do everything." Lovingly filmed through a scrim, the scenes are nothing if not soft pornography; two more such scenes would have earned *Hero* an X-rating and probably a bigger box-office take. The second scene in the bathtub seems to imply that interracial lovemaking requires a symbolic cleansing; a tub spilling over with bubbles turns out to be just the thing.

Basically, Eddie Weller is a nice guy beset by problems and betrayals. At the end of the film he bests two hoods, but he's never a threat to anyone, only a bother, because he has in his possession some bank notes that someone else wants. He gets away, pays off what he owes, provides for his mother, and then goes off with his hooker girl-friend. Maybe they are both outsiders, but that point is never made; both in fact seemed to have staked serious claims to being insiders. American audiences have been trained by now to accept divorcées and ex-girlfriends as being acceptable; they can walk into the sunset with the hero. Hookers haven't quite made it yet, though they may have hearts of gold.

After *Hero*, Pryor set aside the idea of doing another buddy film with Wilder. This one, too, would have been written by Bruce Jay Friedman. *Deep Trouble* went into deep freeze, but things were heating up elsewhere. While movie screens may have shown Kidder riding Pryor, on September 21, 1981, Pryor brought charges against David Franklin. The comedian alleged that Franklin embezzled and misappropriated his money. First lodged in Georgia, the case was ultimately heard in Los Angeles in the rooms of the California State Labor Commissioner. The news hit Hollywood like an earthquake.

At once everyone with an interest in the suit, no matter how remote, took sides. Some black people who considered the comedian to be the epitome of the accolade "his own man" quickly accused Pryor of having been manipulated by the Hollywood Establishment in order to pit him against Franklin, and break up the personal and financial relationship between the two. Millions, they said, had been flowing into the black communities through Pryor's personal philanthropy and also through his business deals. The whites wanted to put a halt to that. These blacks also said there was nothing but great love and respect between Pryor and Franklin. And hadn't Franklin secured better deals for Pryor than had former agents Ron DeBlasio and John Anghardt? No matter that the deals they got for him seemed all right at the time.

"Look," one lawyer said to an interested party, "David Franklin —a *black* attorney—did what the *other* attorneys never did. He made sure that Richard's films employed black people on the screen and behind the cameras. This was built into all his contracts. When the white boys got in, it was something else again. Richard and David had a good relationship. He loved David and probably still does."

Another attorney observed that "Pryor's so rich, he has two sets of lawyers—one for litigations and the other to handle contracts. His kind of money attracts a lot of attention, especially when it's suspected that he was snorting coke to the tune of half a million dollars a year up to the time of the fire. Law is a business, you know, and you gotta get out there and fight for it."

Did that mean that behind the allegations, the real battle was being conducted to see how and with whom Pryor would spend his money?

The response was a grunt and a smile.

In Atlanta, Franklin expressed hurt and surprise, along with a certain weariness. He wondered if the suit was not another attempt by Pryor to gain more publicity. But, with his marriage, and preparations for a new routine he would be trying out at various clubs in Los Angeles, most especially at the Comedy Store, Pryor seemed much too busy to worry about publicity. He agreed to a deal with Columbia to film two performances of a concert at the Hollywood Palladium. Columbia would hand over $4 million to see the job done. Haskell Wexler, most famous for directing and shooting *Medium Cool* (1969), was selected as chief cinematographer. And the comedian was also busy ministering to the needs of the singer Jackie Wilson and his family.

The Motown star had collapsed and remained in a coma; he would die early in 1984. Pryor also began to sponsor Larry Murphy, the Sherman Oaks Burn Center technician who'd worked with him in the hospital, through college; Murphy wanted to be a surgeon. On it went, but the big thing was the new film, and Pryor was nervous.

The first night the concert ended abruptly. Fans in the audience were stunned and hushed and full of pity for the man in the red suit up on the stage. Pryor had started the show close to the end of the routine he'd already put together, talking about the fire. He had nowhere to go but back to the beginning of the performance. He stopped, started, stopped again. "It's hard being up here again," he said. He tried once more, but stopped and left the stage. Later he said, "I wanna stop." He didn't want to finish the concert, the next night's commitment to the fans or to Columbia, but he knew he had to; as a man, as an artist, he had to return. He did, although he was nervous again. He opened, however, with "Let's talk about something serious— fucking." The audience broke up; its response lifted Pryor over the hump and he was off. It was during this legendary performance that he told of suing his attorney, and announced that he wasn't going to say "nigger" anymore. *Richard Pryor Live on the Sunset Strip* hit the screen within weeks of *Some Kind of Hero*. During its first *three* days, playing in 1,277 theaters, it earned almost twice what Columbia had put up to get it in the can.

Nearly all the reviewers remarked on "the new Richard Pryor." *The New York Times'* Janet Maslin wrote "Neither the guards [at the Loews Astor Plaza] nor the packed audience were prepared for the way Mr. Pryor has changed since his accident." Her colleague, Vincent Canby, confessed that it was "not easy to get a fix on Richard Pryor as he performs before a wildly appreciative audience. . . . His speech has the density of a new kind of comic superlanguage." Closer to Pryor's home in Northridge, Sheila Benson of the *Los Angeles Times* suggested that "even longtime Pryor fans will not be quite prepared for the tone of this concert film. This is a deeper and more mellow Pryor than we've ever had before, in performance or on records." Just seventeen days after opening, the film had earned $24 million; Columbia had turned a profit in a record-breaking flash—$17 million after paying Pryor $3 million. Columbia wasn't hurting.

But Pryor was. On Monday, March 1, 1982, hearings began to determine a resolution to the controversy between Pryor and Franklin. Carl Joseph represented the California State Labor Commissioner. Pryor was represented by John H. Lavely, Jr. and Martin D. Singer.

Franklin was represented by Thomasina Reed, with associates Joseph E. Porter III and Robert Pryce. The hearings did not end until May. On March 5, Pryor's friend, John Belushi—a guy he "never imagined with a needle . . . just . . . a guy in a Samurai suit"—died from an overdose. Belushi's death was a sobering reminder of how close Pryor himself had come to death.

On March 9, Jennifer Lee Pryor, already separated from Pryor, filed for divorce, citing "irreconcilable differences." Pryor did not contest and, at least on the record, there was no division of community property and no spousal support awarded. (The divorce became final October 25.) And the Ides of March had not yet arrived.

Although much was going on at the same time in the comedian's life, it was clear to those who stood some distance from it that even if he was not quite the same man who galloped away with *Richard Pryor Live on the Sunset Strip*, he was still a comedian in a class by himself. It was also clear that when Pryor was in total control of his material, when it was his material, he was a far better performer than when the material was someone else's. But he had yet to prove that he was as good an actor as he was a comedian.

Eighteen

The hearings covered the most important years of Pryor's career—from 1975 to 1980—the years Franklin was his agent, manager and attorney; the years that marked the comedian's rise to stardom through the bonding with Gene Wilder in *Silver Streak* (1976) and *Stir Crazy* (1980).

Pryor was not well dressed during the first couple of days of the hearings, and in the witness chair he spoke inaudibly and would not look the attorneys in the eye. Franklin's attorneys frequently questioned the procedures of Pryor's attorneys, sometimes sarcastically. There were documents they hadn't had a chance to see, and new ones were being presented almost every other minute. They asked for a continuance, which was denied because they'd had three earlier ones. The defense attorneys then offered a motion to dismiss because Franklin was an employee of Richard Pryor Enterprises/Indigo Productions, not an outside individual acting alone. This, too was denied.

In labor hearings the rules are almost, but not quite, the same as those in a civil or criminal court. A major advantage for the plaintiff is that the Labor Commission is notoriously artist-oriented; those seeking to settle disputes against agents, accountants and such usually win, and do so quickly, in six months perhaps, as opposed to several years in civil court. It may also be that Pryor's attorneys felt it best not to place the comedian's allegations—that Franklin had misappropriated his money—before either civil or criminal court, fearing that Pryor would be made vulnerable to charges having nothing to do with the present claim. Indeed, there were times when the defense tried to get Pryor to admit that he drank heavily and took drugs during the years under investigation. His lawyers objected, of course, and the hearing officer took pains to instruct Pryor regarding his privilege to take the Fifth Amendment—which the comedian did. There were occasions when the hearing officer remarked that a certain line of questioning belonged more properly in a criminal court. The defense sometimes complained that Pryor, during cross-examination, was not responsive. But he was polite. There were times when he recalled the dates of events accurately, and times when he did not or could not. There were rare times when his responses were cute, as when asked what he'd done in the film *Adios Amigo*. He answered, "The best I could."

During the first and third days of the hearings, Pryor was in the witness chair close to six hours each day. Before the first phase was over on March 25, he traveled to Baton Rouge to begin work with Jackie Gleason on *The Toy*. David Franklin did not appear to testify.

Testimony stated that Pryor had been approached by "others" who wished to represent him. He told Franklin, who suggested that people wanted to "come between them." One of a number of studio executives testified that it was Pryor who "wanted Franklin to be employed" (as executive producer). The same person also said that Franklin's services "exceeded those that an agent would render." However, another studio official said there was nothing unusual about the way the Atlanta attorney had done business.

An attorney familiar with the case said, "David made a mistake by not opening an office in Los Angeles. You can't handle a business like Pryor's or a person like Pryor or any artist from 2,500 miles away. You've got to be there when your client needs you." According to Pryor, Franklin came to Los Angeles twice a month when they first teamed up and then later three or four times a month. This testimony helped the petitioner, Pryor, to establish the fact that Franklin did not practice law in California because he had no state license to do so; therefore, he worked through lawyers who did. However, according to Thomasina M. Reed, who represented Franklin during the hearings, lawyers who acted as talent agents were almost never licensed to do so, even those who practiced law in California.

Pryor's attorneys seemed to have indulged in overkill, dragging into the case—or trying to—rules governing artists' managers as set forth by the Screen Actors Guild (SAG) and the American Federation of Television and Radio Artists (AFTRA). They introduced affidavits and statements to the effect that Franklin had not practiced law in ten years in the one region where he was licensed, Washington, D.C., and also that by not being registered by the Securities and Exchange Com-

JOHN A. WILLIAMS

mission, he was in violation of the Investment Advisors Act of 1940. Franklin's deposition was not admitted into the records until March 25.

Including himself, Pryor had ten witnesses testify over seven days of the first part of the hearings. The defense had three witnesses, including Pryor and Irwin Pomerantz, Pryor's former accountant. Directly after the noon recess on the twenty-fifth, the defense was startled to learn that a complaint by Pomerantz against Pryor, and a cross-complaint by Pryor against Pomerantz, had just been settled. Pryor had sued for damages; Pomerantz because Pryor owed for services already rendered. The hearing officer did not allow the terms of the settlement to go on the record. The defense contended that there was a connection between the Pomerantz/Pryor case and the comedian's claim against Franklin. The hearing officer, in spite of strenuous objections by the defense, would not allow the connection to be made.

During the hearings, Pryor made the point several times that Franklin would not return his calls. The defense asked why he had not confronted the attorney by flying to Atlanta and laying out his suspicions. The comedian answered, "Because I thought it best that I did not do that because I believe that I would have killed him."

Asked then if there was a violent part to his nature, Pryor said, "Especially when someone steals my money."

The hearings continued, with interruptions, briefs and petitions flying back and forth, until May, when Pryor, by then back in Baton Rouge, had to be hospitalized for five days for treatment of a respiratory ailment. By July he was in London doing *Superman III*, after turning down a projected film, *Color Man*, about a sportscaster, for Universal.

On July 2, Liz Smith of the New York *Daily News* wrote: "It's final! Richard Pryor's marriage settlement to Jennifer Lee, his longtime girlfriend and shorttime wife, is $750,000 with no taxes taken out. Jennifer has rented a house in Bridgehampton, Long Island, and says she'll return to her career as actress-songwriter."

If true, this seemed to mean that Jennifer, married almost twice as long to Pryor than Deboragh, was entitled to ten times as much money; Deboragh received only $62,000, and this sparked a racial furor in the black community. The discussions were all the more energetic because Pryor had made the cover of *Newsweek* back in May. Senior editor Jack Kroll wrote: "The wonderful thing about America is that it continues to produce cultural double-crosses that upset the status quo. It's sheer delight that Richard Pryor should have become a cultural hero and a box-office super-superstar in the age of Ronald Reagan, the New Right and the Moral Majority."

During the third week of August, Pryor scored again. California's Labor Commissioner, Patrick Henning, ruled that David Franklin, while serving as the comedian's agent from 1975 to 1980, had "willfully misappropriated" more than $2.3 million of Pryor's money. The commissioner also determined that Franklin was not licensed to act as a talent agent in California, and had to return $753,000 paid to him in fees. Franklin, the commissioner went on, was "guilty of serious moral turpitude," and of actions which constituted "unconscionable and continuing wrongful conduct . . . including numerous acts of embezzlement, fraud and defalcation while acting in a fiduciary capacity." Henning further ordered Franklin to pay interest of 7 percent on $1.8 million of the total award of $3.1 million.

Franklin's refusal to take the hearings seriously, his decision not even to attend, had cost him; the commissioner later admitted to his attorneys that that had been a key factor in the judgment against him. In fact, Franklin had even declined to return his attorneys' phone calls when they sought to inform him of the ruling. He heard about it from an Atlanta newspaper that had called to get his reaction, then called his people in California in a state of utter disbelief. Aside from thinking, wrongly, that the Labor Commission had not the power to render such a judgment, Franklin believed he was insulated because of his unusual position as an officer of Pryor's corporation; he did not take a percentage of the deals he negotiated, as most agents would, but rather received a salary for his services. Another of his unconventional practices had come back to haunt him as well; Franklin never had written contracts with his clients, was arrogant enough to believe he did not need them, and thought, in any case, that was how white managers had always exploited black talent—through bad contracts. Franklin was convinced that others had captured Pryor's ear and persuaded him that the absence of a contract was a shrewd plot on the attorney's part to limit his own liability. "So why did those motherfuckers have contracts?" Franklin asked rhetorically, much later.

Meanwhile Pryor said through a spokesman that he was "very pleased" at the ruling, which was "yet another painful reminder that a person whom [he] had trusted and relied on for five years grossly abused that trust."

Franklin immediately made plans to appeal.

Although the final judgment was yet to be made, Pryor's problems seemed reminiscent of some of Bill Cosby's early career experiences. Of these Cosby once said: "I have this idea that there are always going to be cats walking along with a stick jabbing you in your ass. And there's always going to be another cat who'll smack this cat that's jabbing you in the ass. Just smack him down. Then he'll put his arm around you and begin to jab you in your ass in his own way, while you're busy thanking him for having smacked the other cat."

In November in Miami Beach Pryor was voted Entertainer of the Year, where he said triumphantly, "I have enough money for a black person to live forever."

If that was true, one might wonder why he did *The Toy*, which was released in December, making it his third starring film in a year. One of Pryor's former lawyers, who had no axe to grind because there had been no problems between them, called the film "a metaphor of slavery." While Pryor may have been eager to work with Jackie Gleason, the vehicle itself, adapted from a French comedy with the same title, is high-gloss farce.

It was a movie out of the past, adorned with essentially racist spoofery. If Pryor understood the ramifications of black people *not* being in pictures that portrayed them favorably, then we assume that he also understood the implications of their being in films that showed them negatively. If he had an aversion to portrayals of rape as a violation of body and psyche, then we should expect him to be perceptive enough to see racism in both script and scene. He himself had led us to believe that he was the man who could espy those cinematic nuances and bold presentations that cast him and his people as *Toms, Coons, Mulattoes, Mammies & Bucks*, as per Donald Bogle's book.

In *The Toy*, Pryor played an out-of-work fledgling reporter. He was an out-of-work actor in *Stir Crazy*, and he would be an unemployed computer programmer in *Superman III*. Again circumstances made it necessary for Pryor to take on the job of a waiter, just as he did in *Stir Crazy*. But in this film, Pryor as Jack Brown became a maid, working for the rich U. S. Bates, played by Jackie Gleason, who drew on one of his old characters from his TV show, Reggie Van Gleason. Although Brown masquerades as a maid for only a short time, the publicity photo of Pryor in dress and cap, serving Gleason, was widely reprinted. The desperation that forces Jack to take the maid's job is obscured by slapstick; the movie is, after all, a comedy, and we are not meant to take it seriously. But comedy *is* serious; it creates laughter only as a cloak behind which crouch basic considerations and perceptions.

Even in this film, such considerations were converted into throwaway lines. U. S. Bates says, "We sell everything." His spoiled son, home on vacation from a military school, usually gets everything he wants. This time it is "the black man." Jack Brown's response, "I can be bought, but I can't be wrapped," is a line right out of the 1930s, about as classical as Willie Best's "Feets, don't fail me now!"

It is, however, the feminization of the black man that stamps the film early on as being subversive to the aspirations of the black male. Having to work as a maid seems to be punishment for Brown's wanting to work with words—he must be castrated. The fact that Pryor's mustache remains, even as he is flouncing about in dress and cap, only intensifies both the slapstick—and the intention to de-ball him. He is not therefore a character like the determined actor played by Dustin Hoffman in *Tootsie*; he is a caricature, a fleeting glimpse of the way some Hollywood folk would like the black man to be.

The French and American producers should have read Richard Wright's story, "Man of All Work," in which another desperate black man dons his wife's clothes because she is too ill to work, and he himself has no job. Set in the "Old South" in 1944, Carl Owen as Lucy Owen works for Ann and David Fairchild, where, in short order, he's asked to wash Mrs. Fairchild's back and give his/her opinion of the size of her breasts and hips. He is of course relieved when she dresses and leaves. But only temporarily, for Mr. Fairchild—whose habit was to "wrestle" with the former maid—begins making advances to Carl/Lucy. The balance of the story is both comic and tragic. There is no gloss.

In *The Toy*, we are in the "New South," and the Klan still does business. Reference to the opposition group, Klanwatch, is shoved in to legitimize an otherwise reactionary film. Fast scenes and faster patter make passing reference to larger matters with lines like "He bought a black man." The response is predictable: "I didn't know we sold them," and "This got settled in the Civil War." One scene that might be entitled "Black Man in Flight," also directly out of the 1930s, has Pryor running rapidly on top of water.

In almost every aspect, *The Toy* was a dreadful movie, which was unanimously panned. In two separate "takes," Canby of *The New York Times* turned thumbs down: "My mind wasn't simply wandering during the film—it was ricocheting between the screen and the exit sign." Nine days later, having had some time to think, he zeroed in on Pryor: "It may be that Mr. Pryor will go on forever making third-rate junk like *The Toy* and not lose his public, but I wouldn't bet on it. Of the three films released in 1982, only *Richard Pryor Live on the Sunset Strip* caught the measure of the man's dangerous brilliance, but *Sunset Strip* was a 'concert' film. . . . *The Toy* wants to . . . transform him into a little [white] boy's best friend, a sort of a male mammy."

So, the question would not go away: Why was the comedian accepting such nonchallenging, demeaning parts? Surely he had paid his bill, which was enormous, to the Sherman Oaks Burn Center; and even if greed was running a close second to his self-respect, hadn't he just told people that he had enough money to live forever? And wasn't he due to get back $3.1 million, providing Franklin's appeal failed? Was it ego that made Pryor think he alone could convert bombs into bouquets? Answers were hard to come by. All things considered, in spite of all the Canbys, 1982 had been a good year, and Pryor was still moving, had hardly paused.

With the new year the Hollywood rumor mill was gushing forth an impossible list of projects that Pryor supposedly would be working on. These included *All Day Sucker* (or *Double Whoopee*) with Gene Wilder, *The Charlie Parker Story*, *The Man Who Could Work Miracles*, *Ain't No Heroes*, and *The Music Box*, a remake of a Laurel and Hardy film, with Burt Reynolds. In addition, Pryor was thinking that it was time to gather material for another concert tour and the by now inevitable concert film.

The comedian was now dividing his time between Northridge and the island of Maui, in the Hana area in the eastern side, almost the farthest point away from the port of Lahaina. Haleakala Mountain and National Park, ten thousand feet high, overlooked his home. He fished, flew, jeeped around, and when he grew bored, flew into Honolulu for shopping in the Ala Moana Center, or danced the night down at the Hyatt Regency on Waikiki Beach. Back on Maui, he could sit in the Old Whalers Grog Shoppe in the Pioneer Inn and watch the yachts come in or sail out, and drink the cold beer or eat at Mama's fish House on Kuau Cove. Maui was idyllic but for Pryor by July it would also be boring.

Things were more exciting—and sobering—back on the mainland. There, early in March, Pryor attended the funeral of the five-year-old Patrick Andrew Mason, who had been killed by police officer Anthony Sperl in Stanton, California. The cop thought the boy had a gun. The comedian arrived quietly, offered his condolences to the mother, and left. He characterized himself only as "a concerned citizen," but he had shown similar concern for his own safety in similar circumstances before, in the monologue where he tells a cop: "I am reaching into my pocket for my wallet, 'cause I don't wanna be no motherfuckin' accident!"

Not even the fact that just five days before he had concluded a $40-million-dollar deal with Columbia Pictures could overcome the somber reality that black people, both by accident and design, both physically and psychologically, were being consigned to the beyond. That may be why the comedian seemed to pledge that some of the four films he would make in the deal would be ethnically oriented and "provide opportunities for people who haven't had opportunities to do films in the past."

Pryor would have artistic control over all the pictures and would star in at least three of them. Columbia president Guy McElwaine and chairman Frank Price stood by as Pryor announced that the president of the new company, Indigo Productions, would be Jim Brown. It was also announced that the first two films would be *The Charlie Parker Story* and *Double Whoopee*. The Parker script was already in the hands of Joel Oliansky, who said the film would stretch Pryor "in a different way than he's been stretched" in any other movie. Gene Wilder was working on the *Whoopee* script.

With the news of the formation of Indigo, black Hollywood perked up. Maybe things were about to change. Two *real* bad brothers were in charge of things, it appeared. It was a mythic pairing (more perfect, in fact, than any of the bonding either had done on film), the Signifying Monkey and Stagolee, the Trickster and the Outlaw joining forces to kick Hollywood's ass.

Jim Brown, too, was swamped with calls. He had been summoned from the sidelines; number 32 was back in the game. His appointment was seen as a reward for being "Mr. Nice Guy" during Pryor's tough times at Sherman Oaks. Los Angeles *Sentinel* columnist Maggie Hathaway wrote of that period "I have never seen anything worry him like the hospitalization of his friend Richard Pryor. None of us could reach Jim. He was gone night and day. . . . Jim remained and stuck with Richard through the thunder and lightning; and when it rained, Jim was there to get wet."

In addition to Brown's loyalty, Pryor admired him, said one associate, "for just being that strong specimen of black manhood that white people were scared of." Brown, of course, had had his own share of problems, largely because of that fear he inspired, as well as his steadfast refusal to be programmed, whether at Syracuse, where he was an All-American, Cleveland, where he was an All-Pro, or Hollywood, which had not allowed him to be much more than an actor with a splendid physique.

"You are good when you accept the bullshit," Brown said. "You are bad when you reject the bullshit." He had run afoul of the law at times; the Los Angeles chief of police had Brown's phone number in his files. The former athlete had spent considerable time and energy in the community projects battling racism in Hollywood. He served on the Black Economic Union, the Beverly Hills NAACP, and the Image Awards committee. He once rejected a plea not to introduce Pryor at a public function; there was fear that the comedian would say "nigger." And Brown was also asked not to present an award to minister Louis Farrakhan of the Nation of Islam. He did it anyway. Brown had worked extensively with Fred Williamson and he had been involved in the formations of production companies that did not last long. One of his several ventures outside moviemaking was the formation of SCCROUSA, an oil company with ties to oil-rich Nigeria. (In the winter of 1984, Jim Brown was in the recently invaded Grenada, trying to establish a health club.)

So the bad brothers had a $40-million stake. In Hollywood terms that was not a lot of money for four films—five, some reports said. In fact, it seemed to be an amount calculated *not* to give the comedian a chance to produce a blockbuster film. The figures *sounded* good; they *looked* good, spread out in the papers and magazines. However, as one actor cautioned, "Out here you can talk money from ying to yang. They shove dollar signs wherever they want to, and at the end none of them means a damned thing." Cooking the books was a matter of course.

There was another consideration. Nobody hands over $40 million out of personal admiration; nobody makes such an offer without strings. That simply is not in the nature of man as we know him— especially if that man lives and works in Hollywood. But black actors, writers and directors still hoped, in the face of the obvious, that Tinseltown had undergone a change of heart.

Whatever the negative aspects of the deal, Pryor would be stretching himself even thinner than he already was. He would be in charge of Indigo Productions, responsible for staffing, overseeing and assigning scripts, selecting talent, riding herd on every project, making deadlines and decisions, and perhaps even "hand-holding" actors—all the duties of a superproduction chief. Yet, he obviously would continue to act, and certainly carry on with his comedy in concert and in film. His burden was now immense—if not altogether inhumane. To a distant observer, it was almost as though Hollywood, having failed to destroy him in other ways, was now going to try kindness or generosity.

Was he capable of assuming these expanded responsibilities? His track record, according to journalist Bill Brashler, was none too good in this regard: "Those who work for him describe their routine as unnerving and chaotic. He's likely to remain incommunicado for days, cancel appointments, renege on personal commitments or simply go off somewhere." Of course, this was not a secret. It was well known that in his Reseda and Burbank offices the approach to his person was well-guarded by two faithful lionesses, Margaret Goldsmith and the ever-present Lauren Glassman. They decided who would see Mr. Pryor and when; they booked interviews with writers from major publications and dismissed others; they told countless writers that "Mr. Pryor says when he wants a book done about him, he'll do it himself."

Still, Pryor appeared to be the conscientious "mogul" when he told Stephen Farber of *The New York Times*, "Rarely have I read a good script. Maybe there are some good ones out there, but the scripts that come my way are not very good." Black screenwriters bluntly begged to differ. They wondered if Pryor even read scripts that were passed on to him. Besides, white Hollywood was smirking; Indigo, slow to staff in the first place, was poorly organized, and the chief reader had not even been hired. The seventy blacks in the seven thousand-member Writers Guild prayed this was not because Pryor preferred scripts written by whites. Since Poitier and Harry Belafonte did *Buck and the Preacher* (1972), and Poitier and Cosby did *Uptown Saturday Night* (1974), *Let's Do It Again* (1975) and *A Piece of the Action* (1977), there had not been more than a handful of principal writers who were black.

The odds were against them; "Roots" had not had one black writer among its platoons, and into the 1980s, new series on TV with black characters continued to be created without black writers.

When Jane Ellison was associate executive director of the Guild, she noted that "We've seen a systematic disenfranchisement of nonwhites through recent years. Since I've been in this position at the Guild I've witnessed a kind of silencing, a genocide of ideas. Only about one percent of working screenwriters are black. . . . If all the black characters are written by whites and they intentionally avoid black input, what will I see on screen except a white version of someone black? What are they giving people except their own narrow fantasies of what black people are like?"

So all eyes were on Pryor, as he represented a possible break with existing trends barring nonwhite writers from finding work in film and television. If some Pryor fans were crying "Do it, Richard!" they were not talking about comedy. At about the same time the writers had Indigo and Pryor under the microscope, The Artists and Athletes Against Apartheid, led by Arthur Ashe, Sidney Poitier, Georg Stanford Brown and Bernie Casey, were meeting in New York and in Los Angeles to upbraid entertainers and athletes who had journeyed to the South African enclave of Bophuthatswana, where, apparently, there was no end to the big bucks that could be earned. Celebrity Sun City visitors included blacks and whites; Pryor was not one of them.

Obviously, once again, growing political discontent was fermenting in the Hollywood Hills. The question was, would Pryor be the man to pop the cork? No other black entertainer had so publicly put himself on the line in undisguised, unqualified support of black people, in and out of the industry. The tradition had been one of quiet support, the sudden appearance of a helping hand thrust silently forward. Now, it seemed, was the hour to change the course of the long, straight track of Hollywood.

And the *Los Angeles Times* observed that "Given Pryor's statements about his commitment to helping new talent, especially minorities, it would not be surprising to see this commitment actualized through his production arrangement."

Pryor already had another Grammy tucked away for the best comedy record, *Live on the Sunset Strip*, when he appeared as a cohost on the Academy Award Show in April. With him were Liza Minelli, Dudley Moore and Walter Matthau. Their opening number, "It All Comes Down to This," displayed a quartet whose singing was all but washed away with loud music, and dancing that was pathetic. Pryor told Dudley Moore, who liked his suit, that it was fireproof. The line got a laugh. At another point, a stagehand passed behind Pryor, who was reading from the teleprompter. Out of the corner of his eye, he saw a flame in the stagehand's grasp, turned away from the audience and checked behind a set. "Okay?" Pryor asked. The response was affirmative. The audience laughed. The sight gag went down well, and later, there was a third reference to Pryor's burning, which brought even louder laughs—even if some people in the audience appeared uneasy with the reiteration of the incident. This was not the Pryor people knew; he was subdued, had trouble reading his lines, as nearly everyone did. It was perhaps the mentions of the fire that made people remember the old and dangerous Pryor, and the memory of him—with the fire as focus—was easier to laugh at than the comedian who now stood up there in a tuxedo and red tie looking slightly like a fish out of water.

He seemed far more at ease hosting the "Motown 25" show the next month. Originally billed as a charity show for the victims of sickle-cell anemia, which most affects black people, and some white people from the Mediterranean basin (with Cooley's anemia, a variation of sickle cell), Pryor announced that it was a "Charity, anniversary, reunion, surprise party and salute to the music of Motown." Very little was done to bring attention to sickle-cell anemia; Smokey Robinson did one song-skit with a little girl who appeared to be very uncomfortable. Mostly, the two-hour show as a tribute to Berry Gordy, Jr., the head of Motown. The dancers were of all kinds and colors; the white stars, like Dick Clark and Linda Ronstadt, were thoroughly integrated on the show. It was like watching the Academy Awards; with all the dancers and singers, the presenters, hosts and cohosts, a viewer could come away with the idea that Hollywood was a very well integrated place. The Motown Show, however, was heavier on the black side than on the white, but no one could fault Berry Gordy for not having given it his best shot. Motown was, after all, a black company— even though some people offered the opinion that it was less so than when it began. But it was Motown's 1972 production of *Lady Sings the Blues* which had provided Pryor with his first prominent dramatic role, as Piano Man.

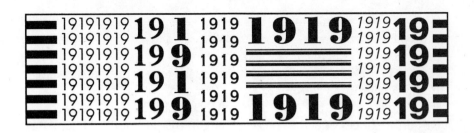

Nineteen

The word was that Pryor did not want to do *Superman III*, but Warner Bros. and the brothers Alexander and Ilya Salkind pursued him until finally he asked for $4 million, hoping the demand would end the chase.

"It was," Pryor said, "the kind of a deal where you take the money and run. Don't look back." However, he also told Johnny Carson on "The Tonight Show" that he was "just kidding around with some people about working in it [*Superman III*]—and I got a job." While there might be some confusion over which of the comedian's versions was closer to reality, there was no bewilderment about the money. Once again Pryor seemed to be wedged between the contradiction of having enough money and being greedy.

He was in London, "on hold all the time, sitting in a hotel room waiting to be called," Pryor told a reporter. And later, in conversation with Bette Davis and Johnny Carson on "The Tonight Show," he related that for one segment, he and Christopher Reeve were strung up with wires so they could "fly," and they were about sixty feet off the ground with nothing beneath them for protection.

"There were no mats or anything?" Miss Davis asked.

"No, ma'am," Pryor replied.

"You're crazy," Miss Davis exclaimed.

Laughing, Pryor came back with, "Yes, that's been said," and Carson, McMahon and Davis joined him in laughter. (In a print interview the comedian said they had him "Hanging ninety feet in the air," and that "scared the hell" out of him.)

I'LL DIE 179

When the film opened in 1983, *Variety* headlined its review of *Superman III* this way: *Unspecial follow-up to 2nd gem, though Pryor should lure lotsa funny business.*

Pryor's role challenged him far, far less than had the part of Eddie Weller in *Some Kind of Hero*. That most of the critics had good things to say about the comedian may be attributed to the unspectacular performances of nearly everyone else in the picture. Villainous Ross Webster, played by Robert Vaughn, is no equal to the crackling cunning and hip villainy of Lex Luthor, played by Gene Hackman in the earlier "red cape" films. Absent too were the lissome Valerie Perrine and the bumbling character of Ned Beatty.

In *Superman III*, an oil crisis, the destruction of coffee crops by satellite, and a temporarily hard-drinking, "evil" Superman make for a plot clearly stitched together from comic books. For this sequel, Lois Lane (Margot Kidder) was jettisoned in favor of another of Superman's alliteratively-named friends, Lana Lang, played by Annette O'Toole.

Pryor is an out-of-work kitchen mechanic who joins a computer trainee program and learns quickly to become enough of a whiz that he is able to use the computer to embezzle so much money that he attracts the attention of the president of the company, the Robert Vaughn character. Between the alternating postures of sambo and savant, Pryor builds Vaughn a computer capable of creating worldwide destruction. This allows the villainous executive to corner the oil and coffee markets. Of course, ultimately Superman saves the day and befriends Pryor, who earlier, in consort with Vaughn, had tried to kill the Man of Steel.

It may be that the opening scenes of the film were more demeaning than Pryor's playing of Gus Gorman. They seemed to deride the comedian's personal holocaust. In the ordered chaos of the opening, one mishap leading to another in a downtown Metropolis street, some toy penguins are bowled over and scattered. One catches fire. The shot is from the rear, thus all we see of the penguin as it waddles aimlessly down the street is its blackness, and flames shooting from its body. This seems to be a mimicking of Pryor's agonized movements along Hayvenhurst Avenue on the evening of June 9, 1980. The fire on the penguin is extinguished by a covert blast of breath by Clark Kent, who happens by on his way to work at *The Daily Planet*.

The film establishes that Gus Gorman is a computer genius. But at the start of the bang-bang ending which centers around the giant computer Gus has built for the villain, Vera, Webster's sister (Annie Ross), and Lorelei (Pamela Stephenson)—described by *Variety* as being the "deceptively dumb bimbo" of Webster—display a sudden and astounding knowledge of computers. *Their* genius has been concealed from us for about 115 of the 123 minutes of the movie. This revelation renders Gus's purported genius null; the two women—and the script—have only let him play at being supersmart. It was all fantasy, and black genius is not present. First you see it, then you don't. It's the old Hollywood habit of substituting slapstick or bathos for realistic revolution.

Although there are moments when Gus and Vera momentarily stroke each other through a glance or two, nothing comes of this. Webster has his "bimbo," Superman his childhood girl, but for Gus (and Vera) nothing. "They cut Richard's nuts off, man," a disgruntled moviegoer complained. "Didn't get near no kinda pussy." His disappointment is of course based upon the Hollywood formula that even second bananas get a girl in the movies. This time, passing through a world of white people, Pryor didn't even wind up with a hooker. Gorman's genius is put into its final, demeaning perspective when Superman asks some workmen if they can find some kind of computer game for Gus to play with.

The recipe for producing a successful movie, director Billy Wilder once joked, is "Get Richard Pryor." But, even within the lines of those good notices the comedian got for *Superman III*, one could detect a certain politeness towards him, perhaps derived from reviewers' habit, and also a letdown, a disappointment that what the audience wanted to happen for Pryor in the Gus Gorman role did not. Some fans asked the question the comedian himself had asked in a monologue:

"How long? *How* long will this bullshit go on?"

Countless newspaper and magazine articles told us that Richard Pryor was the current star among stars, the "crossover" phenomenon; his presence in a film, even a lousy one, earned the various studios from fair to tremendous sums of money. Not a month went by when he was not to be found somewhere on the pages of the print media or on cable or network-television reruns. The impression had been created that he had enormous power and was therefore quite able to influence Hollywood, and by extension the manners and mores of the nation, in a new direction. However, there arose, as it must, the perennial question: Why did he keep appearing in films that did not challenge what we knew to be his considerable talents?

The answer may lie in a brief recapitulation of the way Hollywood often works. Just a few years ago a studio executive was involved in the misappropriation of the funds of actors who'd worked for his company. The official, it turned out, was forging his signature to the checks of the actors, one of whom complained to the authorities. The situation then made the news, appearing off and on for several months. Two of the actors were prominent figures. After blowing the whistle, one of them did not get work for quite some time. His job activity was largely limited to television commercials—and this created the example of someone who should have kept quiet and allowed his victimization to go unnoticed.

Sidney Poitier may have been luckier. He didn't want to do *Porgy and Bess* (1959); he thought the movie an "insult to black people." Harry Belafonte had declined the role of Sporting Life because he considered it demeaning. Norman Zierold writes, however, that Sam Goldwyn's "persuasive powers . . . enabled him to finally sign up Sammy Davis, Jr., Poitier, Pearl Bailey and Dorothy Dandridge." Poitier reports in his autobiography that Goldwyn felt the film was "one of the greatest things that ever happened for the black race."

At the same time Poitier was fending off Goldwyn, Stanley Kramer wanted him to do *The Defiant Ones* with Tony Curtis, but, according to Poitier, Kramer implied that if Poitier was having difficulties with Goldwyn, it would be tough for Kramer to offer the actor the part, "in terms of union regulations and business protocol. . . . In other words, if you can get from Goldwyn an absolute release from the promise he says he's been given, then we've got a deal." Poitier had made no such promise and was furious with his agent, who, without telling him, had. The agent told the actor that Goldwyn was "one of the biggest, most powerful studio heads in the business, and if he chooses to, he can blackball you so you'll never work in a studio again."

Poitier played Porgy.

More recently, another black star, armed with a story scripted by Pamela Douglas and Martin Yarbrough from his plot line, strolled into NBC, where he had starred in two different series and where he still had a deal. This was a strong script—light but accurate in its portrayal of black people— and it had been written by two old Hollywood hands who were themselves black. The network people were glad to see the star. Maybe, they said, they'd consider doing his fresh series if he first took a look at a script they thought was just right for him, a concept series. But the star thought the script was a disgrace, "sambo from the git," and he declined. His script and idea for a series, it followed, did not find a home at NBC. There was not even a discussion.*

Anecdotes like these suggest why Pryor took the roles he did, but change is long overdue. Over ten years ago, Donald Bogle wrote,

---

* Then came "The Cosby Show," with the doctor father and lawyer mother and wonderful kids, one of whom goes to Princeton—a situation at the other extreme of shows where everyone lives in the projects, there is no father, and school isn't especially liked.

"No one knows what the future [of blacks in film] holds. We only know that the black man's past entitles him to a better future."

From all appearances, neither Pryor nor any other black star really shared in Hollywood's exercise of power. In any case, Hollywood simply does not have the vision that black life, expressed beyond comedy or interracial male bonding* can make the huge amounts of money it needs to keep producing garbage under the "greed enterprise" system. Therefore, while we will have *The Fighting 69th*, a film about a predominantly Irish, World War I regiment, it is doubtful that we'll ever have *The Fighting 369th*, about a celebrated black regiment (though in 1989 we had *Glory*, a story of the first black *northern* regiment, the Massachusetts 54th, in the Civil War); we will have *Gone With the Wind* or variations of it forever, but don't count on a *Black Thunder* based on the novel by Arna Bontemps; we will have a *Pasteur* and a *Zola*, but not films about pioneering biologist Ernest E. Just or landmark blood plasma researcher Dr. Charles Drew; we will have a *Silkwood*, but not a *Fannie Lou Hamer*.

Hollywood is in the entertainment business, but it also knows that it manufactures distortions, some of which may be laid at Pryor's door for his portraying characters who lend credence to them.

Perhaps for certain people there is no alternative to greed or the company one keeps, but composer Quincy Jones told *Ebony*'s Charles Sanders in 1979, "It's the stars' fault if they let themselves be insulated and isolated from involvement with their people. How can anyone isolate your mind? If you are a thinking person, an aware person who knows anything at all about the situation which most black people have to deal with, there's no manager or lawyer in the world who can insulate and isolate you from that."

And, as if in response to some innate understanding of his situation, the comedian once again began to mount a concert tour. With these he seemed to cleanse himself; with these he was, no question, the boss; and with these, using whatever language he chose, he could expound on the universe and his most recent experiences, as he could not while clutching Superman's cape. Pryor could sink in the comfortable embrace of Mudbones, his alterego, and there find respite.

But between concert dates there was the promotion to do on *Superman III*, which was premiering in various cities. Some of the cast, including Pryor, went to the White House for a reception and a screen-

* *Heaven help a white (female) star in the thirties who didn't have a loyal, cheery black maid around when times were tough,"* Bogle wrote in Brown Sugar *(1980). The relationship between the madame and the maid, visible in film after film, represented female interracial bonding, prefiguring bonding between black and white males on screen some twenty years later.*

ing of the film. There were initial reports that he was snubbed by the First Family, reports that vanished when *Jet* ran a photo of the Reagans greeting Pryor. That he even attended surprised some people, because two years earlier there was this quote in *People*, attributed to him: "I'm amazed that we live in a country where we have to vote for ERA and civil rights. I'm amazed that an actor is the best qualified person we have to run the country."

His visit to the White House gave him some material for the concert:

> I went to the White House—I met Reagan—we in trouble. [*howls*] I went through that receiving line they had? You know, you go by for this movie *Superman*, y'know . . . I walk in the line 'n' shit, gonna meet 'im, say, Don't be prejudiced—open your mind, see what kinda dude he is. . . . He looks like a dick. *[oooos, howls, applause]* Not even a hard-on. [*howls*] Just a dick with clothes on. That's why he wants those MXs 'n' shit, so he can get off. [*howls, applause*]

The Pryor humor was derived as usual from experience. No doubt Reagan had been called worse things, but never so publicly. Freedom of speech was getting a real workout.

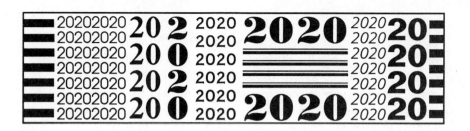

Twenty

In July 1983, *Time* did a cover story on Eddie Murphy, while delivering a nod in Pryor's direction: "Pryor, the most popular black actor in movie history, was one of Murphy's early comedy heroes; as a fledgling professional comic, Murphy used to perform an entire act using Pryor's material, calling it 'A Tribute to Richard Pryor.'"

"Both," *Time* went on, "have won the multiracial mass movie audiences and both have swum in the dark blue undercurrents of ethnic humor." Or perhaps indigo.

The month before, *Ebony* did a spread which also drew the natural comparison between the comedy of the two stars. The articles were within hailing distance of the time when Pryor complained that "they [the studios] keep throwing movies at you; they don't care whether the movies are good or bad. Then after a while you're cool [instead of being the hottest star in town] and you hear people saying 'Eddie Murphy is moving to be the next Richard Pryor.' I don't want to think about things like that." Weeks earlier, in response to Johnny Carson's rave commentary on Eddie Murphy in *48 Hrs.* and *Trading Places*, Pryor said jokingly that Murphy was so good "I'm gonna kill him."

It was obvious that he *had* to think about Murphy; his name was everywhere. Maybe all of Murphy's publicity started Pryor to thinking back on the old days when, while watching Cosby, he decided "ain't room for two niggers." *People*, not surprisingly, also did a cover piece in July—this one featuring both Pryor and Murphy. While Jeff Jarvis and Lois Armstrong were trying to create the impression that Murphy was a follower ("Eddie, twenty-two, aped his idol, Richard, forty-two. If

Richard was cool, Eddie was cooler; if Richard was warm, so was Eddie"), the commentary of both comedians indicated that they were not competitors, but a couple of guys stuck in the same old Hollywood syndrome. Murphy said, "A very militant black woman asked, 'How come no serious black actors get the same kind of deals you get or Richard Pryor gets?'" Murphy answered, " . . . because America is still a racist society." Both comedians observed that "They got a new hotrod every month. One month it's Travolta, one month its Tom Selleck." Black actors, they noted, like Billy Dee Williams or Howard Rollins, just don't get the work. Murphy and Pryor had made it because they're best known as comedians and play mostly in comic films.

"...A white man and a white woman," said Murphy, "can see one of Richard's films or *48 Hrs.* . . . "

"It's not threatening," Pryor said.

"Yeah," Murphy agreed. "and they can just just laugh. A white guy don't have to sit there and worry about his woman seeing me and going 'ooh-ahh.'"

"Eddie and I can go to the top, but we can't carry nobody with us. Can't reach back," Pryor said.

The interview and "photo opportunity" took place at Northridge. Murphy acknowledged his indebtedness to Pryor's material, style and attitude. Pryor graciously responded, although contradicting the "can't reach back," saying that "It goes back to whoever the first comic was who paved the way for the second. Dick Gregory paved the way for Bill Cosby and Bill Cosby paved the way for Richard Pryor. Eddie is paving the way for somebody else."

The relationship of the two should have been viewed as one between a father and son. Pryor's eldest child was five years older than Murphy. But in many publications they were posed subtly as competitors for the job of HNIC (Head Negro In Charge). This kind of positioning was to be expected. The son is expected to destroy the father; the king must die. This expectation presumed that Pryor's ego was so huge that he was already on the way to Murphy's jugular—though they had discussed making a film together (which actors always do, anyway, sort of like saying "Let's have a drink sometime").

Pryor was going away in any case, heading for the City, the Apple everybody was loving, the place where black people "eat you alive if your shit ain't right." He'd be in New York from August 12-21, and his concert-tour publicity man said there would be no interviews, thank you, before, during or after the comedian opened at Radio City Music Hall, which seats 5,582 people. A couple of years earlier Pryor had said,

"I didn't want to work places with 15,000 people. I thought people couldn't see me or something, and it was like a rip-off, so we only did like a couple of those . . . most [of the concerts] were 3500 [seats]."

Even before the ads came out announcing Pryor's concert on August 15 and 16, most of the tickets, priced at $25, $20 and $17.50, were sold out or cornered by scalpers and ticket agents who were selling them for nearly twice the price. Although the concert was announced as being only two days, obviously the Pryor people's plan was to add on other appearances—if all went well—anytime up to August 20. The nineteenth and the twentieth were added as soon as it became clear that the tickets for the first two shows had been snapped up like meat by a starving animal. Richard Pryor, it seemed, was more than a name; he was an entire event.

By 9:15 of opening night (all performances were scheduled for midnight), the scalpers and crowd-watchers were already on the corners of the Avenue of the Americas and 50th Street. They were all young and mostly black and Hispanic. They joked and talked softly in the cooling night that smelled a little like early autumn. The traffic along the avenue was already thinning, rushing up from downtown, in small, headlighted clots. Some of the cars turned off at 50th Street, while others, crossing town from the west, spurted across. They were slowing, seeking parking places, joining an army of automobiles already slowly circling the block bearing passengers from New Jersey and Connecticut and upstate New York. The occupants, once parked either on the street or in a garage, hurried into nearby restaurants.

By 11:15 there were four police vans and three police cars parked across the street from Radio City. Twenty cops leaned against the buildings on the block or strolled insouciantly through the crowd spreading on the sidewalk in front of the theater. The crowd now was mostly black. The whites in it did not look cowed or defensive as much as they looked neutral, or as if they wanted very much to belong. The Hispanics sounded black.

The mass continued to grow and then edged inside the theater to the powder blue ropes inside that held it in check. Platoons of ushers, the majority black and Hispanic, stood on the other side, studying the crowd, trying to judge its mood. The violent robbery spree that had erupted immediately following the Diana Ross concert in Central Park the month before may have been on their minds. But it was the cops, of course, who were better paid to remember such things. However, there was not the slightest indication that what happened in the Park would happen in Radio City; this was another kind of crowd.

A tall white woman, some kind of usher's drill sergeant, sauntered from inside and looked at the crowd. She paused to chat with the lesser ushers. Then a black man strode out, C-H-I-E-F spelled all over his bearing. He talked softly with the tall woman and then moved to the front of the crowd and chatted with a young woman who was accompanied by other women, all of whom looked something like her. It would be another five minutes, the chief told her, before they could let down the ropes. Not a second later an usher behind him shouted that it would be another eight minutes. Someone in the forward section of the mass muttered, "Aw, shit." The chief shrugged and smiled and melted back inside. The tall woman smiled at no one special and said, "As soon as we get the security down here. . . . "

People were still stacking up behind the ropes and spilling deep into the street. There was no shoving; everyone waited with a wary patience. They had been captured by the hour, the investment in the tickets and, it seemed, a definite loyalty to Richard Pryor. Two black men emerged from behind the line of ushers. One was bald. They were both broad, but not very tall. One had two-inch heels on his shoes. They looked bored; they were the security people. An usher with curly hair approached and very politely asked the crowd that it not "flood" him when he let down the ropes. No one responded; the inference to these middle-class folk being cattle was chump talk, not worthy of answer. It was 11:40 when the ropes came down. Most people started for the stairs, but then there was a bunching up before the doors to the orchestra section, which were still closed. An usher apologized. "It'll be another few minutes," he said. People waited or plunged downstairs to the bar. Some returned carrying drinks in plastic cups. People chatted, drank or smoked; no one complained. The calmness seemed an assurance that they all had come to what would turn out to be a great party; there was an air of leashed festivity.

When the orchestra doors were opened, the patrons surged gently but quickly inside. They checked out row numbers, anxiously calculating the distance from their seats to the stage—as well they might. Radio City Music Hall is cavernous. Then began the expectant humming and buzzing, the talking, the laughing, the bantering and other light conversation. People left their seats to go to the bar, to the bathroom, to greet friends, while a five-piece band tuned up on the stage. Three singers, a male and two females, joined them. Cigarette smoke began to rise like a playful blue cloud, some weed-smoke with it. Someone announced over the loudspeaker that New York law prohibits smoking inside the auditorium. No one paid any attention. (We in here now, motherfucker.)

Frankie Crocker came on to introduce Julia McGirt from *Dream Girls*; the band started to play and McGirt began to sing along with her group. It was after midnight then, and the crowd was growing a tad restless. There was more weed-smoke. People were still coming in; they walked in a crouch down the aisles looking for their seats. McGirt and group sang and thumped through approximately two thousand subdued conversations. She sang, it seemed, forever, pausing once for a glass of water, just as Pryor did, at least once during every performance. The band and McGirt seemed to be headed for a finale. The crowd offered up heavy applause and shouts of appreciation. The performers left the stage and the audience seemed to settle in for the heart of the party. It was, after all, 12:30. In the dimmed lights the audience waited. *Richard is next, Richard is on, Richard will come out*, it seemed to be thinking.

Julia McGirt and the band returned, tripping across the stage to their places as the lights came up again. The crowd masked its disappointment; the applause was grudgingly polite. Every third person in the hall, it seemed, rose and hurried to the bar as the band and McGirt pounded out another batch of numbers. And then they were through. A loud ovation was followed with cries echoing above the applause: "See you later!" "Come back soon!" "Thanks a lot!"

A stir rose in the wake of McGirt's exit, a stir like a wind long ago signaled by the bending of the trees way out yonder. What else could be next at this hour *but* Richard?

Striding long out of stage right at 12:50 came the Stroker, wearing a white jacket, black, high-cut overalls, an opened white shirt and white shoes. People rolled up a standing ovation, shouting RICHARD! HEY, RICH! RICHARD! RICHARD! From row Z down to row A people stood. Those nearest the stage reached up for a handshake, and those who could not see listened intently to the exchanges over Pryor's mike, which he had unhooked from its stand: "Hey, Richard! *Newsweek!*" Pryor screamed, "Fuck *Newsweek!*" Howling laughter thundered down the rows. Pryor was heard to shout, "Sit the fuck *down!*" "Sit your ass *down!*" "I'm sorry, man, but you got to sit down. Ain't no handshake worth this ass-whippin' you 'bout to git." "Hey, bitch! Let go my hand!" They loved it in the back and upstairs. They could hear even if they couldn't see. The hall was rocking with whoops, howls, whistles, falling-out laughter and applause. Everyone seemed relieved that Pryor was there and that relief was a catapult to their laughter. It was all like greeting a lover who was wayward but whom you always forgave.

Like a huge, benevolent beast the audience settled down, gathered itself in anticipation. "I'm happy to be here, in the city," Pryor said, and applause greeted the line. Clearly, the audience was primed to applaud almost anything.

The comedian seemed to be measuring the audience, selecting his material, picking his way. The great beast had an instinct; it knew what he was doing. Someone shouted, HEY RICH! DO MUD-BONES! Applause supported the request, but Pryor didn't hear or didn't wish to do Mudbones just yet. He stood near stage left; his body wasn't really into this performance; he seemed almost rooted to the stage. The prowling "red-suited Lazarus," as *Newsweek* had described him, was a comparatively subdued and perhaps tired man. He did a drunk routine in which he posed, as he often does, that conflict between what the mind thinks and what the body can actually do. It was a glimpse of vintage Pryor, the observer who perceives the abyss between dream and deed.

Pryor had always taken the time to introduce his friends to his audience. His prefaces to the introductions were anecdotes. The first was lengthy, about a "man he loves." That brought cries of JIM BROWN! JIM BROWN! It was therefore a surprise when the comedian introduced instead Miles Davis. Davis's wife, Cicely Tyson, was next—with a plug for her current play, *The Corn Is Green*. Then there was the guy Pryor "used to fly around with," Christopher Reeve, and then Eddie Murphy, "A young man who's going to go a long fuckin' way," who was followed by Robin Williams. Pryor told the audience that he'd watched Williams improvise at different times "for an *hour*!" Frankie Crocker's was the final introduction.

It was a good place to pause, for the laughs had been coming about every thirty seconds, rolling up from the front, where people could see and hear without distortion, all the way to the back on all levels. There were disturbances: people talking too loudly, making comments on the monologues; people getting up to go somewhere or people coming back from someplace. The audience was restless.

As almost per usual, Pryor drew the analogy between the behavior of whites and blacks when confronted by the police. The applause certified that his perceptions remained true. And, of course, his relationships with women were well known, and thus fertile ground for the monologue that began with ". . . get drunk, go home and talk to my wi*ves*" who "never understand. DO YOU?" Mock tears followed as he refused to get into the bed because it was moving. "The shit keeps moving. God, don't let me be sick. . . . " The monologue was a working-over of "Nigger with a Seizure," but nobody minded.

It was while drinking a glass of water and bantering with the crowd ("Whatcha drinkin', Rich?" "Water, girl") that he slipped into the persona of Mudbones. There was no preliminary; just a sudden slowing and rounding of speech, a puffing emphasis on certain words, but the audience recognized the character immediately and greeted him with massive applause, shouts and whistles.

Mudbones was to Pryor's audiences what Hal Holbrook's Mark Twain was to perhaps higher falutin' crowds. Only the month before, television viewers had the chance to see what Mudbones *looked* like. In a skit with Arsenio Hall, Pryor played Mudbones as a janitor. His hair and mustache were grayed; a brown felt hat sat almost squarely on his head. He also wore dark pants, an open shirt and a tattered sweater. The ABC studio audience did not recognize the name Mudbones, but the crowd at Radio City did; it was now falling out as Mudbones related an encounter with a kid (which was Pryor's true lead-in to the monologue).

Africa had grown in importance as a subject among Pryor's monologues since his first trip there in 1979. He did a routine on Zimbabwe, which seemed to have become like another home to him. The material deepened the comparison between blacks and whites—in the United States and in Africa. The animals of Africa had become standard fare in this monologue. Pryor did the African routine as he always did, deepening his voice—curiously, because it was what white comics did when they mimicked a black man—and falling easily into the speech pattern recognizable in many parts of Africa.

The comedian then moved to genitalia, men at public urinals. The audience, however, was measuring time—how much was left, and what would he do next, and it sensed that the end of the performance was in sight when Pryor said, "I don't do drugs anymore." The statement brought some thoughtful silences, a couple of very loud boos and some applause, but Pryor was already into a junkie skit, complete with a sprawl on the stage—his second of the evening—and the show was over. With a long, thin stride, he went off, stage right, one arm raised in salute. The rhythmic clapping, the standing ovation, did not bring him back; it was two in the morning and the magic was over.

Only a little of it was recaptured when Pryor went uptown the following Saturday during the day for a brief appearance at the celebrations for Harlem Week.

All in all, the critics were happy with the first performance. *The New York Times'* review by Mel Gussow was one example: "If there is one thing funnier than Richard Pryor's concert films, such as *Richard Pryor Live on the Sunset Strip*, it is Mr. Pryor live in performance...."

his Music Hall show is not entirely structured—at moments he seems to be feeling his way with his material and his audience—but that only adds to the evening's excitement. . . . What we know of Mr. Pryor, of a live lived on the edge of danger, nurtures our appreciation of him as an extraordinary comic actor. His show is not so much a routine as auto-biographical performance art."

Over at the *New York Post*, Clive Barnes was taking the edge off: "Pryor was not as sharp as he was years ago."

But, downtown, in an article entitled "Richard Pryor's Still on Fire," Pablo Guzmán in *The Village Voice* sharpened the edge by defining it as "a high-energy 'outside' gray area most comics, actors and musicians speak of, but few would actually dare live in. A place that feeds the turmoil brought on by your analysis of society's contradictions (and your own) and from where the high-wire artist can liberate audience and self via catharsis. But which usually claims lives."

"Pryor," Guzmán said, "was the first Afro-North American figure I ever saw relate to Puerto Ricans." Guzmán caught the final, Saturday night show, and he believed Pryor was "growing up and daring us to do likewise." But there would always be people, he said, "who want the worst of that 'crazy nigger.'"

There was evidence that Pryor agreed with Guzmán, if only through the title of his filmed concert, *Richard Pryor Here and Now*, which was being readied for distribution in October. The title seemed to suggest that the comedian was asking his fans to check out what he was doing at present and to overlook the past, which sometimes was difficult to do—since Pryor, in the reworking of old material, forced his fans to remember.

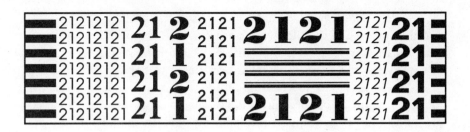

Twenty-One

In September of 1983, Indigo Productions was reported to have gotten its act together and was functioning as a studio. Jim Brown, president and executive producer, was pushing Pryor to purchase the rights to Alice Walker's award-winning novel, *The Color Purple*. Among the scripts that had been submitted, Brown was recommending action on those by actors Paul Winfield, Robert Hooks and Glyn Turman. Later Brown told a reporter that he saw his job as one of gathering all possible information on a project that was being considered for development, putting it together, and passing it on to Pryor. Brown said he was determined to make Indigo exactly what Pryor said it would be.

Columbia Pictures, the parent company, suffered typical Hollywood management upheaval early in October. Frank Price, chairman and one of "the most respected and powerful figures in the movie industry in recent years," said *The New York Times*, was resigning. Price, together with his number two, Guy McElwaine, had godfathered Indigo into existence. McElwaine had been with International Creative Management and then president of Rastar Productions (Ray Stark's company) before joining Columbia. Called the "$10 million man" because that's what he was to earn during four years with Columbia, and because he'd been associated with high-grossing films like *Stir Crazy*, Price reportedly resigned because the new owner of Columbia, Coca-Cola, was trying to bring its management strategies to the movie industry. There were no indications that the resignation would affect Indigo Productions.

During this time, David Franklin was proceeding with his appeal against the California State Labor Commissioner's judgment that the attorney had to pay Pryor $3.1 million.

Richard Pryor Here and Now opened the week of October 20, and the surprise of the film was that it carried Indigo's label and credited Jim Brown as executive producer. Was this to be one of the four or five Indigo films? Was this what was meant to be, as Pryor had said in an interview, "an interesting film," with mass appeal? Was this movie the kind of opportunity Indigo was going to provide "for people who [hadn't] had opportunities to do films in the past"? The fact that it was a film with Pryor as the only black writer and actor indicated that this was not the movie to fulfill Indigo's lofty statement of purpose.

Pryor's performance was filmed before a highly responsive New Orleans' audience—one that at times coughed up disruptive individuals. The film lacked Haskell Wexler's loving expertise that was so visible in *Sunset Strip*. The lighting was poor and the production generally uninspired. The *New York Times'* Janet Maslin saw the camera work as being "occasionally careless." Pryor was listed as director.

Reviewers commented that it didn't meet the cinematic or performance standards of *Sunset Strip*. Many also dealt with the disruptive elements (which by and large were edited out of the recorded and taped performance). Maslin noted that he "mimics people in the audience and very adroitly silences the occasional heckler [and that] no one who gives him any backtalk gets the better of him at all."

However much praised, Pryor seemed to be blamed for the negative audience taunts that marred the overall response to his performance. There was no question but that persons in the audience were trying to bait the comedian. Someone in the audience hurled up that ancient challenge, the gateway to "The Dozens," by shouting, "How's y'momma?"

Pryor was momentarily shaken. "Wh—how's my mama? I beg your pardon. [*laughter*] I'll slap you in the mouth with my dick! [*howls, applause*] One at a time, please. I'ma finish with this motherfucker ask me 'bout my momma. [*howls*] How's *yo'* momma? We be some momma-callin' motherfuckers this evening."

Variety likewise picked up on Pryor's "ad libs or exchanges with the audience [in which] a lot of anger can still be seen lurking," as did Joseph Gelmis of *Newsday*.

Pryor had his supporters. Every time he squelched a heckler, he got applause. And there was a point at which, in anger, he accused the hecklers of being the same people who had tried to disrupt a previous performance, which suggested that he felt that the disruptive individuals in the audience were present for that specific purpose.

Reviewer Jack Kroll, who had done the *Newsweek* cover story on the comedian (May 3, 1982), saw the audience hostility as a sign of Pryor's changing relationship to his audience. Kroll wrote: "A weird thing about this film is the undertow of hostility in the audience that makes Pryor sap his energy and momentum in squashing (or ingratiating) his hecklers. This strange rumbling is significant: Pryor's audience seems to get uncomfortable when they sense Pryor getting too comfortable. They want risk and threat. . . . "

The opening section of the film was tailored for New Orleans, with lines on Creole speech, the weather, slavery, and the alleged penchant for partying. Pryor did not say anything about his grandmother having come from this region—which is what he told interviewers back in the 1960s and 1970s.

Here and Now, as in previous concert films, was based on his latest concert performances. In a real sense, the film was recycled material which, as Kroll put it, "sputters between hits and near misses." For all the critics' reservations, however, Pryor was taking a personal and career risk in having the concert—with or without film—in the Deep South, which maintains its memories, even though it probably has more black quarterbacks on its football teams than the North. Its habits have changed grudgingly. New Orleans is not Atlanta, and certainly not New York, which, far more hip, far more attuned to Pryor's work, had not been hostile at all.

Pryor offered up some stinging lines on the South and on white people generally, and got on a roll when he did the routine on Zimbabwe: "black people kicked ass over there . . . for seven years. They *killed* motherfuckers, Jack. They happy, too."

And, again referring to his African trip, "I know how white people feel in America now—relaxed. 'Cause when I heard the police car, I knew they weren't comin' after me. . . . I slept like a baby . . . I knew the Ku Klux Klan wouldn't be rushin' in on my ass. If they did rush in, they'd be serving something." These lines led to consideration of South Africa: "America helps them motherfuckers, right? We be sendin' 'em shit, napalm 'n' shit, y' know, to help them bomb black people. Fuck that."

He had always been an extraordinary mimic; he did the African speech patterns, the rising and falling rhythms of it, to an unappreciated perfection. The African monologue seemed to be longer on the film than it had been on stage in New York. Pryor must have got a special kick out of doing it in New Orleans.

To those willing to listen, Pryor preached about helping black people the next time "you see us in trouble," about blacks and whites getting along inside the theater, but once outside, "the shit change," and he moved from this and indirectly to talk about nuclear war.

He is, Gelmis wrote, "an outsider to the establishment by reason of race, yet a pop culture hero to the establishment's children.... Like Woody Allen, he cannibalizes his own failures and frustrations ... and transforms the pain into laughter, often at his own expense.... He has the mimetic precision of the great silent film clowns, of Chaplin and Keaton."

The performance was not bad—but Pryor had treated us to better ones—at least that seemed to be the opinion of the critics. Very politely, therefore, they griped. Gelmis of *Newsday* may have supplied the answer for it: "Because Pryor has more creative control over his career than almost anyone in Hollywood. Yet he alternates between the squeaky clean inanities of movies like *The Toy* and *Superman III* and these R-rated cathartic outbursts of talking dirty in person to fans.... Pryor makes his directorial debut with still another concert movie—one that differs little from the standard fare of cable TV networks."

The fall of 1983 brought a series of disastrous events: A South Korean 747 jetliner which had strayed into Soviet airspace was shot down on August 30, then in October there was a terrorist explosion that took 237 U.S. Marine lives in Beirut, and then the U.S. invasion of Grenada. The nation rallied around President Reagan and his foreign policy at about the same time Pryor in concert, and quickly following on film, was denouncing both. The intensity and depth of the comedian's attack on the President was nothing like his comedy about Carter.

In one of those monologues Pryor does a wino who decides to call President Carter. He goes into a phone booth, dials, and says, "Get me Carter. Now listen, this is Tiptoe Johnson, that's who it is. Say, old man, what's going on with this Russian situation? What kind of missiles have we got? Where they at? And what this deficit mean?"

In the autumn of 1983, with the Russians seen behind the Syrians in Lebanon, and the Syrians behind what the press called "Islamic fundamentalist" terrorists, and the Russians also viewed as accomplices to all the antigovernment revolutions in Central America and in Grenada, and complicit also with Cuba, well, as Pryor might have put it, "The shit wasn't funny no more." However, he continued in *Here and Now* with lines like these:

"An' then they try to get everybody mad at the Russians 'n' shit. I ain't mad at no motherfuckin' Russians. [*titters*] I don't even know no Russians. [*titters*] If I seen a Russian in the street, an' he don't have on that hat, I don't know who the fuck he is. [*whoops, laughter, applause*]"

Although Pryor seemed to be outside the anti-Communist whirlwind that was sweeping the nation, not everybody thought his perceptions about Reagan and his foreign policy were wrong.

The second week in December, Howard Koch, who had produced *Some Kind of Hero* and who was now the president and chief operating officer of Rastar Productions, dismissed the four people on the production staff of the company. The move was reported in seventeen lines in *Variety*, but hardly anyplace else. Such dismissals were routine in Hollywood.

On Thursday, December 16, a spokesman for Columbia Pictures, Stan Robertson, who was also a columnist, announced that Richard Pryor had dismissed Jim Brown "due to creative differences," a catchall phrase endemic to Hollywood. The firing was reported in forty lines in *Variety* and was significant enough to command fifty lines in *The New York Times*, which picked up the story from the Associated Press. Three others were dismissed with Brown. The firings had taken place on Pearl Harbor Day, December 7. The Columbia spokesman was, noted *The New York Times*, "the highest ranking black" at Columbia Pictures.

Brown's departure was a bombshell that elicited varying degrees of response in Hollywood and the nation. This was another "Pryor drama." Black Hollywood reeled. The local branch of the National Association for the Advancement of Colored People quickly blamed not Pryor, but Columbia and Coca-Cola. In an assertion that seemed to imply recognition of the powerlessness of black stars, Beverly Hills NAACP executive director Willis Edwards said that Brown's dismissal was "a slap in the face because we were working very hard with Jim Brown. . . . Richard Pryor couldn't just fire Jim Brown by himself. I think they're using Pryor as a scapegoat, making everybody think he did this when in fact it was Coke and Columbia making the move." In Philadelphia, the *National Leader* ran a small piece reporting that Pryor had fired "all Black employees" of Indigo Productions, including the company's president Jim Brown, leaving white staff members "untouched".

Back in Los Angeles, another black paper, the highly respected *Sentinel*, ran a green headline:

In the story by Chico C. Norwood, Edwards's charges were aired once more, and Robertson defended the dismissals, saying, "What bothers me is for blacks to think a major talent like Pryor could be manipulated by Columbia or Coca-Cola. Richard's his own man."

But the black communities of America thought otherwise; he was *their* man, and ultimately Pryor had to respond to the pressure of negative publicity. He said, "Essentially, I'm reorganizing my company. It [the dismissal] was strictly a professional decision. People are fired every day. Contractually, Columbia can't tell me anything. I have complete autonomy. I'm the one who called Jim Brown into my office. I know that I made the right decision."

When asked if there were other factors in the firing that had not been revealed, the comedian answered, "I couldn't do that [respond to the question] and be fair. It would not be the right thing to do."

(The speculation about Columbia's involvement was reinforced eleven months later when Charles Smiley, a black former ABC-TV vice president who had replaced Brown in February, abruptly resigned. "Indigo's relationship with Columbia will necessarily be restructured so that Indigo's activities will be slowed down, with Columbia more actively involved," Smiley was quoted as saying by *Variety*.)

There had been gossip that the dismissal happened because Brown was taking Indigo "too deeply" into the development of minority projects. Pryor denied the rumor. "This is no racial thing," he said. "We are committed to doing minority projects. That's the only reason I started this. I don't want to be self-serving, but it was a sacrifice to myself . . . Jim Brown [is] a decent human being," Pryor continued, but there was "no chance" that he would be brought back into the company.

Brown made no public response other than to say that he had requested meetings with Pryor several times which were turned down. Pryor and Brown had been friends for more than fifteen years.

Seven years later in his book, *Out of Bounds*, Jim Brown made no reference at all to his brief presidency and partnership in Indigo with Pryor.

Indigo, created by the bond of a much-applauded brotherhood shared by two of the most popular black men in contemporary American history, appeared to be coming apart. Never mind that the $40 million was not theirs (but, maybe, it was; reparations for the old days). African-Americans were puzzled and angry—and focused that anger on the white Hollywood establishment. Blacks knew that without their support Pryor never would have made it to the big time. They felt, once again, double-crossed.

There were Pryor-watchers, however, who believed that the comedian was looking for the right moment to discharge Brown when he made that long and loving introduction to the man who turned out to be Miles Davis in Radio City Music Hall. These people say Pryor was testing Brown's popularity, measuring it to see if it was greater than his own. They say that at the point when Brown came to dominate Pryor—in the Sherman Oaks Burn Center—their relationship turned off toward disaster for Brown, just as it had for David Franklin. When Pryor gave Brown the job, that was payback—a rather cozy one, with Brown on the receiving end of a salary estimated to have been between $100,000 and $150,000 a year, perks not included. Pryor, say these folk, giveth and then taketh away.

An observer of Hollywood behavior told a reporter that he didn't know whether or not Columbia and Coca-Cola were involved in Brown's dismissal. "Maybe, maybe not," he said. "But I see Richard going into Jim's office, not the other way around, Richard *summoning* Jim. And Richard saying, 'Jim there's some ego involved here. Yours and mine, and I want my company back. That's it. That's all.' Like Indigo was some toy that Jim had taken from him. Indigo never was *not* Richard's company."

Brown has consistently refused to speak on the record on this subject. He'd received his last paycheck with the dismissal message from Lauren Glassman. The firing seemed to imply that the comedian no longer wished to be indebted to Brown for the former athlete's help in saving his life. That act had given Brown power. Pryor repaid him by giving him a powerful position. The greater power returned to Pryor when he fired Brown.

The incident was not likely to increase the comedian's popularity.

In the aftermath, black Hollywood was left to wonder about what might have been. Some second-guessed whether Brown had been the best choice in the first place; as a jock-turned actor, he had many detractors, and though he had worked hard to gain inside knowledge of the entertainment industry, there had been many others with more expertise. "But," said independent producer Frank Dawson, looking back, "spiritually he was the right guy. He had the kind of relationship with Richard that should have made it work." Certainly, a management team including Pryor, Brown and a more experienced hand might have accomplished much. Even with Pryor's killer schedule and quirky work habits, all he had to do, ultimately, was pick up the phone and say "yes" to any of the scripts raining down on Indigo. He apparently never did. *Richard Pryor Here and Now*, with Brown credited as executive producer, was labeled an Indigo project, as was *Jo Jo Dancer, Your Life is Calling* in 1986. But otherwise the $40 million deal bore no fruit. In fact, Pryor told friend and film executive Thom Mount over Christmas 1985, that he'd had enough. "I ain't never gonna have no more companies," he said in the conversation printed in the March 1986 issue of *Interview* magazine. "No more of *that* shit. I don't have the heart for that. I made more enemies with my little company in the shortest time. . . . Nice try, Rich."

There were those who guessed that Pryor, isolated and insecure, had become immobilized by fear, had fallen prey to whispers that he had too much to lose by backing risky (read "black") ventures; better to do nothing. "Maybe the deal was before its time," mused Dawson. "The industry may not have been any more ready for it than Richard was." Still, there was the possibility that Indigo's failure confirmed the judgment of David Franklin, who observed that Pryor, for all his talent, was a follower, not a leader, who didn't want the pressure of being a role model—and that he was a self-professed coward condemned to destroy that which he treasured most.

Franklin spoke from bitter personal experience. His own long-running legal dispute with Pryor remained unresolved until after the Indigo shake-up. By that time, Pryor's attorneys had obtained confirmation from a California superior court judge of the $3.1 million Labor Commission finding, without benefit of a court hearing on the facts of the case. With that, they sought a court order in Georgia in an attempt to freeze Franklin's Atlanta-based assets. Franklin, meanwhile, finally opened his records for a thorough examination by auditors, who found that expenditures Pryor had claimed no knowledge of during the hearings, such as real estate investments, had indeed been made legitimately on his behalf through an escrow account set up by Franklin. (Pryor had taken his ignorance to an extreme, insisting he had no idea how much money he had made on any given film or in any given year, though he had signed his tax returns for those years.) With the matter at last heading for trial in early 1984, Pryor's attorneys approached Franklin for a settlement, and the former manager agreed to pick up some of the comedian's court costs. Franklin refused to confirm the rumored figure of $300,000 but suggested that it was much less; a confidentiality clause shrouded the details of the settlement.

Pryor had already spent twice that amount in legal fees going after Franklin. For him, clearly, it was an emotional thing, a matter of pride. "It was basically a divorce," said Franklin's attorney Thomasina Reed of the dispute, "where Richard Pryor, who loved David Franklin very dearly as a brother or father or whatever, was upset because Franklin didn't want to deal with him anymore. He did not appreciate that upwards of half a million dollars a year of Pryor's income was going to drug dealers."

Pryor's full-court press of legal retaliation struck many as overkill, perhaps encouraged by reports of white handlers who found Franklin too "uppity." What better way to bring him down, went that way of thinking, than with his own superstar? Franklin, for his part, never subscribed to the theory of a Hollywood conspiracy against him, though he was keenly aware of the unusual power he wielded in the form of his clientele. Yet the experience, which he described as "a nightmare," left him drained. The suicide of his first client, Donny Hathaway, the year before Pryor's holocaust, had shaken him, and he took Pryor's assault as a sign to get out of the business. If there *had* been a scheme to wrest power from Franklin, it couldn't have worked better. By the end of the decade he retained only one entertainment client, singer Peabo Bryson, and concentrated on international business deals, making money, he explained, "in things where the money wouldn't talk back."

With Pryor, Franklin said after the fact, "you know your turn is coming." Franklin was sued, and then Brown was fired. They were the two people—two black men—most closely associated by the public with Pryor's career; both claimed to have spent the better part of their respective relationships with the comedian "protecting" him and "covering his ass." Yet other associates remained willing to do so, demonstrating a fierce loyalty, despite Pryor's history of contentious relations, that seemed to take on an air of self-protective paranoia. Such behavior had the effect of fortifying his isolation. By the time Franklin had been dealt with, it was implied, the whites really had hold of Pryor—he never again had black representation—and would use him up, bleed him, drain his talents in ventures that would ultimately erase the impact he'd had on so many people for so many years.

The most troubling sign of Pryor's public life after ending his associations with Brown and Franklin was the absence of fresh comedy material. No more concert films; no albums after the Grammy-winning *Rev. Du-Rite* in 1981 and the recording of the *Sunset Strip* set. It may have been that he was simply plowing the more lucrative field of film.

It may also have been the result of an ironic kind of destabilization. If he did free himself of drugs and alcohol, as he claimed to have done by 1983, that personal recovery could well have cost him his street-level bearings. "Success is a comedian's biggest danger because there's no pain," observed Keenen Ivory Wayans. For Pryor, more than most, it seemed the absence of pain would be the kiss of comic death, even though it might be the only way of preserving his life. "I really love being funny," Pryor said in 1986. "But I don't want to go through what I had to go through to do it. *That's it.*" On this leg of his career, being successful, being clean and sober, and being without the guidance of some key advisers threatened to turn a once-transcendent genius into just another comedian.

This latest incarnation appeared in a most unexpected form. In September 1984, Pryor returned to network television with the Saturday morning children's series, "Pryor's Place." It presented the rambunctious comedian as a somber, earnest figure, a dark Mister Rogers, hosting the wholesome adventures of two black boys, young Richie and his buddy, Wally. All this took place on a Sesame Street set peopled with producers Syd and Marty Krofft's puppets and Pryor characters like the Mudbonish Bummer, who lived in an alley and delivered mush-mouthed wisdom. The show gently sermonized on themes like the importance of reading and the pain of divorce; for children's entertainment, it was a thoughtful alternative to cartoon commercials like the Smurfs, and recalled traditional fare like "Captain Kangaroo." For television, it was also a minor racial breakthrough. Very much like "The Cosby Show" that debuted the same month, "Pryor's Place" accepted the blackness of its central characters as an unremarkable fact and went on about its business. That, and the extremely low key of its humor, may have doomed it; the series did not return the following year.

By then, Pryor was back to his old antics, although clearly at less than full force. *Brewster's Millions*, a 1985 Universal release, cast him as yet another jittery, good-hearted dupe, a minor-league baseball pitcher required to squander $30 million in order to collect a $300 million inheritance. A remake of a 1945 film, *Brewster* demanded some changes. Apparently it was deemed more plausible that an old white curmudgeon would have Pryor's Monty Brewster as his only heir than that a multimillionaire could be black.

The romantic interest proved a further complication. An attorney, played by black actress Lonette McKee, is engaged to another lawyer, played by white actor Stephen Collins. Not to worry: Collins's character is a snobbish preppie bad guy who fancies himself McKee's

Pygmalion. Brewster conveniently engineers a reunion with the lawyer's equally snotty white exwife, removing the specter of interracial romance and clearing the decks for a Pryor-McKee pairing at the end.

Since the happy ending is never in doubt, there is little for Pryor to do but try to sustain the thin premise through the power of his own animation. "Watching Richard Pryor as he forces himself to cavort with simulated abandon," wrote Vincent Canby in *The New York Times*, "is like watching the extremely busy shadow of someone who has disappeared." But such notices, which were becoming depressingly routine, could not have mattered much at the time to Pryor, who was looking ahead to perhaps his greatest film challenge.

Jo Jo Dancer, Your Life Is Calling was more than Pryor's directorial debut (not counting the concert film *Richard Pryor Here and Now*); it was his attempt to make sense of his own life in a medium that had consistently denied him an opportunity to express his full range. While his other film roles had picked up on pieces of the Pryor persona, Jo Jo Dancer *was* Richard Pryor. The story line is unambiguous autobiography. As quoted in *Interview* magazine, Pryor explained to Thom Mount that he had meant to write a straight comedy, but that the events of his own life had taken over; he felt that it was something he had to do.

Told in flashback after the character, a comedian, is badly burned in a cocaine-smoking accident, the film recounts much of the Pryor legend: the childhood in a brothel with a strong grandmother (played by singer Carmen McRae); the early-career struggles with second-rate material, followed by stardom; the failed marriages; the self-destructive behavior. All this is angled in a determinedly upbeat direction. "I am the ruler of my destiny," chants the opening theme, "I can determine what becomes of me." Jo Jo chooses life. His ghostly alter ego, in a plot device reminiscent of the one used by Bob Fosse in his equally autobiographical *All That Jazz*, returns to his hospitalized body and Jo Jo is reborn, a new man.

Pryor himself was evidently in much the same frame of mind as he wrapped the project, which he also produced and cowrote. He took pride in his effort to become more involved in his film projects and to open doors for blacks working behind the scenes. And he was optimistic about his own life. "I'm in a good place now," he told *Ebony*'s Charles Whitaker. "I'm working with people and vulnerable to them. I think if I hadn't done *Jo Jo* I wouldn't be able to do all that." He was also philosophical about his past. "Nobody made Richard Pryor do what he did to himself, but him," he said. "It's nobody else's fault."

But if *Jo Jo Dancer* worked as therapy—"Maybe this project is more like basket weaving," Pryor confessed to Mount—it was somewhat less successful as art. Paul Attanasio wrote in *The Washington Post*: "The long list of directors who haven't figured out a way to yoke Richard Pryor's genius to a narrative frame now includes Richard Pryor." It was not that the film included no bright spots; it had many. The problem was that the brightest, the places where the Jo Jo character comes to life, are the stand-up comic performances, and those had already been done, better, by Pryor in concert.

One scene in *Jo Jo*, for instance, depicts the young comic trying to force a crooked nightclub owner to pay him and his colleagues their due. The same anecdote shows up in *Live on the Sunset Strip*, but there Pryor's depiction of the owner, patronizingly impressed by the comic's chutzpah, far outshines the more literal reenactment. While the film recognizes that only a powerful metaphor, like Pryor's accident, is worthy of his tragicomic karma, the decision to recycle old material said as much about the film community's lack of imagination as it did about Pryor's own insecurity.

The take for *Jo Jo* fell far below that for either *The Toy* or *Brewster's Millions*, which no doubt sent a message to the studios and maybe to Pryor himself. The ambitious, personal stuff hadn't worked well and neither had Pryor's hands on the controls. Other star actor-filmmakers had flops, lots of them, and came back strong; *Ishtar* didn't prevent Warren Beatty from doing *Dick Tracy* But for whatever reason, one got the feeling that Pryor had had his chance (though maybe he didn't *want* another). The years following *Jo Jo Dancer* saw a return to the old formula: frantic comedies and star bonding. But first, there were some personal issues arising.

In October 1986, Pryor appeared on "The Tonight Show" and shocked viewers with his emaciated appearance. "I was worried about those diseases around," he said. "I thought I had one of them and I was going to die." He said that he'd had his blood checked and was okay, but given the times, morbid speculation was inevitable. Within weeks, Pryor was back on the air, this time with Barbara Walters, to scotch the ominous rumors about his health. He'd had sinus problems, he said, and other unnamed illnesses, but nothing worse than that. And, as if to show that things were looking up, he appeared with his fifth wife, twenty-three-year-old Flynn BeLaine, whom he had married secretly in October, and their two-year-old son. Apparently, he had changed his mind shortly after telling *Ebony* there would be no Number Five

JOHN A. WILLIAMS

because it's "not as easy getting married sober." If so, he changed it again; soon after the Walters interview, Pryor filed for divorce.

The issue of his health was not resolved as easily as his marriage. Pryor's appearance became a matter of frequent comment for both fans and reviewers from that point on. With a five-year lapse since his last comedy album, few public appearances, and only low-impact film roles, there seemed little else to talk about. Janet Maslin wrote in *The New York Times* in 1987 that Pryor "looks haggard" in *Critical Condition*, which she pronounced "a frantic mess of a movie." A year later, reviewing *Moving*, she observed that Pryor "appears to be working at something less than full throttle."

Both films were undistinguished, the kind that disappear quickly from theater screens to fill the shelves of video rental stores, and they marked a dubious accomplishment for Pryor. He was now appearing in generic comedies that could as easily have been vehicles for the likes of Chevy Chase or Bill Murray, two of the more ubiquitous of the "Saturday Night Live" alumni who came to dominate film comedy in the 1980s.

Critical Condition features the comedian in a Murray-style role, with Pryor as fast-talking Eddie Linehan, who cons his way into a mental ward after being wrongly convicted of a crime and then breaks loose during a hospital blackout. Impersonating a doctor as he seeks to escape, he ends up guiding the staff through the crisis and proving his worthiness. (Murray, of course, would have at least kissed the female lead, a person of indeterminate race, played by Hispanic actress Rachel Ticotin.) In *Moving*, Pryor does a Chase turn as Arlo Pear, a smug New Jersey suburbanite who is fired, lands a new job in Boise, Idaho, and suffers every improbable misfortune in the process of relocating. (The "high concept" here, evidently, is the notion of a *black* family going to Idaho, somebody's idea of surefire comedy.)

It seems hardly to have mattered, if indeed it occurred to anyone, that Pryor was unlike those other genial film comics, the Murrays and Chases, Dan Aykroyds and Steve Martins, and that such boilerplate material was wholly beneath him. Yet even as he moved ghostly through those films, audiences knew he could follow the precedent set by Robin Williams. Williams, maybe the only contemporary comic who possessed anything like Pryor's power on stage, was able to build movie credibility with starring roles in *The World According to Garp*, *Moscow on the Hudson*, *Good Morning, Vietnam* and *The Dead Poets Society*. These allowed him to show muted flashes of his own high-energy style, along with more dramatic moments in a serious human context. In other words, they were precisely the sort of roles Pryor had been mostly lacking since the days of *Blue Collar* and *Which Way Is Up?* a decade earlier. Much of the blame must be laid on Hollywood's enduring image of blacks in film as either isolated comic characters or part of a milieu that reflects white filmmakers' skewed ideas of black life.

Undaunted, Pryor rebounded—at least at the box office—in 1989 with *See No Evil, Hear No Evil,* a one-more-time romp with Gene Wilder. In this round the pairing depends more than ever on predictable gags as the blind Pryor hooks up with a deaf Wilder after they witness, sort of, a murder. The timing of its release, however, made that film simply an appetizer for a more anticipated team-up, that of Pryor and Eddie Murphy in Murphy's *Harlem Nights.*

Obviously, Murphy had done well since the 1983 poolside meeting with Pryor, with *Trading Places* (1983), *Beverly Hills Cop* (1984), *Beverly Hills Cop II* (1987), *Coming to America* (1988), and *Eddie Murphy Raw* (1987), the last a concert film directed by Robert Townsend, which never came close to even the worst Pryor "live" films. Murphy's leap to stardom on "Saturday Night Live" had provided him a built-in crossover audience. His debut bonding with Nick Nolte in *48 Hrs.* (1982) had been the second coming of *Silver Streak,* and he commanded nearly as much fan devotion (if not the same respect) and apparently more clout than Pryor had at his peak. *Black Film Review* noted that, however much Murphy's films were criticized for lack of substance, the actor had "reached such icon status that he could turn a profit by reciting the alphabet."

Murphy's joining with Pryor seemed perfect, a filmgoer's dream come true, and it appeared to mean just as much to the younger actor. "I've been working towards this moment since I was fifteen," he said at the time. "If I dropped dead tomorrow, at least I'd know I finished what I set out to do. He's the reason I'm Eddie Murphy." The career stakes were high for both of them. Pryor needed the lift Murphy's hot hand might provide.

The expectations may have proved too great. A sleek-looking period piece about a Harlem after-hours club, the film drew early criticism for avoiding shooting on New York's streets in favor of a Hollywood back lot. Pryor plays Murphy's father (a nice touch enhanced by the presence of sidekick Redd Foxx, representing a third generation of black comedy), but the film has no spark. Pryor, indeed, is more wooden than ever; he seems hardly ever to move, and delivers many of his lines in deadpan earnest. Veteran singer-actress Della

Reese—whose character, according to Murphy, was based on an old Pryor routine—earns most of the laughs. By the time Murphy's crew takes on crooked cops and the mob and, of course, wins, all hope for a high-voltage family reunion of black actors has faded.

That apparently held true on the set as well. In a 1990 *Spin* magazine interview with Spike Lee, Murphy professed disappointment in his working experience with Pryor. "Richard doesn't like me," said Murphy, because he assumed Pryor believed the younger comedian responsible for short-circuiting his career. "He's not himself," offered Lee, reflecting the prevailing view about Pryor at the time.)

Harlem Nights did well enough at the box office, better than all but two of Pryor's previous efforts, but within the film community it threatened to dull some of Murphy's glow. The *Cop* films had done serious business, which the more black-oriented *Coming to America* had failed to match. *Harlem Nights,* just as "black," less critically satisfying and bringing in far fewer dollars, presumably had Hollywood executives concerned that "Golden Child" Murphy was sliding in the wrong direction. In the spring of 1990, he was back on screen with Nolte in a heavily promoted sequel, *Another 48 Hrs.* And to the disappointment of many blacks in Hollywood, he reportedly shelved a black cowboy project because it was considered financially risky, and he was aware of his need to, in the words of one insider, "hit a home run."

If the all-star jam of *Harlem Nights* did little for Murphy, where did it leave Richard Pryor? Scrambling for safe shores, apparently, and trying to stay alive. March of 1990 brought mixed reports of another heart attack, suffered either while skin diving or on the golf course at the Sanctuary Cove Hyatt Regency resort near Brisbane on Australia's Gold Coast. He may have sustained two attacks, and he was placed in intensive care in critical condition at Wesley Hospital, which specializes in coronary care. Pryor soon stabilized and was released, but not before Guy McElwaine—friend, confidant, former colleague at Columbia, Rastar and other film companies, and now agent at ICM—flew to his side. Another visitor, soon after Pryor returned to Los Angeles, was Flynn BeLaine, his fifth wife who became his sixth when they remarried in April. That reunited the actor with their son, Steven, by then six, and their daughter, Kelsey, three. (Not included in the new family picture was Franklin Matthew Pryor, the 1987 product of a union with a *Jo Jo Dancer* extra to whom Pryor had been ordered to pay child support.) Once again Pryor's new-old bride, a Jehovah's Witness, stood ready to offer stability, now at a time of apparent ill health, signalled by his wan appearance and obviously limited mobility.

Pryor's poor health, according to Tri-Star, forced him to withdraw in the summer of 1990 from the film *Look Who's Talking Too*, for which he had agreed to dub the voice of a toddler. (He was replaced by comedian Damon Wayans.)

Still the show must go on. "Now you know what I'll go through," the recovering Pryor said after his attack, according to McElwaine, "to create new material." What he had planned, however, sounded anything but new. By fall of 1990 he was filming a fourth duet with Gene Wilder, appropriately titled *Another You*.

To many it remained puzzling that Pryor consistently played roles bereft of much redeeming value. Greed simply couldn't have been *that* overpowering. David Franklin attributed some of Pryor's preferences—before, during and after their time together—to a basic lack of taste. "You can put a pound of shit here and a pound of gold," he said, "and Richard, for some perverse reason, will take the shit every time." That choice is more likely, of course, when far more shit than gold is offered, but a perceptive artist must begin to make the distinction at some point—or his audience, sooner or later, will. From the mid-1980s on it seemed that Pryor played one-dimensional roles in which he strained to fit the character so often that the pictures melted into each other and became one, which was released over and over again. They made enough money for producers to return to the well; Pryor's audience, perhaps because of the tremendous affection it had for him, didn't seem to mind that he'd stopped growing as an actor and a comic who, even in bad, earlier films, had moments and scenes that promised greatness. The record of Pryor's films in the 1980s, however, suggests a declining public confidence in his ability to carry a picture on his own. And even those precious moments that once enlightened mediocre films were seldom present during this period. Pryor, fifty in December 1990, after forty-one films, was still somewhere between the caterpillar and the butterfly. Of course, he knew (he and Murphy discussed it publicly) that black actors were more readily accepted in comic roles than in serious roles, but it was Pryor, more than any other black actor (and there had been some) who had voiced his disgust over the way Hollywood worked, indeed, had played that disgust and fury so well that he was feared not because of his "craziness," but because everyone knew he had the right to make the claims he did.

An older generation of African-Americans (perhaps half a generation younger than Mudbones) remembers that over fifty years ago, the marquees of movie houses like the Apollo in New York and the Regal in Chicago proudly carried the names of the black actors who were given star status on the signs, but were not stars in the films: Bill Robinson, "starring" in *The Little Colonel*; Dooley Wilson, in *Casablanca*; Hattie McDaniel and Butterfly McQueen, in *Gone With the Wind*; Canada Lee, in *Lifeboat*, and so on.

So urgent and powerful was the need to have the black image reflected on screen, even if radically out of focus, that black communities raised to stardom almost any black person appearing on it. A great actor like Paul Robeson, however, refused to accept any more demeaning roles after he had made five American films. (Robeson's roles in films made in England, such as the 1940 *Proud Valley*, were far superior to anything he made in the U.S.) Canada Lee was never given roles that allowed him to exploit his full potential as a serious actor. Black actresses suffered similarly, except when cast, as Lena Horne and Dorothy Dandridge frequently were, in exotic, sexually suggestive roles.

Hollywood did reach the point when serious black actors (roles for black comics remained essentially unchanged: demeaning) were given parts that were not degrading as much as out of focus. This occurred just about when filmmaking was being widely considered an art form. As such, film was then open to criticism on several levels, so it was inevitable that the degradation, even if in new clothing, would begin to show through, like a garment worn too comfortably for too long.

For many black Americans, even the forward-looking films such as *Imitation of Life* (1934), *Home of the Brave* (1949, which earlier on Broadway had a Jewish, not a black protagonist), *The Defiant Ones* (1958, with its symbolic chain that linked the black and white prisoners), and a few others, failed at point of resolution. As a case in point, the love story of the elderly people that frames *Driving Miss Daisy* (1989) is never given voice (nor did critics mention it), and is not so much resolved as abandoned. All films of this type demand great sacrifices from the black characters. The white characters, and the audience, expect this sacrifice. The central problem of resolution derives directly from the white scriptwriters' concepts of black life, how it is lived, what conflicts are faced, and how they are resolved. While it is certainly probable that some white writers can (or already have) handled these considerations realistically, the majority have not or will not.

It was, perhaps, this key problem people hoped Pryor and Indigo Productions and Jim Brown could turn around, and that is pre-

DENNIS A. WILLIAMS

cisely why the black newspapers and magazines of Los Angeles and elsewhere were inundated with calls about the breakup. Pryor had become a symbol for more than he ever could have realized; he was that misfit black man we knew so well, that rebel, that swaggering, glamorous American black man portraying the down-home father figure, Mudbones, offering caustic commentary on human nature—and with Jim Brown blocking!

The game was called off. Time for another assessment of Richard Pryor.

Few people knew what he stood for; they had to go along with what he said he stood for. His life and career continued to be contradictions. While that may have been true for any number of other stars, black people looked for Pryor to come through the Hollywood crucible as he had overcome his holocaust. To even appear on the screen, small or large, is an event shrouded in the mystique of power. People wished to see that power exercised by the man who said he could use it well and wisely. Pryor/Zagreus would return. He always did. This concept of power is so ancient and universal—that death, real or symbolic, is just a stopover—that it must be given some credit for the enduring popularity of film, which allows an actor to die in one picture and return quite alive in another.

In the ten years after "the Fire," however, Pryor's career, in a dozen films, showed little of the phoenix. On one level, that fade illustrated the limits of an actor's power, even one who is a proven draw and especially one who is black. Moreover, neither Indigo Productions nor his frequent contributions as a writer and, more briefly, as director and producer, enabled Pryor to become, like Jo Jo Dancer, the ruler of his destiny. Instead, that hope has passed to another generation of black filmmakers, whose concerns have been to rearrange black life more truthfully, more basically, without bonding black and white, and without worrying about the crossover routes. In short, they accomplish what Pryor's routines, but not his films, do; they ignore white people. Spike Lee set the pace with his independently produced *She's Gotta Have It* (1986), followed by *School Daze* (1988), *Do the Right Thing* (1989) and *Mo' Better Blues* (1990). Those efforts were joined, most noticeably, by Robert Townsend's send-up of black film stereotyping in *Hollywood Shuffle* (1988); Keenen Ivory Wayans's blaxploitation spoof *I'm Gonna Git You Sucka* (1988), and Reginald and Warrington Hudlin's teen-oriented *House Party* (1990).

Although these projects were created free from the big-bang demands of the studios, their unexpected success commanded the industry's attention. That was not, of course, because they illuminated previously hidden corners of black life, but because they did the right thing by Hollywood standards: delivered sizable profits on ludicrously small budgets. *She's Gotta Have It*, made for $175,000, returned $7 million; *Hollywood Shuffle* earned $5 million on a $200,000 budget; *House Party* cost $2.5 million and raked in more than $26 million. And so, even as Pryor's film career stalled and Murphy's sought to maintain its trajectory, black-made films came to be seen as something of a growth industry. "Every studio wants to be in business with a hot young black filmmaker, and they're all hoping they've got the right one," said a black Hollywood observer.

Still, Hollywood inevitably hedged its bets. Wendell B. Harris won the 1990 Sundance Film Festival in Park City, Utah, with his *Chameleon Street*, which he wrote, directed and starred in. But the studios, fearing that it lacked commercial value, were reluctant to distribute the film. Warner Bros. reportedly offered to buy the rights—to remake it as a big-budget vehicle for a more established black actor. Charles Burnett's independently produced family drama, *To Sleep with Anger*, received modest funding from Sony but languished before being released in the fall of 1990 by The Samuel Goldwyn Company; but for the presence of star Danny Glover it might never have seen the light of day. Tri-Star gave the go-ahead to USC film-school grad John Singleton's first feature, *The Boys in the 'Hood*, a story of teen gangs that, whatever its merits, struck some black insiders as a typically limited depiction of black life. And meanwhile, skeptics were waiting to see whether Lee's *Mo' Better Blues*, a serious film, would justify its $10-million budget (about twice the typical black-film budget, but less than half the average funding for a white feature). It took in about $14 million in its first five weeks, respectable but not overwhelming, and potentially just the kind of evidence reluctant studios needed to confirm their fears. As one black entrepreneur was told by a talent agency, despite the impressive track record of recent black films: "As soon as there's one dud, it's probably going to close up the whole shop."

It is possible that Hollywood was more afraid than impressed by the black-film bonanza, which threatened to expose the bloat that afflicts the film industry. In straight business terms, even the most modest profits turned by thin-budget black films represented a solid investment, and in truth most performed spectacularly. But high studio overhead demanded big-budget features, even if many were paper losers, as long as an occasional *Batman*-sized winner came along to balance the books. (Some charged that sleight-of-hand accounting was a deliberate effort to thwart those whose contracts called for a percentage of net profits.) While studios could afford to back marginally profitable or break-even projects if they chose to, some high-rising black filmmakers considered themselves more restricted. Unable to afford losing ventures, they felt pressure to score big, which often meant comedies, however faithful to the black experience.

But there were, and are, alternatives. Warrington Hudlin, who helped found the Black Filmmakers Foundation in 1979, predicted that noncommercial markets, such as museums and public television, would nurture the next generation of black filmmakers. (*Daughters in the Dust*, a debut feature on Gullah life by Julie Dash—whose work was encouraged by the foundation—was financed by PBS, which planned to air the film after its theatrical run.) Others actively sought direct financing from black backers to help establish a competing film industry freed from the Hollywood profit structure. The timing felt right: Films had proved to be a profitable investment, the new breed of director-writer-producers seemed willing to work outside the system, and there were enough experienced behind-the-camera black film folk to sustain the effort.

That entrepreneurial spirit might also benefit from a broader focus. Most of the multitalented young black filmmakers write, act, produce and direct, often at the same time. Yet creative weaknesses can develop when one person has too much control and is spread too thin. Few, if any, of the new crew have availed themselves of the untouched treasures in black literature, which has been around since the middle of the eighteenth century. Even if Hollywood itself often forgets, young filmmakers might remember that many of the best films have been made from books, and there remains a vast store of unclaimed African-American material. (Al Young's protagonist, Sidney J. Prettymen in *Sitting Pretty*, for example, is nothing if not the Pryor character Mudbones.)

On the other hand, Ernest J. Gaines' *A Gathering of Old Men* (1987), which was written for television by Pulitzer Prize-winning playwright Charles Fuller, represents an unnoticed landmark—a novel and movie script done by two black people. The black actors had a white director, but it is the script that gives the director his playing field. Two out of three isn't bad; usually it's nothing out of nothing.

It may well be that the times have passed Richard Pryor by; he has always seemed more comfortable as a *performer*, acting out the visions of others, even when he has made a significant contribution in concept or in script. He has not, at least in the majority of his films, done as much as the younger filmmakers to advance the cause of African-Americans. The need still exists for such advancement, as he well knows. To paraphrase his monologue on Vietnamese orphans, "We got thirty million black people here need to have their story told."

It is, of course, such insights, delivered in the context of his own act, that have secured Pryor's place in American popular culture. It is the comedy, not the comic acting on film, which, according to Aristotle, pictures men worse than average so that we may laugh them to an upper level. Pryor's pictures are of winos, junkies, cunning clergymen, and blustering chicken-hearts in whom there are elements of tragedy. These elements do not depict suffering on levels higher than those to be found in reality; rather, Pryor's tragedy is rooted in America's particular tragic past. When the comedian does pure comedy, when he does not preach, but simply *is* the character, he is performing in the finest tradition of a comedy particular to his society.

He has also, almost singlehandedly, updated that tradition for a contemporary mass audience. Pryor has long been likened to Lenny Bruce (whom he has acknowledged as a limited influence), in the rawness of his language and, more significantly, in the use of that language to convey truth and pain. But Pryor's reach, even completely disregarding the non-concert films, has proven far greater than Bruce's was. They were of different times: As Pryor hit stride in the mid-1970s, society had already become more comfortable with public expressions of sex and profanity, the twin taboos that haunted Bruce. And they were of different cultures: The African-American perspective of Pryor's visions provides its strength, revealing unseen flaws in the larger society as if holding a picture up to black light.

Pryor begat generations of black comics who have continued to enrich the culture with their dark-side perceptions. "He's Yoda, the Jedi master," says Keenen Ivory Wayans, who argues that Pryor laid the groundwork for all that he and his contemporaries do. And in the general explosion of stand-up comedy reflected in the proliferation of clubs, frequent concert films and extensive cable-television programming, it is clear that Pryor has liberated white comics as well. The class-based womanist screeds of a Roseanne Barr, the howling rage of a Sam Kinison, the sexist virulence of an Andrew Dice Clay are all nearly inconceivable without the revolutionary precedent of Pryor.

The profound effort—and responsibility—of truth-telling may have taken its toll. Yet every prophet has his day and no more; it is left to the faithful to draw continuing sustenance from the prophecy. Though it would be hard to imagine an America without a Richard Pryor, cursed and blessed though he is, it would be harder still to imagine, or endure, life if there had never been a Pryor, teaching us to laugh, and, by laughing, to see.

Word Up: An Afterthought

Richard Pryor was right on time.

I didn't need him before. Bill Cosby's gentle childhood humor had tied a bow on my own background—and that of millions of others, black and not—and allowed me to set it carefully aside as I lurched into adolescence. It gave me a sense of security as I, and we, then tumbled through the late 1960s and saw each other through sharp new eyes. (Yes, we could remember if we cared to, we all started out as children.)

Very soon, though, that memory was not enough. Lines were drawn: black and white, hawk and dove, have and have-not. It was easy enough to determine in which quadrant of the grid one stood. (The tricky part was finding any common ground with those whose flags were planted in other squares.) We knew what we believed and knew the correct arguments to defend our positions. As a college student in the early 1970s, I even knew well the cultural threads that held black people together and wove us inextricably into the fabric of what Jesse Jackson would later call the American quilt. Langston Hughes, Ralph Ellison, W.E.B. Du Bois and countless other voices offered testimony of our African and American pasts, our struggle and survival, dignity and humor, uniqueness and individuality. More contemporary heroes like Malcolm X and Amiri Baraka and Sonia Sanchez provided righteous ammunition. And James Brown stayed around to help us keep the beat. There was no shortage of cultural resources or intellectual vitality to help us promote the cause. But even in that fervent time, most of the messengers were somehow sterile, their teachings things that many of us studied and believed but did not always feel personally, even when their ideas propelled us into action.

Then, like a rumor, there was Pryor's record *Craps: After Hours*. A fresh voice, rhythmic and entertaining as a party, socially perceptive as a political tract, familiar as the fellas, wherever they were—in the pool hall or the plant, the dorm or the office. The voice on the record was transportable and transcendent, a common language that bogarted its way up from the underground. It gave brothers like me who had done little time in the streets a new, hip way of expressing ourselves, and a license to do so. At first it didn't have anything to do, really, with progressive politics or culture studies, but as an entertaining diversion it seemed to carry more import than most; its phrases became part of ordinary discourse in a way that Malcolm would have envied.

The record *That Nigger's Crazy* tore the roof off the sucker. I was in grad school by the time I caught up to that one, and I realized this Pryor character, who'd been hanging around for years as just another cute comic before transforming himself into a ghetto griot, was not an accidental phenomenon. He was a force. He told the truth, and in the process had us rolling on the floor, gasping for breath and wiping away tears of laughter that could just as easily have been tears of sorrow. It was the word made real. All the speeches and dissertations on The Community paled in comparison to his evocation of its inhabitants. Triumph, struggle, despair? It was all there. Contempt for government and its institutions? He had that down cold. Yet by working from the inside out, he conveyed all that from the most human, and humane, perspective.

There was something else, a combination of his own genius and the timing of his comic assault. There had been generations of black comics who talked directly to black folks partly because they had no alternative; their performances and recordings were confined to a largely segregated black market. Others spoke to whites about us in racially restricted clubs, or, later, in the new integration of the 1960s, on television and in trendy nightclubs. Pryor spoke directly to us, in our native language—there was no mistaking that—but he did it in a way that was slyly accessible to any white who dared eavesdrop. He was telling "them" off and taking them to school even as he taught and entertained us. And he didn't give a damn what anybody thought. His progression, from marginal record labels with "X-rated" notations like an old-timey Redd Foxx "party" record, to platinum double albums on mainstream labels and concerts with multiracial audiences in places like Radio City Music Hall, reflected no change in his tone or approach. It was the same stuff, political and personal, sexual in a way that was never really just about "doing it"; the profane prophecy of a been-there brother barely able to conceal (and hardly trying to) his own anger and aching vulnerability. Everyone wanted to hear it. Even today, people who would quickly be at each other's throats about Louis Farrakhan, Jesse Jackson, Al Sharpton or Marion Barry would gladly sit side-by-side to hear Pryor's judgments.

The pitch and timing of Pryor's message worked not only across racial lines. He burst into the national consciousness at the moment that African-Americans were distilling themselves into now familiar groupings: the affirmative-action "new middle class" and the slowly sinking "underclass." Never mind that any given black family tree had branches reaching in both directions; the split was real and painful on both sides. As a driven entrepreneur pushing into white markets, Pryor represented one branch; as a steady-cussing, throw-down chronicler of lowly life, he championed the other. His humor cut both ways, and, more important, he provided a common language and cultural reference that bridged the gap. Richard belonged to all of us, and reminded us as clearly as a family reunion that we, still and forev-er, belonged to each other.

He was cross-generational, too. Pryor's age landed him neatly between my father and me, and his insights bonded us by decoding the wisdom I was meant to receive. His routines evoked the streets from which my father escaped and over which he helped to propel me. But we both knew those characters; every black American does. Moreover if, as James Baldwin wrote, every black man has a Bigger Thomas in his head, we each have a Richard Pryor in our hearts, a crazy mother-fucker who will not bludgeon you with mute, brute force but *read* your ass to death. His weapon—not the dissipated grumbling of the thunder but the pinpoint lightning of The Word—spoke not just to personal adversaries but to all the oppressive forces that have weighed on us black men. Fuck *you*, yes, but also Fuck It, a spitting in the eyes of capricious gods, an age-old declaration of manhood and of being.

But Pryor's own apparent greed and that of the entertainment industry demanded that such a potent force be contained, packaged, marketed. We didn't mind. We couldn't get enough of him, and because he came to matter to us so deeply, we wanted to see him do well, and gain power. He would be our Trojan Horse, remembering his roots—how could this man not?—as he carried his righteous message to the American public. Movie star? Go ahead, Rich. Multimillion-dollar deals? Kick ass, my brother.

He showed undeniable drawing power on the screen, yet much was often lost in the transition. Film critic Donald Bogle, in the revised edition of his *Toms, Coons, Mulattoes, Mammies & Bucks*, wrote: "With the exception of Dorothy Dandridge, it is doubtful if any other black film star, even Poitier or later Eddie Murphy, has ever connected with the black audience in quite the intense way that Pryor did." But there was a catch, a huge one, that Hollywood has yet to fathom. No American movie star's career has ever depended *less* on his on-screen performances. In Pryor's case, only a few have been memorable, a few more touching, several fleetingly funny, and most extremely frustrat-ing. For years we have kept waiting for Pryor, our Richard, to break through one of those silly roles and *talk to us*. He has rarely done so. In *Lady Sings the Blues*, before his big comic surge, he proved himself a first-rate second banana, an impression mightily strengthened when he rode off with *Silver Streak*. His star vehicles, on the other hand, have been mostly unaffecting. We tolerate them, though, used to anticipate them, because of the comedy. As long as there were fresh routines, maybe a concert film in the offing, something going on in his live act, we could go along with the rest. Is it surprising that his biggest-grossing film, *Stir Crazy*, was released shortly after he nearly died?

When I first heard of that accident, Pryor's holocaust, my immediate reaction was sharp sorrow and a sense of yawning emptiness (very much like what I felt when I heard about Stevie Wonder's near-fatal car crash, though I knew that wasn't his fault). My second reaction, which followed within seconds, was to hope he would survive—because I knew the routine would be a bitch. It was. Other comedians play What If; they think of something funny, something that would be absurd or outrageous, and tell the story. Pryor, like a great blues singer, had lived it—at least some of it, we knew—enough to give all his stories the credibility of a survivor bearing witness. When he cried out from those hopeless places, where the loving was too good, the dope too strong, the white folks too stupid, he wasn't telling jokes; he was testifying. By 1980 he had been to the brink of death twice, first, apparently, through heart failure, and then by fire, and he brought back such bright, purifying truth that he stood alone among mortal men as a reason to believe in resurrection. Who else would you want to tell you about the Other Side? After another heart attack in 1990, Pryor was quoted as saying that it showed what he'd do to come up with new material. For the first time, though, I felt doubt about whether he would, or could, deliver.

That doubt is what has shadowed his career for the past decade. Is there, still, a commitment to reflecting life as we know it, truth as he sees it, or has he simply become a man privately trying to stay alive while publicly trying to make a living? If so, I wish him well, as always, and happiness, but almost wish he would take his "rich, happy, black ass" on home. I have never believed that brilliant artists were not entitled to die a natural death; no one should be forced to live on the edge until he falls off, purely for the sake of art. On the other hand, it is nearly as sad to watch an immensely gifted man lapse into constant self-parody with little sign of recovery. It has happened. By the end, millions thought of the great Louis Armstrong as little more than a clown, but who wants to see Richard Pryor become a latter-day Stepin Fetchit (or even a black Elvis)? "In Living Color," a television show that like much contemporary comedy owes something to Pryor, has depicted him in his typical movie hysteria as being "scared for no reason," and that cut was uncomfortably deep. He might once have been counted on to make such a piercing observation, especially about himself. Check Mudbone's insightful and unforgiving commentary on Richard Pryor in *Live on the Sunset Strip*, which, delivered in past tense, takes on the air of a eulogy. Increasingly, the evidence suggests that he meant it.

Art, however, can outlast both productivity and celebrity. Film, tape, vinyl and laser disc retain the power of the comic genius who joined us and lifted us and gave us voice. Now and always, that shit is funny as a motherfucker. And it's deep, too.

D.A.W.

THE BUSY BODY   Paramount (1968)
Producer & Director—William Castle.   Writer—Ben Starr.   Starring—Sid Caesar,
Robert Ryan, Anne Baxter, Kay Medford, Jan Murray, Richard Pryor.   Comedy. 102
minutes.

THE GREEN BERETS   Batjac/Warner Bros. (1968)
Producer—Michael Wayne.   Directors—John Wayne, Ray Kellogg.   Writer—James
Lee Barrett.   Starring—John Wayne, David Janssen, Jim Hutton, Aldo Ray, Raymond St.
Jacques; billed nineteenth is Richard "Cactus" Pryor.   War Drama 141 minutes.

WILD IN THE STREETS   AIP (1968)
Producers—James H. Nicholson, Samuel Z. Arkoff.   Director—Barry Shear.
Writer—Robert Thom.   Starring—Shelley Winters, Christopher Jones, Diane Varsi, Ed
Begley, Hal Holbrook, Millie Perkins, Richard Pryor.   Drama/Comedy/Satire. 96 min-
utes.

THE YOUNG LAWYERS   (1969)
Information not available

CARTER'S ARMY   (1969)
Information not available

THE PHYNX   Cinema Organization/Warner Bros. (1970)
Producers—Bob Booker, George Foster.   Director—Lee H. Katzin. Writer—Stan
Cornyn.   Starring—A. Michael Miller, Ray Chippewan, Dennis Larden, Lonny Stevens,
Lou Antonio, Mike Kellen, Joan Blondell, Martha Raye; Richard Pryor makes a cameo
appearance.   Comedy. 91 minutes.

**YOU'VE GOT TO WALK IT LIKE YOU TALK IT
OR LOSE THAT BEAT**   J.E.R. (1971)
Producer, Director & Writer—Peter Locke.   Starring—Zalman King, Allen Garfield,
Suzette Green, Richard Pryor, Bob Downey, Liz Torres.   Darma/Comedy. 85 minutes.

DYNAMITE CHICKEN   EYR Programs (1972)
Producer & Director—Ernie Pintoff.   Starring—Joan Baez, Richard Pryor, Ron Carey,
Marshall Efron, Lisa Ryan, Peter Max, John Lennon, Ondine, Andy Warhol, Malcolm X.
Variety/Performance. 76 minutes.

LADY SINGS THE BLUES   Motown-Weston-Furie/Paramount (1972)
Producers—Jay Weston, James S. White.   Director—Sidney J. Furie. Writers—Terence
McCloy, Chris Clark, Suzanne DePasse.   Starring—Diana Ross, Billy Dee Williams,
Richard Pryor, James Callahan, Paul Hampton.   Biography/Drama. 144 minutes.

WATTSTAX   Stax Films-Wolper Pictures/Columbia (1973)
Producers—Larry Shaw, Mel Stuart.   Director—Mel Stuart.   Starring—Richard Pryor,
The Dramatics, The Staple Singers, Kim Weston, Jimmy Jones.   Performance. 102 minutes.

HIT
Paramount (1973)

Producer—Hary Korshak.   Director—Sidney J. Furie.   Writers—Alan R. Trustman, David M. Wolf.   Starring—Billy Dee Williams, Richard Pryor, Paul Hampton, Gwen Welles, Warren Kemmerling   Crime.   134 minutes.

THE MACK
Cinerama (1973)

Producer—Harvey Bernhard.   Director—Michael Campus.   Writer—Robert J. Poole.   Starring—Max Julien, Don Gordon, Richard Pryor, Carol Speed, Roger E. Mosley, Dick Williams, Juanita Moore.   Crime.   110 minutes.

SOME CALL IT LOVING
CineGlobe (1973)

Producer, Director & Writer—James B. Harris.   Starring—Zalman King, Carol White, Tisa Farrow, Richard Pryor, Veronica Anderson.   Fantasy.   103 minutes.

UPTOWN SATURDAY NIGHT
First Artists/Warner Bros. (1974)

Producer—Melville Tucker.   Director—Sidney Poitier.   Writer—Richard Wesley. Starring—Sidney Poitier, Bill Cosby, Harry Belafonte, Flip Wilson, Richard Pryor, Rosalind Cash.   Comedy.   104 minutes.

ADIOS AMIGO
Atlas (1975)

Producer, Director & Writer—Fred Williamson.   Starring—Fred Williamson, Richard Pryor, Thalmus Rasulala.   Comedy.   87 minutes.

THE BINGO TRAVELING ALL-STARS & MOTOR KINGS
Motown-PanArts/Universal (1976)

Producers—Rob Cohen.   Director—John Badham.   Writer—Hal Barwood.   Starring—Billy Dee Williams, James Earl Jones, Richard Pryor, Rico Dawson, Sam Briston. Comedy.   110 minutes.

CAR WASH
Universal (1976)

Producers—Art Linson, Gary Stromberg.   Director—Michael Schultz.   Writer—Joel Schumacher.   Starring—Franklyn Ajaye, Sully Boyar, Richard Brestoff, George Carlin, Prof. Irwin Carey, Richard Pryor.   Comedy.   97 minutes.

SILVER STREAK
Twentieth Century Fox (1976)

Producers—Thomas L. Miller, Edward K. Milkis.   Director—Arthur Hiller.   Writer —Colin Higgins.   Starring—Gene Wilder, Jill Clayburgh, Richard Pryor, Patrick McGoohan, Ned Beatty, Clifton James, Ray Walston.   Comedy.   113 minutes.

GREASED LIGHTENING
Third World Cinema/Warner Bros. (1977)

Producer—Hannah Weinstein.   Director—Michael Schultz.   Writers—Kenneth Vose, Lawrence DuKore, Melvin Van Peebles, Leon Capetanos.   Starring—Richard Pryor, Beau Bridges, Pam Grier, Cleavon Little, Vincent Gardenia, Richie Havens.   Drama/ Comedy.   96 minutes.

WHICH WAY IS UP?
Universal (1977)

Producer—Steve Krantz.   Director—Michael Schultz.   Writers—Carl Gottlieb, Cecil Brown.   Starring—Richard Pryor, Lonette McKee, Margaret Avery, Morgan Woodword, Marilyn Coleman.   Comedy.   94 minutes.

BLUE COLLAR

T.A.T. Communications Co./Universal (1978)

Producer—Don Guest. Director—Paul Schrader. Writers—Paul Schrader, Leonard Schrader. Starring—Richard Pryor, Harvey Keitel, Yaphet Kotto, Ed Begley Jr., Harry Bellaver. Drama. 110 minutes.

THE WIZ

Motown/Universal (1978)

Producer—Robert Cohen. Director—Sidney Lumet. Writer—Joel Schumacher. Starring—Diana Ross, Michael Jackson, Nipsey Russell, Ted Ross, Mabel King, Lena Horne, Richard Pryor. Musical. 133 minutes.

CALIFORNIA SUITE

Columbia (1978)

Producer—Ray Stark. Director—Herbert Ross. Writer—Neil Simon. Starring— Alan Alda, Michael Caine, Bill Cosby, Jane Fonda, Walter Matthau, Elaine May, Richard Pryor, Maggie Smith, Gloria Gifford, Sheila Frazier. Comedy/Drama. 103 minutes.

RICHARD PRYOR: LIVE IN CONCERT

Special Event Entertainment (1979)

Producers—Del Jack, J. Mark Travis. Director—Jeff Margolis. Starring—Richard Pryor. Performance. 78 minutes.

RICHARD PRYOR IS BACK LIVE IN CONCERT

Hillard Elkins-Steve Blauner Productions/Special Event Entertainment (1979)

Producers—Del Jack, Tony Conforti. Director—Jeff Margolis Starring—Richard Pryor. Performance. 78 minutes.

THE MUPPET MOVIE

ITC Entertainment/Associated Film Distribution (1979)

Producer—Jim Henson. Director—James Frawley. Writers—Jerry Juhl, Jack Burns. Starring—Kermit the Frog, Miss Piggy, Fozzie Bear; cameos include—Charles Durning, Austin Pendleton, Mel Brooks, Milton Berle, Dom DeLuise, Elliot Gould, Bob Hope, Madeline Kahn, Steve Martin, Richard Pryor, Telly Savalas, Orson Welles, Carol Kane. Comedy/Fantasy. 98 minutes.

WHOLLY MOSES

Columbia (1980)

Producer—Freddie Fields. Director—Gary Weis. Writer—Guy Thomas. Starring —Dudley Moore, Laraine Newman, James Coco, Paul Sand, Jack Gifford, Dom DeLuise, John Houseman, Richard Pryor. Comedy. 109 minutes.

IN GOD WE TRUST

Universal (1980)

Producers—Howard West, George Shapiro. Director—Marty Feldman. Writers— Marty Feldman, Chris Allen. Starring—Marty Feldman, Peter Boyle, Louise Lasser, Richard Pryor, Andy Kaufman. Comedy. 97 minutes.

STIR CRAZY

Columbia (1980)

Producer—Hannah Weinstein. Director—Sidney Poitier. Writer—Bruce Jay Friedman. Starring—Gene Wilder, Richard Pryor, Georg Stanford Brown, Jobeth Williams, Miguelangel Suarez, Craig T. Nelson Comedy. 111 minutes.

BUSTIN' LOOSE
United Artists (1981)

Producers—Richard Pryor, Michael S. Glick.   Director—Oz Scott.   Writer—Roger L. Simon (based on an adaptation by Lonne Elder III of a story by Pryor).   Starring—Richard Pryor, Cicely Tyson, Alphonso Alexander, Kia Cooper, Edwin DeLeon.   Comedy.   94 minutes.

SOME KIND OF HERO
Paramount (1982)

Producer—Howard W. Koch.   Director—Michael Pressman.   Writers—James Kirkwood, Robert Boris.   Starring—Richard Pryor, Margot Kidder, Ray Sharkey, Ronny Cox, Lynn Moody.   War Darma/Comedy.   97 minutes.

RICHARD PRYOR: LIVE ON THE SUNSET STRIP
Columbia (1982)

Producer & Writer—Richard Pryor.   Director—Joe Layton.   Starring—Richard Pryor. Performance.   82 minutes.

THE TOY
Rastar/Columbia (1982)

Producer—Phil Feldman.   Director—Richard Donner.   Writer—Carol Sobieski. Starring—Richard Pryor, Jackie Gleason, Ned Beatty, Scott Schwartz, Teresa Ganzel. Comedy.   99 minutes.

SUPERMAN III
Warner Bros. (1983)

Producer—Pierre Spengler.   Director—Richard Lester.   Writers—David Newman, Leslie Newman.   Starring—Christopher Reeve, Richard Pryor, Jackie Cooper, Margot Kidder, Annette O'Toole.   Fantasy/Adventure.   123 minutes.

RICHARD PRYOR: HERE AND NOW
Columbia (1983)

Producers—Bob Parkinson, Andy Friendly.   Director & Writer—Richard Pryor. Starring—Richard Pryor.   Performance.   94 minutes.

BREWSTER'S MILLIONS
Universal (1985)

Producers—Lawrence Gordon, Joel Silver.   Director—Walter Hill.   Writers— Herschel Weingrod, Timothy Harris.   Starring—Richard Pryor, John Candy, Lonette McKee, Stephen Collins, Jerry Orbach, Pat Hingle, Tovah Feldshuh, Hume Cronyn. Comedy.   101 minutes.

JO JO DANCER, YOUR LIFE IS CALLING
Columbia (1986)

Producer & Director—Richard Pryor.   Writers—Rocco Urbisci, Paul Mooney, Richard Pryor.   Starring—Richard Pryor, Debbie Allen, Art Evans, Fay Hauser, Barbara Williams, Carmen McRae.   Drama/Comedy.   97 minutes.

CRITICAL CONDITION
Paramount (1987)

Producers—Ted Field, Robert Cort.   Director—Michael Apted.   Writers—Denis Hamill, John Hamill.   Starring—Richard Pryor, Rachel Ticotin, Ruben Blades, Joe Mantegna, Bob Dishy, Sylvia Miles.   Comdey.   99 minutes.

MOVING
Warner Bros. (1988)

Producers—Stuart Cornfield, Kim Kurumada.   Director—Alan Metter.   Writer— Andy Breckman.   Starring—Richard Pryor, Beverly Todd, Dave Thomas, Dana Carvey, Randy Quaid.   Comedy.   89 minutes.

SEE NO EVIL, HEAR NO EVIL

Tri-Star (1989)

Producer—Marvin Worth. Director—Arthur Hiller. Writers—Earl Barret, Arne Sultan, Eliot Wald, Andrew Kurtzman, Gene Wilder. Starring—Gene Wilder, Richard Pryor, Joan Severance, Kevin Spacey, Alan North. Comedy. 103 minutes.

HARLEM NIGHTS

Eddie Murphy/Paramount (1989)

Producers—Mark Lipsky, Robert D. Wachs. Director & Writer—Eddie Murphy. Starring—Eddie Murphy, Richard Pryor, Redd Foxx, Danny Aiello, Michael Lerner, Della Reese, Arsenio Hall. Action/Comedy. 115 minutes.

ANOTHER YOU

Tri-Star (1991)

Producers—Ted Zachary, Ziggy Steinberg. Director—Maurice Phillips. Writer—Ziggy Steinberg. Starring—Richard Pryor, Gene Wilder, Mercedes Ruehl, Stephen Lang, Vanessa Williams, Phil Rubenstein. Comedy. 98 Minutes.

JOHN A. WILLIAMS

Discography

RICHARD PRYOR (1969, Reprise)

CRAPS AFTER HOURS (1971, Laff)

PRYOR GOES FOXX HUNTING (1973, Laff)

THAT NIGGER'S CRAZY (1974, Reprise)

DOWN-N-DIRTY (1975, Laff)

IS IT SOMETHING I SAID? (1975, Reprise)

RICHARD PRYOR MEETS RICHARD & WILLIE & THE S.L.A. (1976, Laff)

BICENTENNIAL NIGGER (1976, Reprise)

L.A. JAIL (1976, Tiger Lilly)

ARE YOU SERIOUS??? (1977, Laff)

RICHARD PRYOR'S GREATEST HITS (1977, Warner Bros.)

RICHARD PRYOR LIVE (1977, World Sound)

WHO ME? I'M NOT HIM (1977, Laff)

BLACK BEN THE BLACK SMITH (1978, Laff)

THE WIZARD OF COMEDY (1978, Laff)

OUTRAGEOUS (1979, Laff)

WANTED: LIVE IN CONCERT (1979, Reprise)

INSANE (1980, Laff)

HOLY SMOKE (1980, Laff)

RICHARD PRYOR'S GREATEST HITS (1980, Reprise)

REV. DU-RITE (1981, Laff)

LIVE ON THE SUNSET STRIP (1982, Warner Bros.)

HERE AND NOW (1983, Warner Bros.)

JOHN A. WILLIAMS is the author of twelve critically acclaimed novels, including *Jacob's Ladder* and *The Man Who Cried I Am*. He has also written seven nonfiction books, among them *The Most Native of Sons: A Biography of Richard Wright*; and has edited or co-edited six collections of writing. He is Paul Robeson Professor of English at the Newark campus of Rutgers University.

DENNIS A. WILLIAMS is a former *Newsweek* reporter and editor whose work has appeared in many other publications, including *Essence*, the *Village Voice*, *Emerge* and the *Black Scholar*. His first novel, *Crossover*, was published in 1992. He teaches writing at Cornell University in Ithaca, New York.

John A. Williams and Dennis A. Williams are father and son. *If I Stop I'll Die* is their first collaborative book.

Index